Brain Quest®

Dear Parent,

"It's Fun to Be Smart!" That's not just our slogan, it's our philosophy. For over twenty years we've been adding a big dose of "fun" into learning—first with our bestselling Q&A Brain Quest card decks; then with all the licensed games and products bearing the Brain Quest brand; and, of course, with Brain Quest Workbooks.

At Brain Quest we believe:

- All kids are smart—though they learn at their own speed.
- All kids learn best when they're having fun.
- All kids deserve the chance to reach their potential—given the tools they need, there's no limit to how far they can go!

Brain Quest Workbooks are the perfect tools to help children get a leg up in all areas of curriculum; they can hone their reading skills or dig in with math drills, review the basics or get a preview of lessons to come. These are not textbooks, but rather true workbooks—best used as supplements to what kids are learning in school, reinforcing curricular concepts while encouraging creative problem solving and higher level thinking. You and your child can tackle a page or two a day—or an entire chapter over the course of a long holiday break. Your child will be getting great help with basic schoolwork, and you will be better able to gauge how well he or she is understanding basic course material.

Each Brain Quest Workbook has been written in consultation with an award-winning educator specializing in that grade, and is compliant with most school curricula across the country. We cover the core competencies of reading, writing, and math in depth—with chapters on science, social studies, and other popular units rounding out the curriculum. Easy-to-navigate pages with color-coded tabs help identify chapters, while Brain Boxes offer parent-friendly explanations of key concepts and study units. That means parents can use the workbooks in conjunction with what their children are learning in school, or to explain material in ways that are consistent with current teaching strategies. In either case, the workbooks create an important bridge to the classroom, an effective tool for parents, homeschoolers, tutors, and teachers alike.

Learning is an adventure—a quest for knowledge. At Brain Quest we strive to guide children on that quest, to keep them motivated and curious, and to give them the confidence they need to do well in school . . . and beyond. We're confident that Brain Quest Workbooks will play an integral role in your child's adventure. So let the learning—and fun—begin!

—The editors of Brain Quest

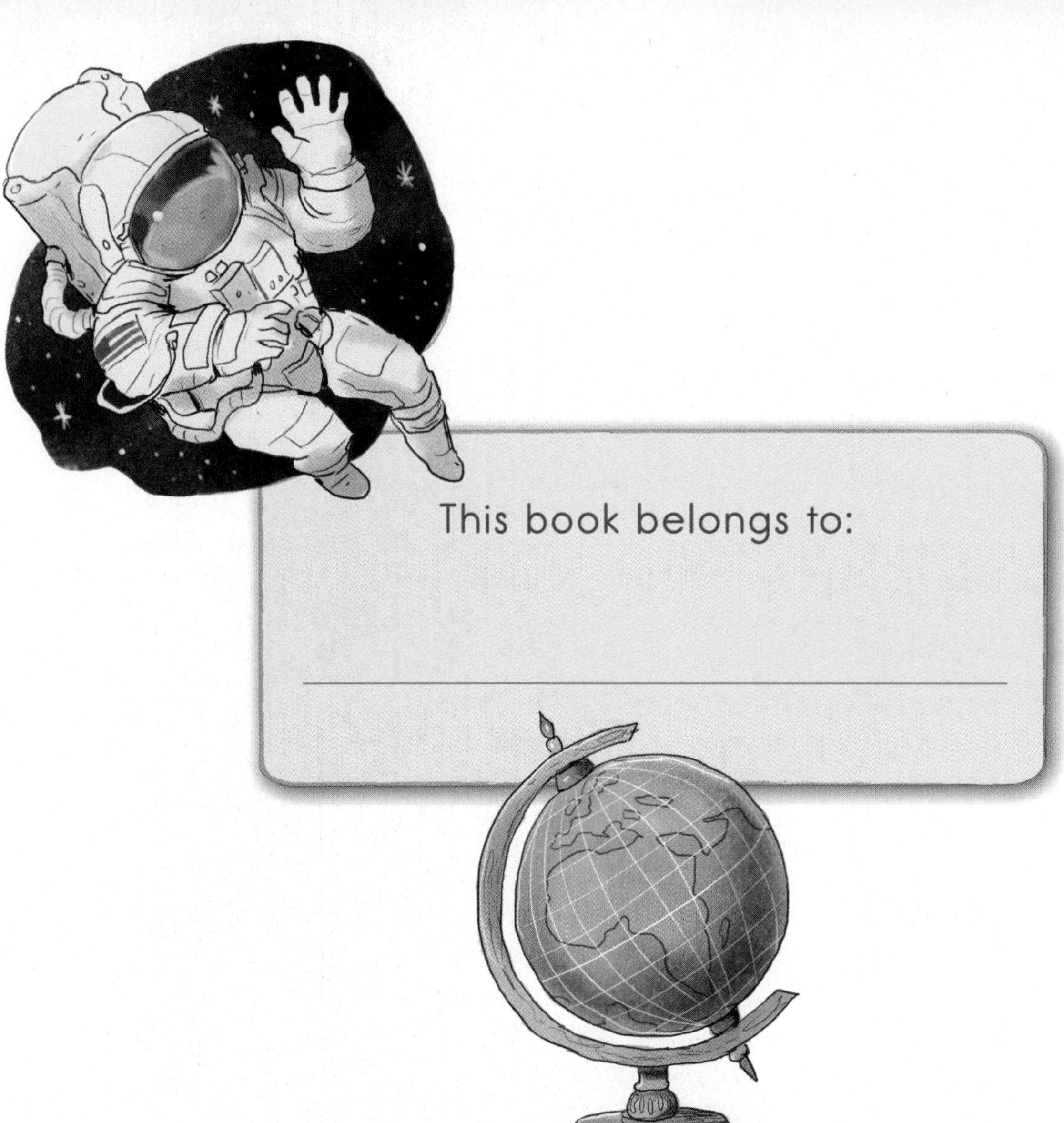

Library of Congress Cataloging-in-Publication Data is available.

ISBN 978-0-7611-8278-8

Workbook series design by Raquel Jaramillo
Illustrations by Matt Rockefeller

Workman books are available at special discounts when purchased in bulk for premiums and sales promotions as well as for fund-raising or educational use. Special editions or book excerpts also can be created to specification. For details, contact the Special Sales Director at the address below, or send an email to specialmarkets@workman.com.

Workman Publishing Co., Inc.
225 Varick Street
New York, NY 10014-4381
workman.com

Printed in the United States of America
First printing April 2015

Brain Quest® Grade 5 Workbook

Written by Bridget Heos

Consulting Editor: Kim Tredick

WORKMAN PUBLISHING

NEW YORK

Contents

5

Spelling and Vocabulary

6

Start at the Beginning

Choose the correct **prefix** from the cards to complete each word.

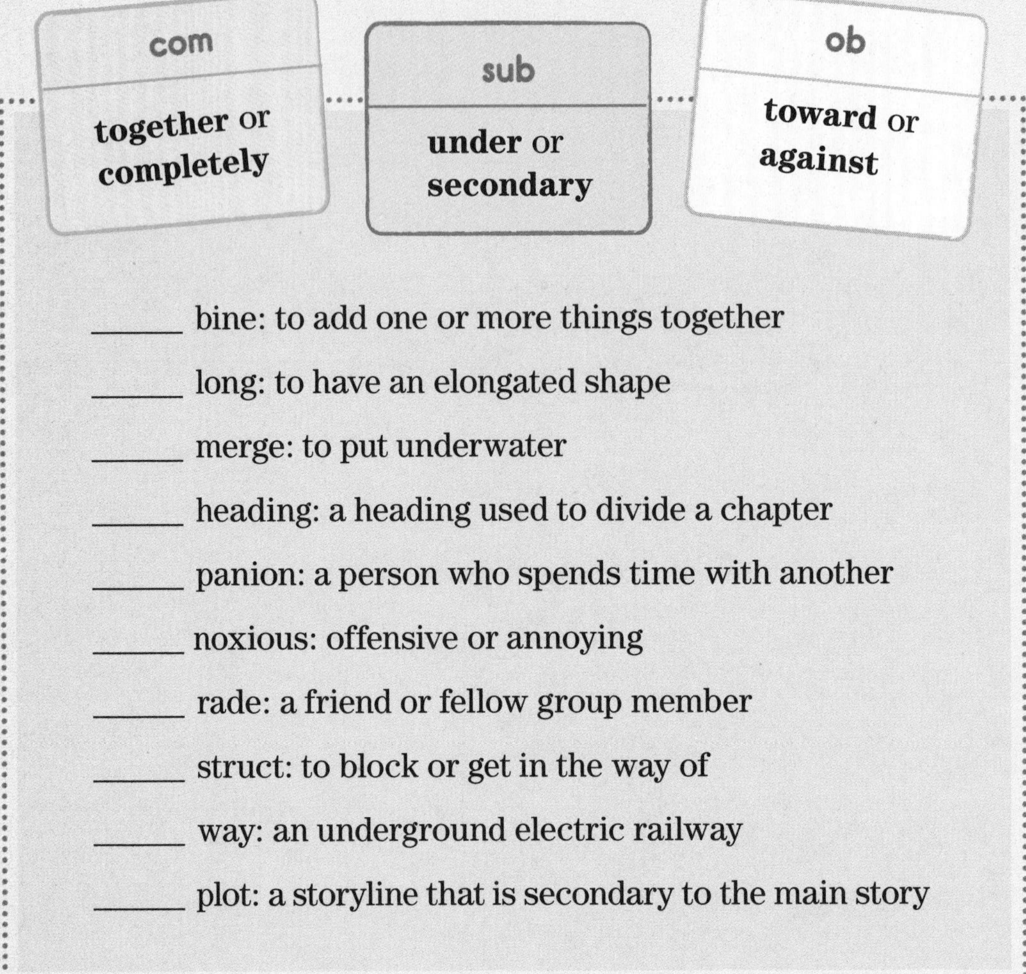

_____ bine: to add one or more things together

_____ long: to have an elongated shape

_____ merge: to put underwater

_____ heading: a heading used to divide a chapter

_____ panion: a person who spends time with another

_____ noxious: offensive or annoying

_____ rade: a friend or fellow group member

_____ struct: to block or get in the way of

_____ way: an underground electric railway

_____ plot: a storyline that is secondary to the main story

Spelling and Vocabulary

Prefixes

Brain Box

A **prefix** is a word segment that changes the meaning of a word when added to the word's beginning.

Write a letter to a restaurant manager, politely asking for your money back because you found a fly in your soup. Use as many of the **sub**, **ob**, and **com** words above as possible.

Building Opposites

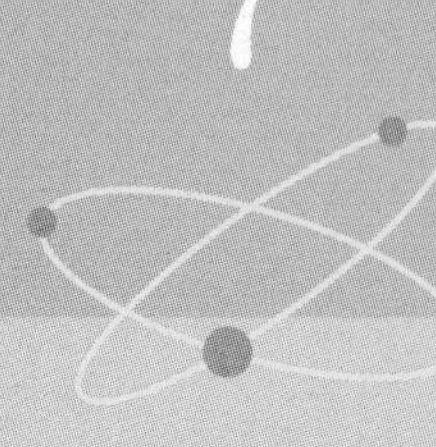

Spelling and Vocabulary

Prefixes

Add the correct prefix from the box to make a new word. Then write the definition of the new word.

un	dis	in

approve	to accept as satisfactory
disapprove	**to deem unsatisfactory**

adequate	acceptable
________	____________________

advantage	a situation that gives one an edge over others
________	____________________

accurate	correct or exact
________	____________________

timely	happening at a convenient time
________	____________________

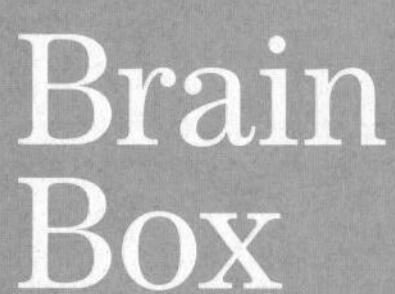

Brain Box

The prefixes **un**, **dis**, and **in** can create words that are the opposites of the root words.

A Doable Activity

Spelling and Vocabulary

Suffixes

Word	Word with Suffix	Meaning
do	**doable**	able to be done
break	**breakable**	able to be broken

When the root word ends with **e**, drop the **e** before adding **able**.

Word	Word with Suffix	Meaning
love	**lovable**	observing love
note	**notable**	worthy of notice

Finish each sentence by adding **able** to the highlighted word and writing it in the blank.

Pigeons **adapt** well to city life. They are ____________.

Careful! That porcelain penguin will **break** easily. It is ______________________.

The cozy sweatshirt provides much **comfort** to Carlos. It is ______________________ .

The customers **desire** chocolate fudge sundaes. The sundaes are ______________________.

You can **distinguish** between the fraternal twins. They are ______________________.

The lifeboats **inflate**. They are ______________________ .

Who doesn't **love** floppy-eared rabbits? They are absolutely ______________________.

Note that detective stories date back to ancient China. The fact is ______________________ .

Mike hasn't jumped off the high dive before, but his friends **believe** he can do it. It is __________.

Write four additional words ending in **able**.

______________ ______________

______________ ______________

Brain Box

A **suffix** is a word segment that changes the meaning of a word when added to the word's ending. The suffix **able** changes the word to mean "able to be (the word)."

Are You Able or Ible?

Circle the 10 words that have incorrect **able** and **ible** endings in this letter.

Hey Charlie,

I just heard the horrable news that your cupcakes were stolen. That's terrable! I hope there is tangable evidence pointing to whoever is responsable! I always felt comfortible leaving my food unattended, but not after this unbearible event. I guess none of us is invincable. We are all susceptable to thievery. The sad thing is: the cupcakes probably had incredable frosting.

Sincerely,

Your Lovible Dog, Junior

P.S. Please excuse the crumbs.

Write the misspelled words correctly.

____

____

____

____

____

____

____

____

____

____

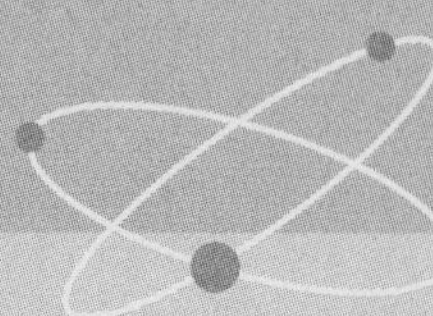

Spelling and Vocabulary

Suffixes

Brain Box

The suffix **able** is more common than the suffix **ible**. The roots of words ending in **able** are usually complete words. Examples: **preferable** **comfortable** The roots of words ending in **ible** are less likely to be complete words. Examples: **terrible** **incredible**

10

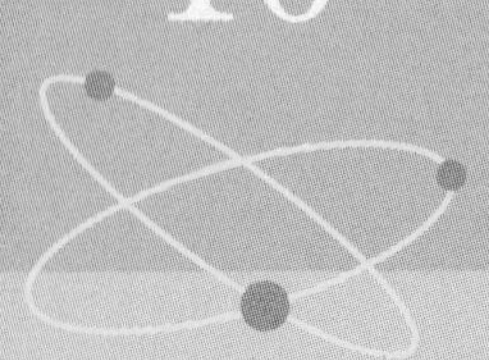

Spelling and Vocabulary

Suffixes

Fun with Shun

Fill in the blanks with the correct word from the word box. Then read the sentences aloud.

collision	addition	division	nation	revision
duration	persuasion	ambition	decision	editions

The moon was most likely formed by a _________ between Earth and a Mars-size object.

Our _________ guarantees the right to life, liberty, and the pursuit of happiness.

They stayed for the _________ of the dull movie in the hope that it would improve as it went along.

A fraction can also be described as a _________ problem.

To convince her parents to adopt a puppy, Bea would need the power of ___________________.

The foreign _________ of the Harry Potter books are written in various languages from French to Japanese.

They spent all summer working on a new _________ to the tree house, which included a whole second floor and a ladder.

The poorly written story was in need of _________ before it was published.

The jury could not reach a _________.

His lifelong _________ was to study penguins in Antarctica and eventually write a book.

TION

SION

Brain Box

The **shun** sound at the end of words is usually spelled **tion** or **sion**. Sometimes the two endings sound slightly different, as in **division** and **addition**. Other times, you must memorize the correct ending.

Happy Endings

Write the **ed** and **ing** form of each verb by first doubling the consonant. Then find the **ed** and **ing** verbs in the word search.

admit	admitted	admitting	refer	_______	_______
transfer	_______	_______	expel	_______	_______
control	_______	_______	regret	_______	_______
equip	_______	_______	tap	_______	_______
permit	_______	_______	commit	_______	_______

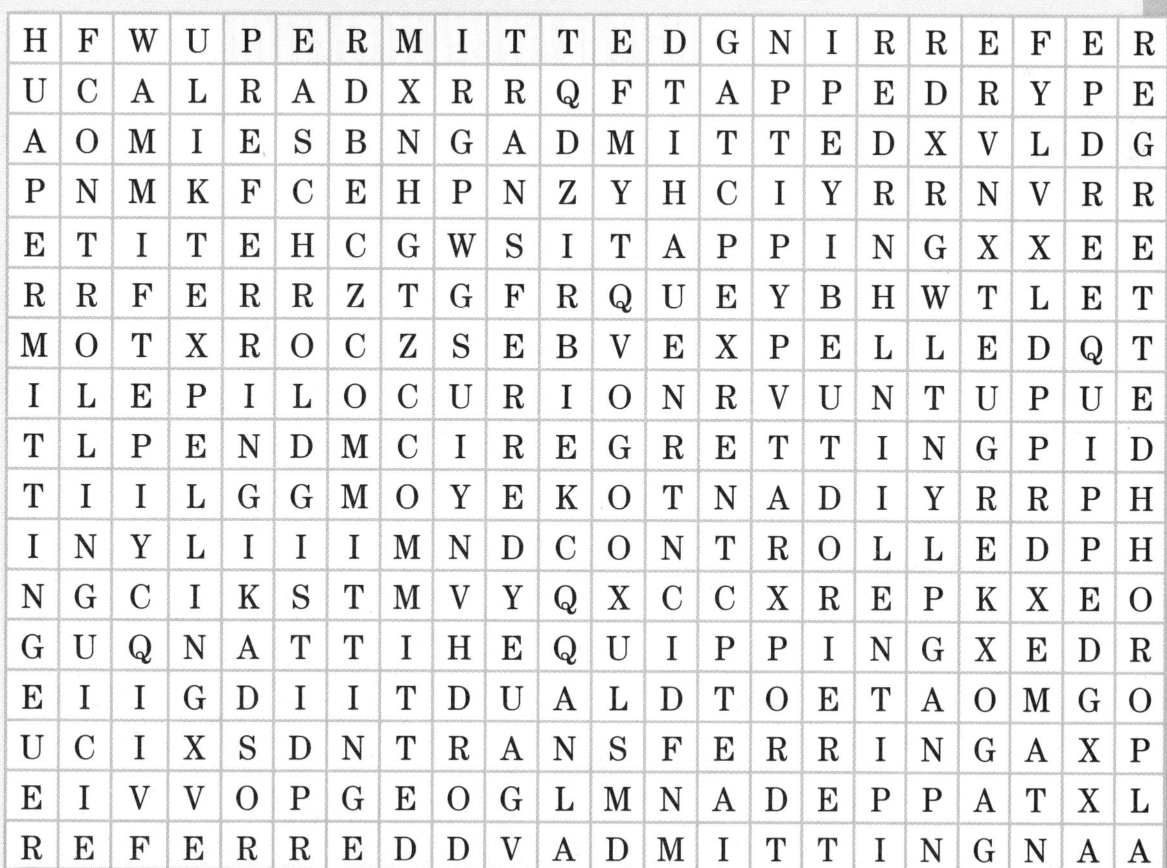

H	F	W	U	P	E	R	M	I	T	T	E	D	G	N	I	R	R	E	F	E	R
U	C	A	L	R	A	D	X	R	R	Q	F	T	A	P	P	E	D	R	Y	P	E
A	O	M	I	E	S	B	N	G	A	D	M	I	T	T	E	D	X	V	L	D	G
P	N	M	K	F	C	E	H	P	N	Z	Y	H	C	I	Y	R	R	N	V	R	R
E	T	I	T	E	H	C	G	W	S	I	T	A	P	P	I	N	G	X	X	E	E
R	R	F	E	R	R	Z	T	G	F	R	Q	U	E	Y	B	H	W	T	L	E	T
M	O	T	X	R	O	C	Z	S	E	B	V	E	X	P	E	L	L	E	D	Q	T
I	L	E	P	I	L	O	C	U	R	I	O	N	R	V	U	N	T	U	P	U	E
T	L	P	E	N	D	M	C	I	R	E	G	R	E	T	T	I	N	G	P	I	D
T	I	I	L	G	G	M	O	Y	E	K	O	T	N	A	D	I	Y	R	R	P	H
I	N	Y	L	I	I	I	M	N	D	C	O	N	T	R	O	L	L	E	D	P	H
N	G	C	I	K	S	T	M	V	Y	Q	X	C	C	X	R	E	P	K	X	E	O
G	U	Q	N	A	T	T	I	H	E	Q	U	I	P	P	I	N	G	X	E	D	R
E	I	I	G	D	I	I	T	D	U	A	L	D	T	O	E	T	A	O	M	G	O
U	C	I	X	S	D	N	T	R	A	N	S	F	E	R	R	I	N	G	A	X	P
E	I	V	V	O	P	G	E	O	G	L	M	N	A	D	E	P	P	A	T	X	L
R	E	F	E	R	R	E	D	D	V	A	D	M	I	T	T	I	N	G	N	A	A

Spelling and Vocabulary

Spelling verb endings

Brain Box

When adding **ed** or **ing** to a verb ending in a consonant, you should double the consonant when the verb ends with one vowel and one consonant, and the stress is at the end of the word.

Example:
mop
mop**ped**
mop**ping**

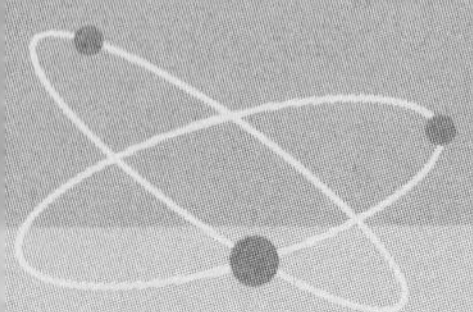
12

Double or Nothing

Write the **ing** form of each verb. Decide whether or not to double the consonants.

Spelling and Vocabulary

Spelling verb endings

		Double the consonant?	
interest	________	yes	no
forget	________	yes	no
appear	________	yes	no
treat	________	yes	no
stop	________	yes	no
act	________	yes	no
explain	________	yes	no
exit	________	yes	no
begin	________	yes	no
edit	________	yes	no

Brain Box

Do not double the consonant before adding **ed** or **ing** when:

- The verb ends with two vowels in a row followed by a consonant.

  Examples: peal, pealed, pealing
- The verb ends with two consonants in a row.

  Examples: arrest, arrested, arresting
- The verb ends with one vowel and a consonant and the stress is at the beginning of the word.

  Examples: target, targeted, targeting

Write four sentences using the **ing** verbs above.

____

____

____

____

Surprise Endings

Spelling and Vocabulary

Altered sounds

Finish each sentence by choosing the word from the box that is an altered form of the highlighted word. Then read the sentences aloud, noting how the pronunciation of the word changes.

signaled	circumstantial	criticized	financial	publicity
criminal	electricity	authenticity	residential	influential

The flashing walk **sign** and the loud beeping _________ that the light would soon turn red.

The restaurant **critic** _________ the food for being too salty.

Though he had committed a **crime**, Robin Hood did not consider himself to be a _________.

Electric cars run on batteries powered by _________.

After studying **finance**, Taylor became a _________ advisor.

The sign said "**authentic** gold," but the ring was so cheap that Delaney questioned its _________.

Eloise **resided** in a _________ suite at the Plaza Hotel.

The bakery made a **public** apology for selling day-old pastries, but it seemed insincere and resulted in more negative _________.

The **circumstances** indicated that he was guilty. Unfortunately, the jury was skeptical of the _________ evidence.

The doctor's grandmother **influenced** his early studies. Some say she was the most _________ person in his life.

Brain Box

When the endings of root words change, the pronunciation of the root word may also change. For instance, **define** has a **long i**, but **definition** has a **short i**.

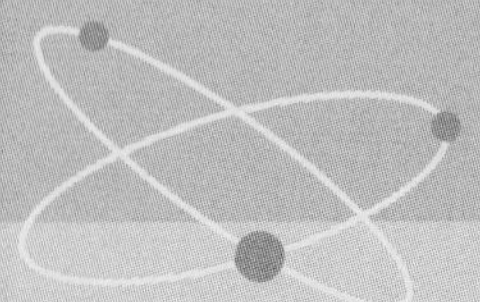

Spelling and Vocabulary

Homographs

Twin Words

Read the word, definition, and sentence. Circle whether the ending of the word sounds like **it** or **āt**.

alternate	to take turns	it / āt
The altos alternate in singing solos.		
associate	a partner or coworker	it / āt
My associate Bob and I are hard at work on a project.		
articulate	able to speak clearly	it / āt
The toddler was articulate for his age.		
graduate	to complete a course of study	it / āt
My cousin will graduate from college this spring.		
separate	divided from each other	it / āt
Keep the animals in separate compartments.		

Brain Box

Homographs are words that are spelled alike, but differ in meaning and sometimes pronunciation. Sometimes the noun or adjective form ends with a **short i** while the verb form ends with a **long a**.

Example: The teacher was an advocate for the poor. (**Advocate,** the noun, ends with an **it** sound.)

We should advocate for more art classes. (**Advocate,** the verb, ends with an **āt** sound.)

Circle whether the highlighted homographs differ in meaning, pronunciation, or both.

The conductor, who wore a bow tie, turned to bow to the audience.

Meaning **Pronunciation** **Both**

The circus performer couldn't bear to wrestle another bear.

Meaning **Pronunciation** **Both**

Park your car on the west side of the park.

Meaning **Pronunciation** **Both**

We can't waste another minute arguing about minute details.

Meaning **Pronunciation** **Both**

"I shall contest the results of this pie contest!" roared the baker.

Meaning **Pronunciation** **Both**

Multiple Meanings

Spelling and Vocabulary

Homographs

Read the two definitions and the scrambled word.
Then write the word that could be used for both definitions.

a player at bat	OR	a mixture for making cakes	tarbet batter
a steep slope	OR	a company that keeps money	anbk ________
new and unusual	OR	a long, fictional book	volen ________
to mislead	OR	a cliff	bfluf ________
a shoemaker	OR	a dessert made with fruit and dough	creblob ________
a weaving machine	OR	to be near and threatening	molo ________
pieces of ice that fall as precipitation	OR	to greet	hali ________
a large wading bird	OR	a machine that lifts heavy weights	necra ________
able to wait calmly	OR	a person receiving medical treatment	tenapit ________
to look closely	OR	a person who is an equal	eerp ________

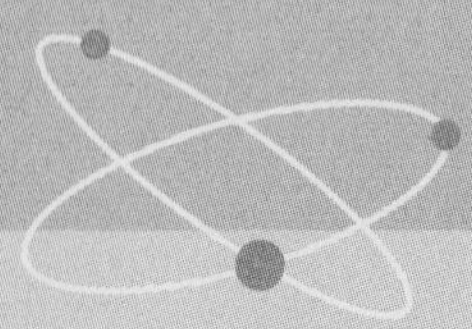

Correct the Comments

Your big sister posted a vacation picture on social media. Some of the commenters have confused the words **its/it's**, **their/they're**, and **your/you're**. Circle the misspellings.

Spelling and Vocabulary

Spelling

Sylvie

I love you're hat. Its so cute!

Chris

I didn't know you went to Silver Beach this summer! Its my favorite place!

Maley

Your so photogenic!

Antonio

Did you ever get ice cream at Mimi's? Its across the street from the beach.

Molly

Where did you're family buy they're great sunglasses?

Kaitlyn

My cousins live in that town. We stayed at they're house last year.

Antonio

Kaitlyn, I played beach volleyball with you're cousins. Their cool.

Chris

Let's all meet up next summer if your around when I am.

Write the words correctly below.

Brain Box

Commonly confused words include **its** and **it's**, **their** and **they're**, and **your** and **you're**. **Its**, **their**, and **your** are possessive pronouns. **It's**, **they're**, and **you're** are contractions for **it is**, **they are**, and **you are**.

One Hot Dog

17

Spelling and Vocabulary

Vocabulary

Use the words in the first column to fill in the blanks. Some answers may be used interchangeably.

If you say:	You mean:
However	I am going to contradict my previous thought.
Although	My next thought will contradict this one.
Similarly	This thought will resemble my previous thought.
Moreover	This thought will add to my previous thought.
In addition	This thought will add to my previous thought.
For instance	This example will support my previous thought.
Therefore	This conclusion will be based on my previous statements.

Dear Charlie,

____________ I do enjoy hot dogs, I did not eat the hot dog off your plate tonight. ____________, I did not appreciate being blamed for that. I counted three other individuals in the room when the hot dog was eaten. It could have been any one of them. ____________, your dad loves hot dogs, so it might have been him. ____________, your sister said before sitting down to dinner that she was "famished." That means that she was very hungry and might have eaten your hot dog.

I know that your mom said she saw me eat the hot dog. ____________, eyewitness accounts can be very unreliable. ____________, have you ever known me to steal food? I didn't think so. I feel that I have been wrongly accused. Frankly, my feelings are hurt. ____________, I think I deserve an apology. And nothing says "sorry" like a hot dog. Think about it.

Love,
Junior

Brain Box

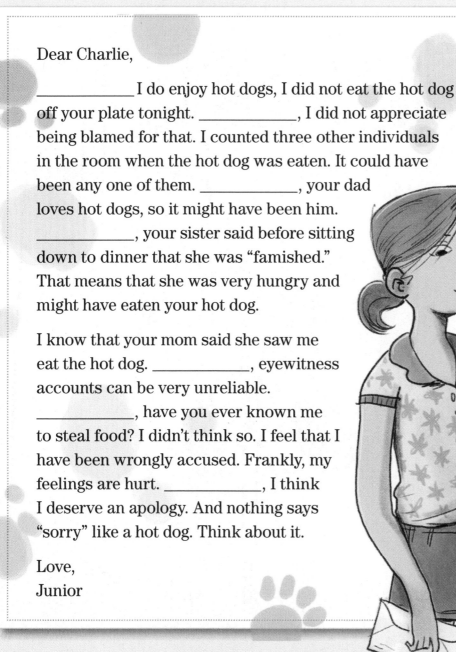

Words such as **however**, **moreover**, and **for instance** show the logical relationships between thoughts.

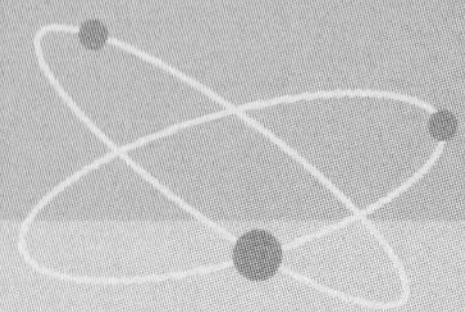

Spelling and Vocabulary

Vocabulary

It's All Greek to Me

Read the meaning of each Greek and Latin prefix and suffix.

Prefix/Suffix	Meaning
astro-	Greek: (astron) a star
photo-	Greek: (phot) light
-ology	Greek: a field of study
ambi-	Latin: both
tele-	Greek: far off
aero-	Greek: (aer) air
anti-	Greek: opposed
-phobia	Greek: (phobos) fear
audi-	Latin: to hear
-meter	Greek: (metron) to measure
amphi-	Greek: on both sides

Brain Box

Many English prefixes and suffixes come from Greek and Latin words. Knowing what these suffixes and prefixes mean can help you understand the correct meanings of many words.

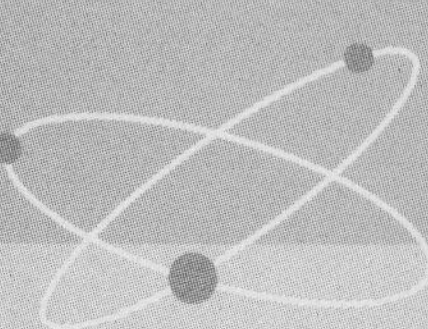

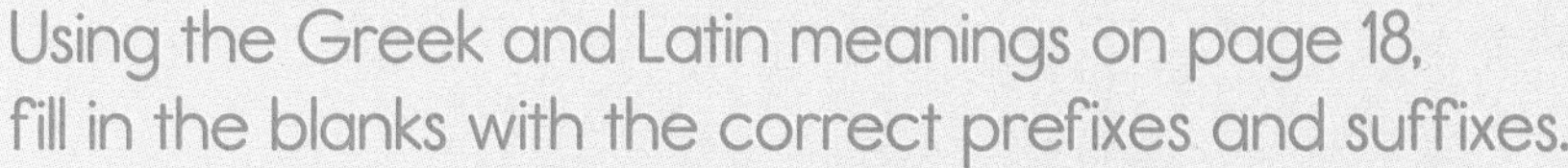

Using the Greek and Latin meanings on page 18, fill in the blanks with the correct prefixes and suffixes.

astro	logy	tele	anti	audi	photo
ambi	aero	phobia	meter	amphi	

In the old days, people wanting to send a message to a distant place quickly would send a __________ gram.

A device that measures temperature is a thermo__________.

Plants convert sunlight into energy in a process called __________ synthesis.

When a person can use both the right and the left hand with equal skill, he or she is __________ dextrous.

When something is equally suited for water or land, it is __________ bious.

The science of air travel is known as __________ nautics.

Proteins produced by white blood cells to fight infection are called __________ bodies.

If you are able to hear something, it is __________ ble.

The study of life is bio __________, and the study of space is __________ nomy.

Arachno __________ is the fear of spiders.

Match the correct word endings and beginnings. Fill in the blanks with three complete words.

geo	valent	phobia	ambi	logy	claustro

__________________ is the study of the Earth.

__________________ is the fear of small spaces.

When you both love and hate something, you are __________________ toward it.

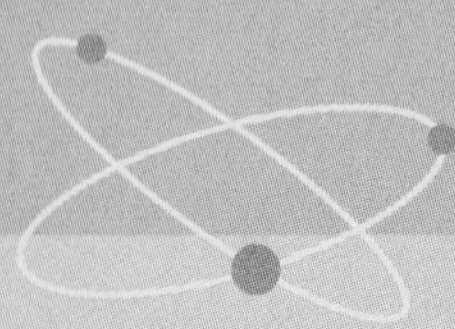

Extra! Extra!

Read the passage.

Spelling and Vocabulary

Vocabulary

Newsies

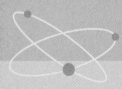

Can you imagine working all day instead of going to school? In big cities in the 1800s, this was not a **rarity**. Many children—especially boys—were newsies. They sold newspapers for about 2 cents per copy. Most newsies were 10 to 13 years old, but some were as young as 7.

The newsies **purchased** newspapers from wholesalers for about $1\frac{1}{2}$ cents each. The newsies were not **reimbursed** for copies that didn't sell. So they had to **predict** how many they would sell each day. If there was a big story, such as a disaster or a murder trial, they would buy more copies that day. The most industrious newsies could earn 3 dollars on big news days. Usually, newsies earned about 25 cents per day, which meant they sold around 10 to 12 newspapers.

While many newsies shared their earnings with their families, others chose to **sever** ties with parents or were orphaned. With no **kin** to turn to, these newsies lived on the filthy city street. This was not only **unsanitary** but also incredibly dangerous!

Orphaned newsies were not alone, however. They formed groups that would huddle together in doorways or on steps to sleep. Though **deprived** of the comforts of home, the newsies enjoyed being **independent**. They were their own bosses by day and often had free rein at night, too. After work, they would go to plays, and drink coffee in "coffee and cake" shops past midnight. Some newsies went on to be **influential** city leaders. For instance, "Big Tim" Sullivan was a newsie who grew up to be a powerful New York politician. Would you like to be a newsie in the 1800s?

Brain Box

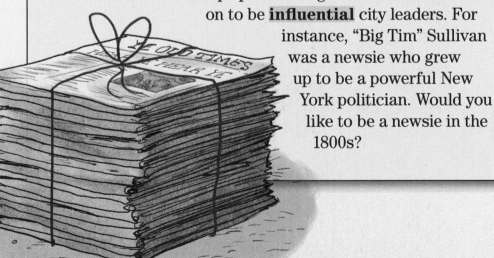

You can often determine the meanings of words from clues in the sentence and paragraph. These are called **context clues.**

Circle the correct definition for each word using **context clues** from the passage.

rarity

a plan of action
the top of a mountain
something unusual

sever

to separate
to join
to embrace

reimburse

to separate
to repay money spent
to stop working at a certain age

deprive

to be given orders
to have recorded information
to have taken away

purchase

to buy
to make fun of
to stop

kin

food
work
family

unsanitary

very good
dirty and unhealthy
not easily seen

independent

entertaining
doing things on one's own
wise

predict

to guess what will happen in the future
to ease one's worry
to keep safe

influential

having the power to affect others' decisions
easily having one's mind changed
handsome

22

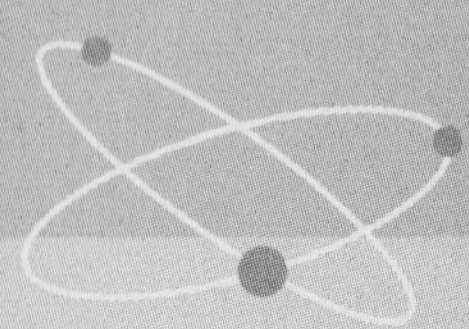

Spelling and Vocabulary

Vocabulary

Jargon Talk

Read the following sentences. Then on the next page, draw lines to match the highlighted **jargon** with the correct definitions.

In World War II, the United States, Great Britain, France, the Soviet Union, China and other countries cooperated to win the war. They were **allies**.

The **Treaty** on the Non-Proliferation of Nuclear Weapons was an agreement among 190 nations to stop the buildup of nuclear weapons.

Explorer Ferdinand Magellan set off on a voyage to **circumnavigate** the globe in 1519.

If you travel around the world at **latitude** 23 degrees north, you will cross Mexico, northern Africa, Saudi Arabia, India, and southern China.

Following **longitude** 30 degrees east, you would pass through Europe, Africa, and Antarctica.

The heart is an **organ** that pumps blood throughout the entire body.

Together, muscle cells known as myocytes form muscle **tissue**.

The **vascular** system is the network of arteries, veins, and capillaries that carry blood throughout the body.

Arteries have thick walls that can handle the strong flow of blood as it is pumped out of the heart.

Blood flowing through **veins** from the feet to the heart must flow against gravity.

Brain Box

Jargon is language that is mainly used in a specific field, like medicine, law, or engineering.

Jargon can be hard to understand at first, but often you can figure out the meaning by context clues.

tissue	an imaginary line around the Earth that is perpendicular to the equator
circumnavigate	an imaginary line around the Earth that is parallel to the equator
vascular	a collection of similar cells that together share a common function
treaty	a thick vessel through which blood from the heart flows to the rest of the body
organ	a formal agreement between two or more parties, usually countries
ally	a vessel through which blood flows from a part of the body back to the heart
longitude	a person or group of people cooperating with another person or group
artery	to travel around something, usually the globe
vein	a part of the body with a specific function
latitude	related to blood vessels

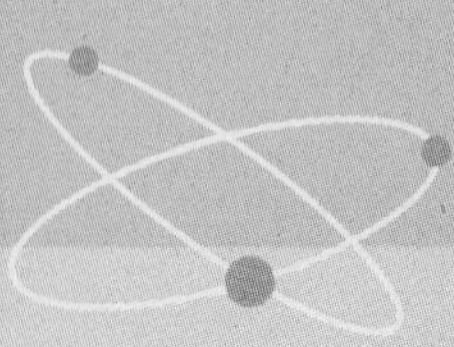

Pirate Dictionary

word pronunciation

pirate ('pī-rət)

part of speech definition synonym

1. *noun* one who robs ships; *synonym:* raider
2. *verb* to reproduce a work without permission

how it is used in a sentence

Major Steed Bonnet was nicknamed the Gentleman *Pirate* because he was a wealthy landowner before he began his criminal career on the high seas.

ahoy (ə-'hȯi)

interjection a call used to signal a boat or to say hello

Ship ahoy! Ahoy, matey!

avast (ə-'vast)

interjection (slang) stop

matey ('mā-tē)

noun a friendly form of address; *synonym*: buddy

pardon ('pär-d^{ə}n)

1. *verb* to forgive.
2. *noun* an act of forgiveness

parley ('pär-lē)

verb to discuss with an enemy

plank ('plaŋk)

noun a long, thick board

plunder ('plən-dər)

1. *verb* to rob and destroy by force; *synonym*: pillage
2. *noun* goods taken by force *synonyms*: loot, booty

scalawag ('ska-li-ˌwag)

noun a rascal

Spelling and Vocabulary

Dictionary skills

Answer the questions about the dictionary page.

Is the first syllable of **matey** pronounced with a long or short a?

____

Is **scalawag** a noun, a verb, or both?______________

Write a sentence example for **parley**.

____

What is a synonym for the noun **plunder**?

____

What part of speech is **ahoy**?

____

If someone yells **avast**, what is he or she telling you to do?

____

What could be added to the **matey** entry as a synonym?

____

What part of speech is **plank**? ______________

If the word **buccaneer** were added to this dictionary, between what two words would it go?

____

Brain Box

A **dictionary** can give you a word's spelling, pronunciation, part of speech (the type of word it is), definition, synonyms, and usage (the way it is used in a sentence).

Write definitions for these p words. Use a dictionary if you need help, but write the definitions in your own words.

pasture ______________________________

____

perish ______________________________

____

petrify ______________________________

____

protagonist ______________________________

____

26

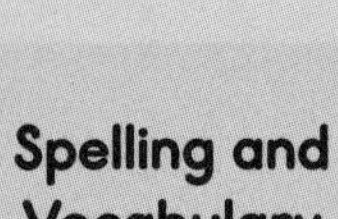

Spelling and Vocabulary

Idioms

What's That Supposed to Mean?

Read the **idioms.**

cool as a cucumber calm; not nervous

pie in the sky unrealistic

in a pickle in a bad situation

have a cow be upset

bee's knees excellent

bell the cat to complete an undesirable or impossible task

apple of my eye the one I love

the whole nine yards all of it

dressed to the nines dressed very nicely

piece of cake easy

Fill in the blanks with the correct idioms from above.

When asked if he wanted marshmallows, whipped cream, or sprinkles in his hot cocoa, James said, "I'll take ____________________."

Although some students were nervous during the spelling bee, Mari was ____________________.

"You are the ____________________," said Romeo before kissing Juliet.

Tickets to the concert sold out fast because everybody thought the band was the ____________________.

Although not everyone studied, the whole class aced the test because it was such a ____________________.

Tommy ran home, knowing that if he was late his parents would ____________________.

My 4-year-old sister asked for a unicorn for her birthday, which was a ____________________ request if I ever heard one.

Though she usually wore soccer clothes, Madeline was ____________________ for the party.

Standing up to the giant was a great idea, but who would ______________?

Mickey was babysitting until 5 p.m. but remembered he was supposed to meet Avery for ice cream at 2 p.m. He was ____________________.

Brain Box

An **idiom** is an expression that means something different from its literal meaning. For instance, "You are the cat's pajamas" means that you are awesome.

The Party

Circle the **simile**, **metaphor**, or **hyperbole** in each sentence. On the line, write an **s** if it is a simile, an **m** if it is a metaphor, or an **h** if it is hyperbole. Some sentences have multiple answers.

The Party

Aleia, it is a tragedy that you were out of town for Sierra's birthday party! _____

Sierra lit up the room in her bright pink dress. _____

There were a million kids there from all different schools. _____

We were all dancing like maniacs. _____

Then the lights temporarily went off. We were as blind as bats until they came back on. _____

Afterward we were as hungry as bears! _____

So the 20 cheese pizzas were a gift from heaven. _____

Then they brought out the cake, and it was as big as a house. _____

Time flew by, and before we knew it, it was time to go home. _____

For party favors, Sierra gave us toy kittens, which were as cute as buttons. _____

Brain Box

A **simile** is a comparison that includes the words "like" or "as." Example: busy as a bee.

A **metaphor** is a comparison that does not include "like" or "as." Example: You are my sunshine.

Hyperbole is exaggeration used to make a point. Example: There were a billion people at the zoo today.

28

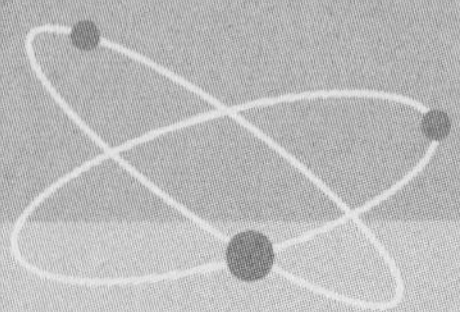

Spelling and Vocabulary

Proverbs and their meanings

Wise Words

Read the following **proverbs**.

A stitch in time saves nine.
Fixing a problem quickly can help prevent it from becoming worse.

Actions speak louder than words.
People's feelings and intentions show more through what they do than what they say.

Don't look a gift horse in the mouth.
Don't complain about gifts or charity.

Fortune favors the bold.
Those who are willing to risk failure are more likely to achieve their goals.

If it ain't broke, don't fix it.
If something is working, changing it unnecessarily may cause it not to work as well.

No man is an island.
People need each other.

Practice makes perfect.
Hard work can lead to improvement.

Rome wasn't built in a day.
Big jobs take time to accomplish.

The early bird gets the worm.
If you start a job early, you can beat the competition.

You catch more flies with honey than with vinegar.
A person is more likely to give you what you want if you ask nicely instead of rudely.

Brain Box

A **proverb** is an expression of wisdom that has significance beyond its literal meaning. For instance, "There is no use crying over spilled milk" means there is no use getting upset about a mistake that has already been made.

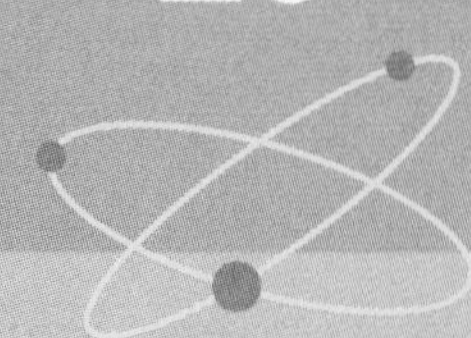

Choose the **proverb** that offers the best advice for each situation.

Alex shot several air balls on his first day of practice. "Forget it," he said. "I'm terrible at basketball."

____

Mr. Paul planned to fix the leaky toilet later, not knowing that the water would soon damage the ceiling below.

____

Ava said she was Sophia's best friend, but she completely ignored Sophia when other kids were around.

____

Brooklyn planned to sell cookies in the neighborhood at 10 a.m., but Mia had set her alarm so that she could sell cookies at 8 a.m.

____

Harry was struggling with the pressures of school, sports, and friends, but he refused to ask for help.

____

Maeve was frustrated that after a day's work, she had completed only one page of the 10-page project.

____

Dalen made 75 percent of his free throws, but he was thinking about changing his form.

____

Nick's teacher had marked a test question wrong that should have been correct. He planned to demand angrily that she change his grade immediately.

____

Audrey's grandparents gave her a sweater for her birthday, but she hated that it was so out of style!

____

Luke badly wanted to be on the student council but worried that he might flop at giving a campaign speech.

____

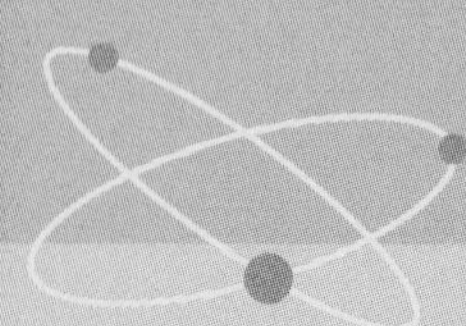

Spelling and Vocabulary

Synonyms and antonyms

Crossword Puzzle

Read each clue. Write the answer in the crossword puzzle.

Across

2 synonym for annoy

5 antonym for huge

6 synonym for accomplishment

10 antonym for enter

11 antonym for hot

12 antonym for exciting

14 antonym for fast

Down

1 synonym for buy

3 synonym for obvious

4 synonym for sparing

7 antonym for different

8 synonym for avoid

9 antonym for arctic

13 antonym for silence

Brain Box

Synonyms are two different words that have the same or nearly the same meaning. **Antonyms** are words that have the opposite meaning.

Language Arts

32

Language Arts

Prepositions

Over Under

Read the common **prepositions**. Then underline the **prepositional phrase** in each sentence.

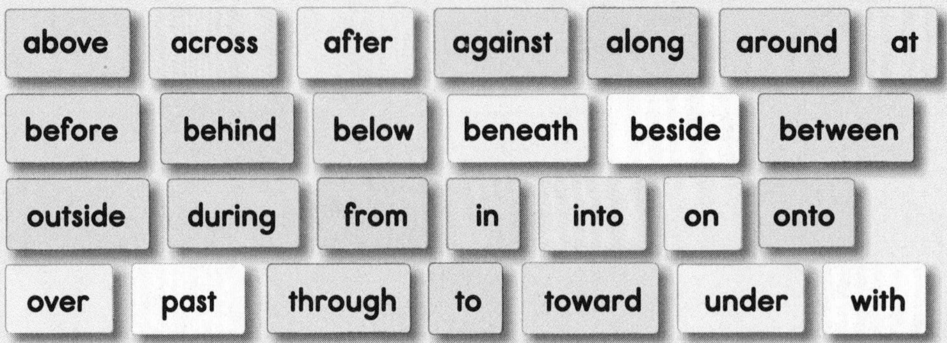

above
across
after
against
along
around
at
before
behind
below
beneath
beside
between
outside
during
from
in
into
on
onto
over
past
through
to
toward
under
with

Brain Box

A **preposition** shows how nouns and pronouns relate to other words in a sentence. They often show where something is or when something happened.

Example: We skated **on** the icy lake.

Together, a preposition and a noun make up a **prepositional phrase**. Any words used to describe the noun are also part of the phrase.

Example: We jumped **off the high diving board**.

The key is hidden above the door.

We'll settle this at sundown.

The puppy got stuck under the blanket.

The pitch was outside the strike zone.

Follow the man with the eye patch.

The diver swam toward the shipwreck.

I rowed along the shore.

Never try to swim against a rip current.

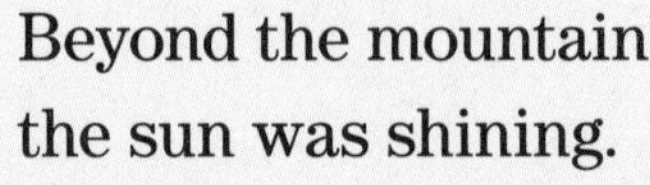
Beyond the mountain, the sun was shining.

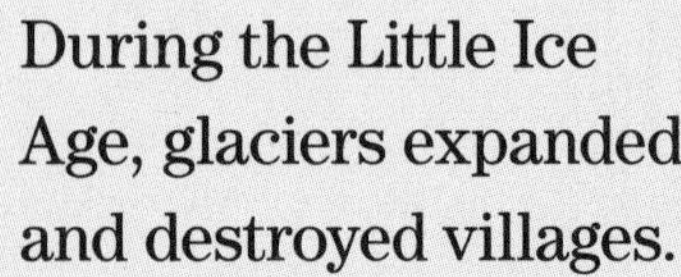
During the Little Ice Age, glaciers expanded and destroyed villages.

Where's Furious?

On the line, write the prepositional phrase that describes where the guinea pig Furious is. Use prepositions from the list to the left.

Underline the prepositional phrases in this verse from the poem "Over the River and Through the Wood" by Lydia Maria Child.

Over the river, and through the wood,
To grandfather's house we go;
The horse knows the way,
To carry the sleigh,
Through the white and drifted snow.

Uh-oh! Vampire Bunnies!

Underline the **interjections**.

Wow! It's a vampire bunny.

Uh-oh! It's a hundred vampire bunnies.

Stop, vampire bunnies!

Hey, help me get away from these vampire bunnies!

Oops! I tripped.

Ouch! A vampire bunny bit my arm.

Well, I'm sure I'll be fine.

Yikes, I'm not feeling so well.

Zoinks, I'm a vampire bunny!

Yum. Carrots taste delicious.

Write four more sentences that have interjections.

Language Arts

Interjections

Brain Box

Interjections are words of protest, command, or excitement. They can stand alone as a sentence with a punctuation mark, or they can be followed by a comma in a longer sentence. Examples:

Stop! This isn't the right movie theater.

Oh no, my sandwich is soggy!

The Pizza Shop

Read the **conjunctions.** Fill in each blank with the correct conjunction.

and
but
or
so
yet
if
unless
although
while
because

"I'd like a large pizza with pepperoni, green peppers, _________ black olives, please."

"Would you like any cheesy toast _________ garlic bread with that?"

"No, thank you, _________ maybe next time."

"They are delicious, _________ do keep them in mind for next time."

"Will do. We don't need any tonight _________ we have to save room for birthday cake."

"I'd like to wish you a very happy birthday, _________ it's somebody else's birthday."

"It's actually our cat's birthday. _________ she doesn't eat cake, the rest of us do."

"What do you give the cat, _________ you don't mind my asking?"

"We give the cat anchovies, _________ I wasn't able to find any at the grocery store."

"You're in luck. We have anchovies. I'll put some in a container _________ you wait for your pizza."

Brain Box

Conjunctions link phrases, clauses, or sentences.

36

Language Arts

Conjunctions

Pep Talk

In each sentence, the **correlative conjunction** is missing its matching word. Fill in the blank with the correct matching word.

both . . . and	either . . . or	whether . . . or
neither . . . nor	not only . . . but also	not . . . but
not so much . . . as		

You are **both** ready ______________ able to win this race.

You have trained **not only** hard ______________ smart.

You'll start out in **either** second ______________ third place.

You should pass **neither** at the start ______________ on the curve.

Then it will be **not so much** a matter of taking the lead ______________ a matter of keeping the lead.

Remember, it's **not** the dog in the fight ______________ the fight in the dog.

Whether you win ______________ lose, I'll be proud of you.

Rewrite these sayings correctly.

Neither a borrower or a lender be.

____

____

Either you are with us nor you are against us.

____

____

Brain Box

Correlative conjunctions are words that pair up in a sentence to link words or phrases. For instance, **either** pairs with **or**, and **neither** pairs with **nor**.

Perfect! Just Perfect!

Fill in each blank with the **perfect tense verbs**.

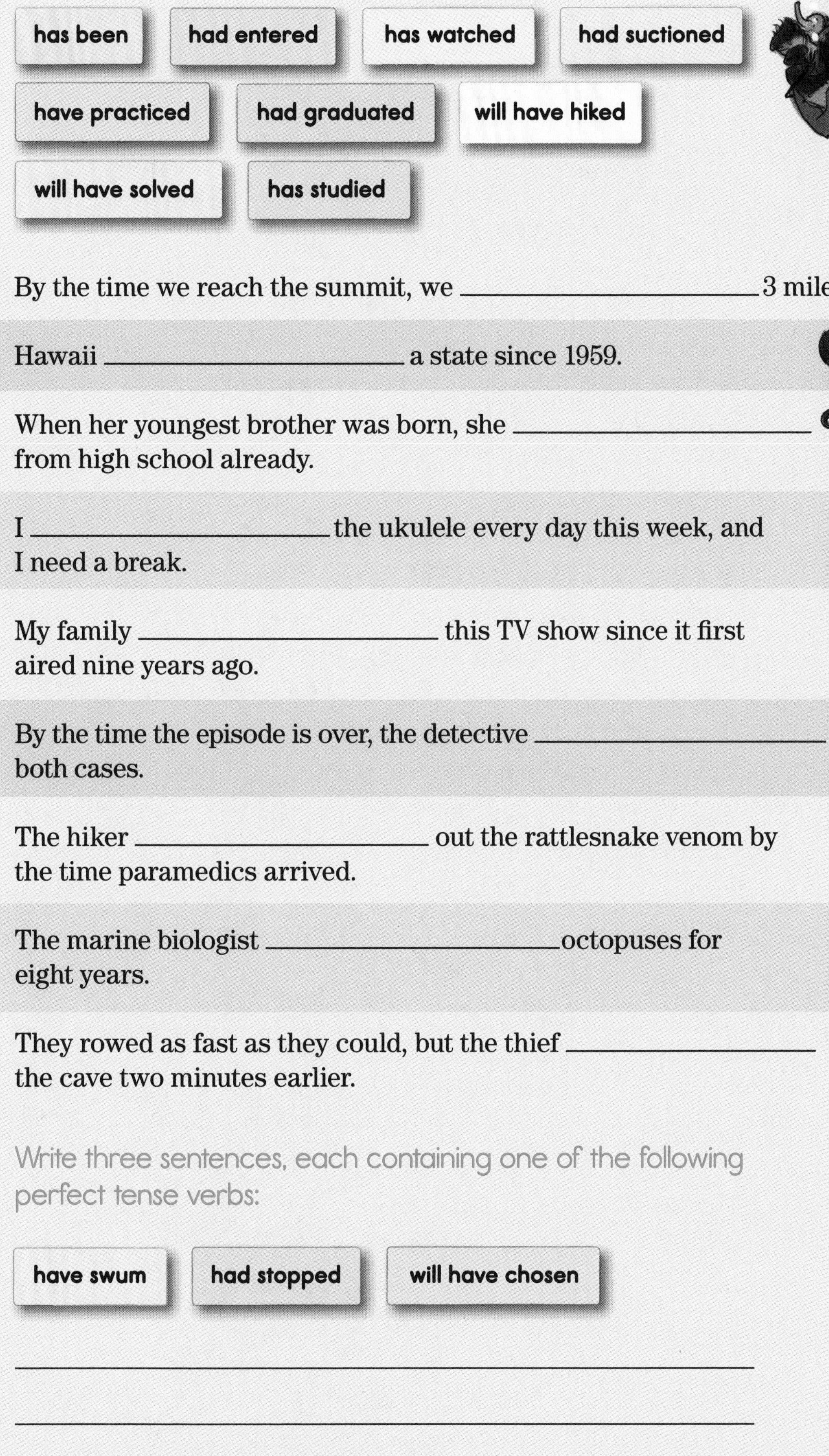

has been | **had entered** | **has watched** | **had suctioned** | **have practiced** | **had graduated** | **will have hiked** | **will have solved** | **has studied**

By the time we reach the summit, we ______________________ 3 miles.

Hawaii ______________________ a state since 1959.

When her youngest brother was born, she ______________________ from high school already.

I ______________________ the ukulele every day this week, and I need a break.

My family ______________________ this TV show since it first aired nine years ago.

By the time the episode is over, the detective ______________________ both cases.

The hiker ______________________ out the rattlesnake venom by the time paramedics arrived.

The marine biologist ______________________ octopuses for eight years.

They rowed as fast as they could, but the thief ______________________ the cave two minutes earlier.

Write three sentences, each containing one of the following perfect tense verbs:

have swum | **had stopped** | **will have chosen**

____

____

____

Language Arts

Verb tense

Brain Box

In the **perfect verb tenses**, the words **have**, **had**, or **will have** come before the main verb.

Present perfect shows that something occurred at an indefinite time or is still occurring. Example: I **have played** volleyball since third grade.

Past perfect shows that something happened before another past action. Example: The movie **had started** by the time we arrived.

Future perfect shows that an action will occur before another action. Example: By the end of the summer, I **will have read** twenty novels.

38

Leave the Past in the Past

Circle the verbs that are in the incorrect **tense**.

Language Arts

Verb tense

Brain Box

When a sentence is about something that happened in the past, the verb should be in the past **tense**. If a sentence is about the present, the verb should be in the present tense. A story can have both past and present tense verbs. However, it is important to have a reason for shifting tenses. Example: Sarah **went** to see *Flowers for Flora.* It **is** rated PG. Sarah saw the movie in the past, but the movie is rated PG in the present, so it is correct for the verbs to shift tense.

What I Did on My Summer Vacation

This past summer, I worked for my aunt at the Blue Bonnet Café. It is a vegetarian restaurant downtown. My aunt is the chef and owner.

My job was to fill water glasses and clear plates. I also washed dishes. Sometimes I chop vegetables, too.

One day, another worker was sick, so I substituted as a server. I wrote orders on a notepad. I have to write neatly so that my aunt knows what to cook. I also have to bring the customers their food quickly. Even though I was in a rush, I don't drop any plates.

Working at the restaurant was fun. I especially liked being a server. I am going to ask my aunt if I can be a server next summer.

Hottest, Coldest, Biggest, Tallest

Each of the following sentences has at least one **capitalization** mistake. Draw 3 lines under letters that should be capitalized. Draw a diagonal line through letters that should not be capitalized.

The longest River in the world is the nile river.

However, the amazon river is the largest river by volume.

From its base, which is far below sea level, to its summit, mauna kea is the tallest mountain in the world.

Measuring from sea level to summit, Mount Everest is the highest Mountain.

With an average temperature of 93°F, the Danakil Desert in ethiopia is the world's hottest Desert.

The highest temperature on earth—134°F—was recorded in Death Valley, california.

The record was set on july 10, 2013.

Only two u.s. states have never surpassed 100°F: Alaska and hawaii.

The lowest temperature ever—negative 136°F—was recorded in antarctica.

The coldest town in the world is oymyakon, Russia, where the average temperature is negative 58°F.

Language Arts

Capitalization

Brain Box

Proper nouns, such as people, places, and things, should be **capitalized**.

Always capitalize:

- the names of people, buildings, schools, businesses, streets, towns, cities, states, countries, continents, rivers, lakes, oceans, and mountains.
- the titles that come before people's names, as in Dr. Flood or Professor Plum.
- the days of the week and the months of the year.

Never capitalize:

- words such as school, river, mountain, or doctor unless they are named.
- the names of animals, plants, or foods unless they have a proper noun in their name. For example, Italian in Italian dressing is a proper noun and, therefore, capitalized.

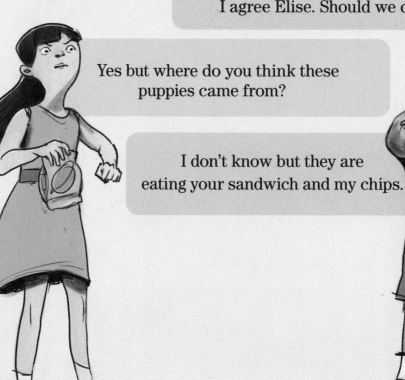

Language Arts

Commas

Comma Drama

Add **commas** to the story. You need to add 13 **commas** in all.

We meet again Marcos.

What an unpleasant surprise Elise!

Hand over the PB&J and don't try any funny business.

I'll give you your PB&J but you have to give me back my chips first.

If you think I'm here to negotiate you are sorely mistaken.

Well if that's how you feel then say good-bye to your sandwich.

Wait what's that noise?

Look it's a bunch of puppies.

It's hard to stay mad while looking at puppies Marcos.

I agree Elise. Should we call a truce?

Yes but where do you think these puppies came from?

I don't know but they are eating your sandwich and my chips.

Brain Box

Use **commas** in a series of three or more words. **Example:** I'd like a burger, fries, and a drink. Use a comma after an introductory word or group of words. **Example:** If you like french fries, you'll love sweet potato fries. Use a comma in a compound sentence. **Example:** I'll search the alley, and you check the fire escape. Use a comma to offset an interjection or name. **Example:** Yes, I'll also search the corridor, Bill.

Lions and Hunters and Commas! Oh, My!

Add commas to the story.

Living with Lions

What if your neighbors were lions? That is true for the San people of the Kalahari Desert. The San are hunters and gatherers. They work play and eat outside. They also share their land with lions. Usually the San are able to avoid the lions. Lions generally hunt at night and the San hunt and gather during the day. The San still sometimes encounter lions by day. In that case the people calmly walk away from the lions. The lions usually walk away too.

At night lions can be heard roaring and they sometimes visit the people's camps. The San tell the lions in a stern voice to go away. If the lions do not leave the people wave flaming branches at the giant cats. This does not hurt the lions but it scares them off. What about when the San are sleeping? They sleep in shelters made of grass and sticks so the lions are unable to attack them from behind. This is the lions' preferred method of attack. Therefore the lions tend to leave the San alone even when they are sleeping.

The San are afraid of lions and it's easy to see why. A lion can easily kill a person. In some situations groups of lions have been known to attack people. The lions that live with the San rarely attack. By avoiding the lions by day confronting them with fire in the evening and sleeping in shelters at night the San have managed to stay safe. As for the lions they have learned not to see people as easy prey. For both the San and the lions being neighbors is a way of life.

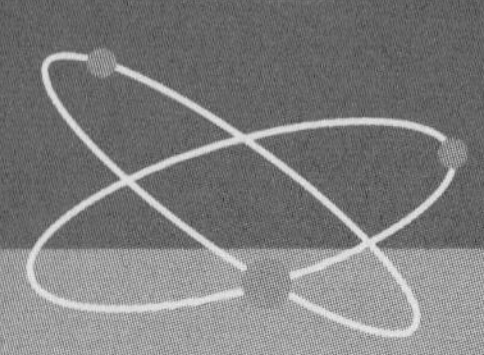

My Favorite Things

List your five favorites in each category. Underline **titles** of movies, books, and TV shows. Put titles of songs in quotation marks.

my TOP 5

My Top 5 Movies

My Top 5 Books

My Top 5 TV Shows

My Top 5 Songs

Bonus: My Top 2 Plays/Musicals

Language Arts

Titles

Brain Box

The titles of movies, magazines, TV shows, plays, newspapers, and books should be underlined or formatted in italics. Examples: *The Lord of the Rings* The Lord of the Rings Put quotation marks around titles of songs and articles.

The Flip

Language Arts

Quotation marks

Write in the missing **quotation marks** in the story.

Giana and her friend Rose were taking turns going off the high and low diving boards. Giana did a flip off the low dive after Rose did one off the high dive. Now it was Giana's turn to do a flip off the high dive. But she was scared.

Let's both jump instead of doing a flip, said Giana. I'll jump off the high dive, and then you jump off the low.

Why? Are you scared to do a flip off the high dive? asked Rose.

No, said Giana.

It's okay if you're scared, said Rose. I won't make fun of you. I promise.

Okay, said Giana. I'm scared.

What are you afraid of? asked Rose.

I'm afraid of doing a belly flop, said Giana.

How about you jump this time, but while you're in midair, you picture yourself doing a flip, said Rose. Then maybe you'll be ready to do a flip next time.

Giana jumped off the high dive, closed her eyes, and pictured herself doing a flip.

Rose asked, So are you ready to do a flip this time?

I think so, Giana said.

Giana jumped, flipped, and landed on her belly, but it didn't hurt too much.

Now it was Rose's turn to flip off the high dive. She hesitated. Now I'm scared *I'm* going to land on my belly, she said, backing away from the edge.

Brain Box

Quotation marks can show what a person says. Place quotation marks before the first word and after the ending punctuation of each quotation.

Whose Shoes?

Write whose items appear in these pictures.

librarians' shoes

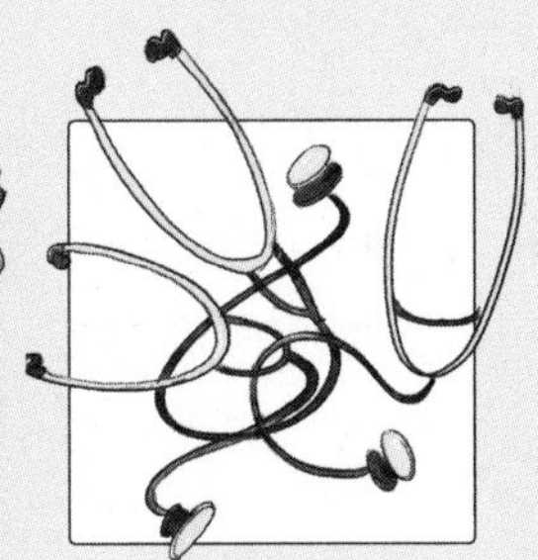

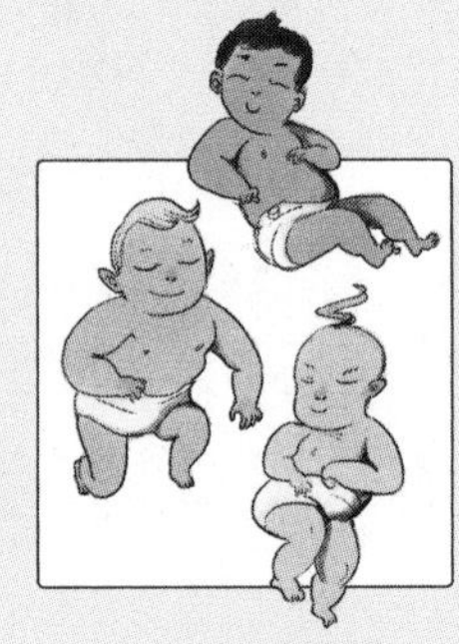
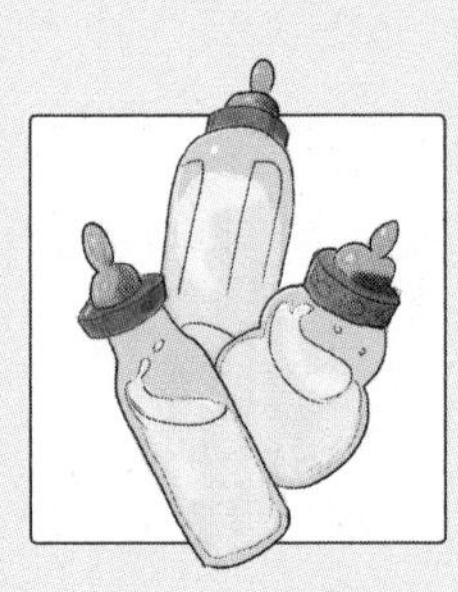

Language Arts

Plural possessives

Brain Box

Plural nouns are made **possessive** by adding an apostrophe after the s.

Example: librarians'

If the plural noun does not end in s, add apostrophe s.

Example: women's.

Dear Diary 1876

Write the **paragraph** symbol ¶ where a new paragraph should begin.

May 10, 1876

Dear Diary,

Today, I went to the Centennial Exposition—the first World's Fair ever to be held in America. And to think, it was held right here in Philadelphia! President Ulysses S. Grant, the emperor of Brazil, and pretty much everybody in Philadelphia were there—not to mention folks who traveled from far and wide. I can't describe all the exhibits, but I'll tell you the highlights. There was tomato ketchup. Very tasty! I also drank root beer made with 16 roots and berries. Not only was it delicious, the poster said it is also good for your blood. I'm feeling healthier already! Second best to the food and drinks was the telephone. This device allows you to talk to your friend without either of you ever leaving home! It was made by Alexander Graham Bell, an American. Not everything at the World's Fair was American, of course. The Italian exhibition had statues of men, women, and children. They looked so real! As for the British, they brought bicycles. These are machines with two wheels—a giant one in front and a tiny one in back. The man demonstrating how they worked sped downhill and appeared to be flying! When the wheel hit a tree root, he really did go flying through the air, over the bicycle, and onto the grass. I wonder if I will ever be so brave as to ride a bicycle. As I write, my mind is full of possibilities. I feel like the world must be full of such things as bicycles. I hope to see them all!

Another innovation that was shown at a World Fair is the hot air balloon. Write a paragraph to describe a hot air balloon to someone who has never seen one.

____

____

____

____

____

Language Arts

Paragraphs

Brain Box

Start a new **paragraph** to begin a new topic, introduce a new speaker, or skip to a new time or place.

46

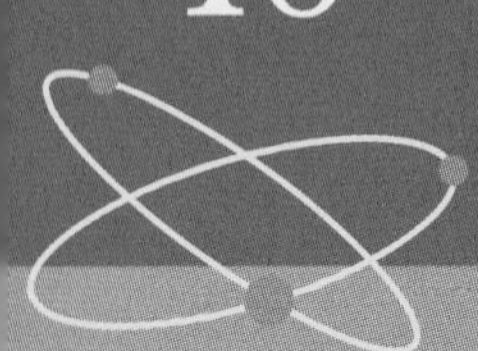

All About Animals

Use your own words to rewrite each **incomplete sentence** as a **complete sentence**. Rewrite each **run-on sentence** as either two sentences or a compound sentence.

If a rat can squeeze through a hole the size of a quarter

Did you know dolphins gossip they chat about good places to find food?

The bats under the bridge

Most monarch butterflies live for only 8 weeks the generation that migrates to Mexico each fall lives for 8 months.

When ants find crumbs

Language Arts

Sentences

Brain Box

A complete sentence needs a subject and a verb. Even with a subject and a verb, a dependent clause by itself is an **incomplete sentence**, or **fragment**.

Example: If you study for the test

Two sentences combined without a conjunction make a **run-on sentence**.

Example: We bicycled to the movies then we played in the park.

Peanut Butter and Jelly

Rewrite the sentences as **compound sentences**.

Modern jelly was invented in the Middle Ages. What we think of as modern peanut butter wasn't invented until the late 19th century.

____

____

At first, peanut butter was served at fancy parties. It was served not with jelly, but with other foods, such as pimientos or watercress.

____

____

Then a businessperson began to sell peanut butter in jars. It became affordable for families.

____

____

In 1928, presliced bread began being sold. That helped kids to make their own sandwiches.

____

____

Peanut butter and jelly sandwiches have been popular ever since. Peanut butter also goes with bananas, apples, or bacon on sandwiches.

____

____

Many children are allergic to peanuts. Some schools do not allow peanut butter in the lunchroom.

____

____

In Europe, children do not eat much peanut butter. They eat a similar spread made of hazelnuts.

____

____

Language Arts

Compound sentences

Brain Box

Short sentences can be combined with a **conjunction** to make **compound sentences**. Examples of conjunctions: and, but, for, nor, or, so, yet

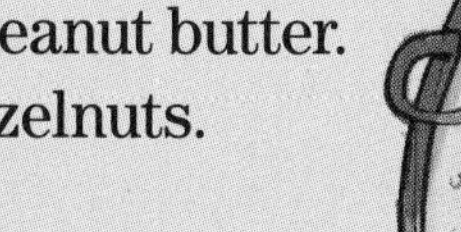

You Be the Teacher

Circle the mistakes on the homework. Look for errors involving commas, capital letters, italics/underlining, quotation marks, plural possessives, sentence fragments, and run-on sentences.

Language Arts

Grammar review

Name: Conrad Cates

Homeroom: 5H

Opossum Facts

Opossums are the only marsupials that live in north america. Other marsupials, including Kangaroos and Koalas, live in australia, new zealand, or south america. All marsupials give birth to extremely small babies twenty baby opossums would fit in a single teaspoon. Once born, baby opossums climb into their mothers pouch, where they drink milk. When they are bigger, they ride around on their Mother's back. Opossums eat a variety of foods, including mice insects birds and slugs. They also scavenge in trash cans for this reason, some people think of opossums as pests. However, usually Raccoons, Dogs, or Cats knock over the garbage cans opossums just eat what they find afterward. In fact, opossums are so harmless that they usually play dead. When they feel threatened.

Write a note to Conrad explaining the capitalization rules he needs to use in his writing.

Reading Comprehension

I ♥ Facts

Read the **nonfiction** essay about the heart shape.

The Heartfelt History of Hearts

Did you know that 10,000-year-old heart-shaped drawings have been found in prehistoric caves? Archaeologists don't know what the heart shape meant to the Cro-Magnon people living at the time, but an ancient coin offers a clue.

A heart shape appears on a very old coin from the African city-state of Cyrene. In this case, historians know that it represents the heart-shaped silphium seed, which was valued for medicinal purposes. Beyond the silphium seed, the heart shape is ubiquitous in nature. Heart-shaped leaves grow on many plants, including squashes, rosebud trees, and morning glory vines. There are also heart-shaped flowers called bleeding hearts. So perhaps the Cro-Magnon people were simply drawing something that they saw in nature.

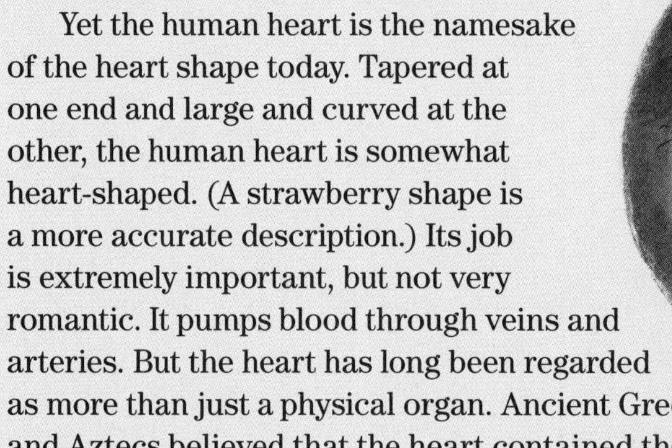

Yet the human heart is the namesake of the heart shape today. Tapered at one end and large and curved at the other, the human heart is somewhat heart-shaped. (A strawberry shape is a more accurate description.) Its job is extremely important, but not very romantic. It pumps blood through veins and arteries. But the heart has long been regarded as more than just a physical organ. Ancient Greeks and Aztecs believed that the heart contained the human soul.

In the Middle Ages, the heart also came to represent love. Men during this time period tried to woo ladies by singing songs, reciting poetry, and offering presents. This practice was called courtly love. Tapestries and illustrated manuscripts show men giving women their hearts (in the form of the heart shape).

Today, the heart shape still symbolizes love, and heart-shaped cards and candy are popular gifts on Valentine's Day. Perhaps you have even doodled a heart in the margin of a notebook. In that way, you share something with people who lived 10,000 years ago.

Write five new facts that you learned from the essay.

____

____

____

____

____

Reading Comprehension

Informational texts

Brain Box

Whether **nonfiction** is read for an assignment or for fun, its purpose is to teach new information.

The Sami

Read the nonfiction story about the reindeer herders.

The Sami: Reindeer Herders

The Sami live in Norway, Sweden, Finland, and Russia, but they are a culture unto themselves. They have their own language, style of clothing, and specific way of making a living.

The Sami are reindeer herders. They follow the herds across the Arctic tundra as the reindeer migrate from their winter to summer grazing grounds. While on the journey, the Sami sleep in cone-shaped tents that can endure 50-mile-per-hour Arctic winds. They wear warm wool clothing and hats that are known for their bright colors and intricate designs.

The reindeer are the Sami's livelihood. The Sami have traditionally eaten the meat, made tools and toys with the antlers, and used the skins for clothing. They even used the tendons as thread. Today, the Sami sell the reindeer to butchers, who use only the meat.

The Sami way of life is changing. They now must maintain fences so that their reindeer do not roam onto private property. Many Sami live in towns and have jobs other than reindeer herding. Few speak the traditional Sami language. But some families continue to herd reindeer and to follow the traditions of their ancestors.

Write the **main idea** MI and **supporting details** SD for each paragraph above.

First Paragraph

MI ____________________

SD ____________________

Second Paragraph

MI ____________________

SD ____________________

SD ____________________

Third Paragraph

MI ____________________

SD ____________________

SD ____________________

Fourth Paragraph

MI ____________________

SD ____________________

SD ____________________

Reading Comprehension

Supporting details

Brain Box

A **main idea** is explained and supported by details. Every good paragraph has one or more **supporting details.**

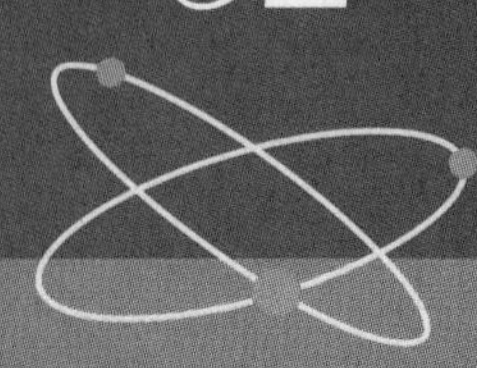

Reading Comprehension

Maps

What a Deal!

This **map** shows the area of the 1803 Louisiana Purchase on top of a modern **map** of the United States. Study the map and answer the questions.

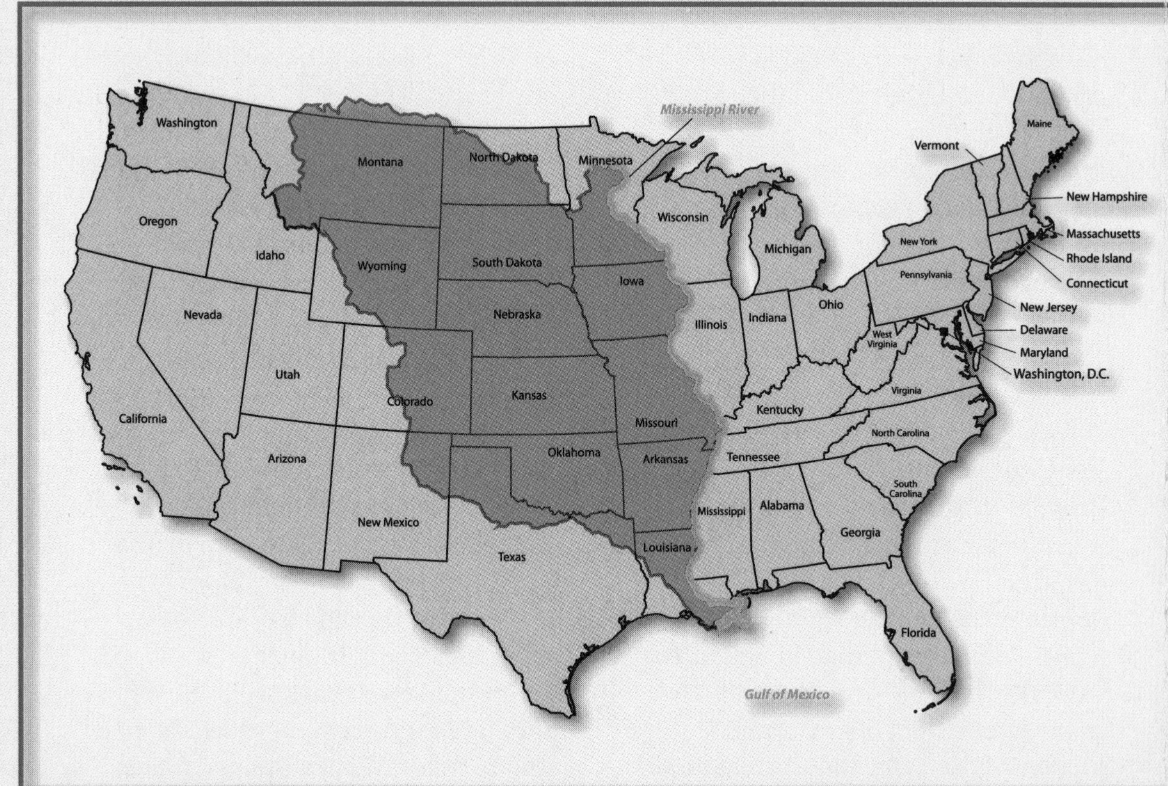

What modern-day states were part of the Louisiana Purchase?

___

What river marks the eastern boundary of the purchase?

___

Was the western or eastern half of Colorado part of the purchase?

___

What large body of salt water borders a part of the purchase?

___

Were any of the Great Lakes part of the Louisiana Purchase?

___

Brain Box

Maps can show **political territories, physical characteristics** (mountains, lakes, etc.), and more, including climate, economics, or resources.

Coming to America

Read the **chart** about immigration and population. Then answer the questions.

Year	U.S. Population	Number of Immigrants
1820	9,638,453	143,439
1830	12,860,702	599,125
1840	17,063,353	1,713,251
1850	23,191,876	2,598,214
1860	31,443,321	2,314,825
1870	38,558,371	2,812,191
1880	50,189,209	5,246,613
1890	62,979,766	3,687,564
1900	76,212,168	8,795,386

Did the population decrease or increase from 1820 to 1830?

____

How many people lived in America in 1840?

____

How many more people lived in America in 1900 than in 1820?

____

In what year did the most immigrants arrive?

____

Based on this chart, how might you explain the large increase in population from 1820 to 1900?

____

____

Reading Comprehension

Charts

Brain Box

A **chart** presents **data** in an organized format so that the data is easy to understand and analyze.

54

Energy Sources

Read the **pie chart** and answer the questions.

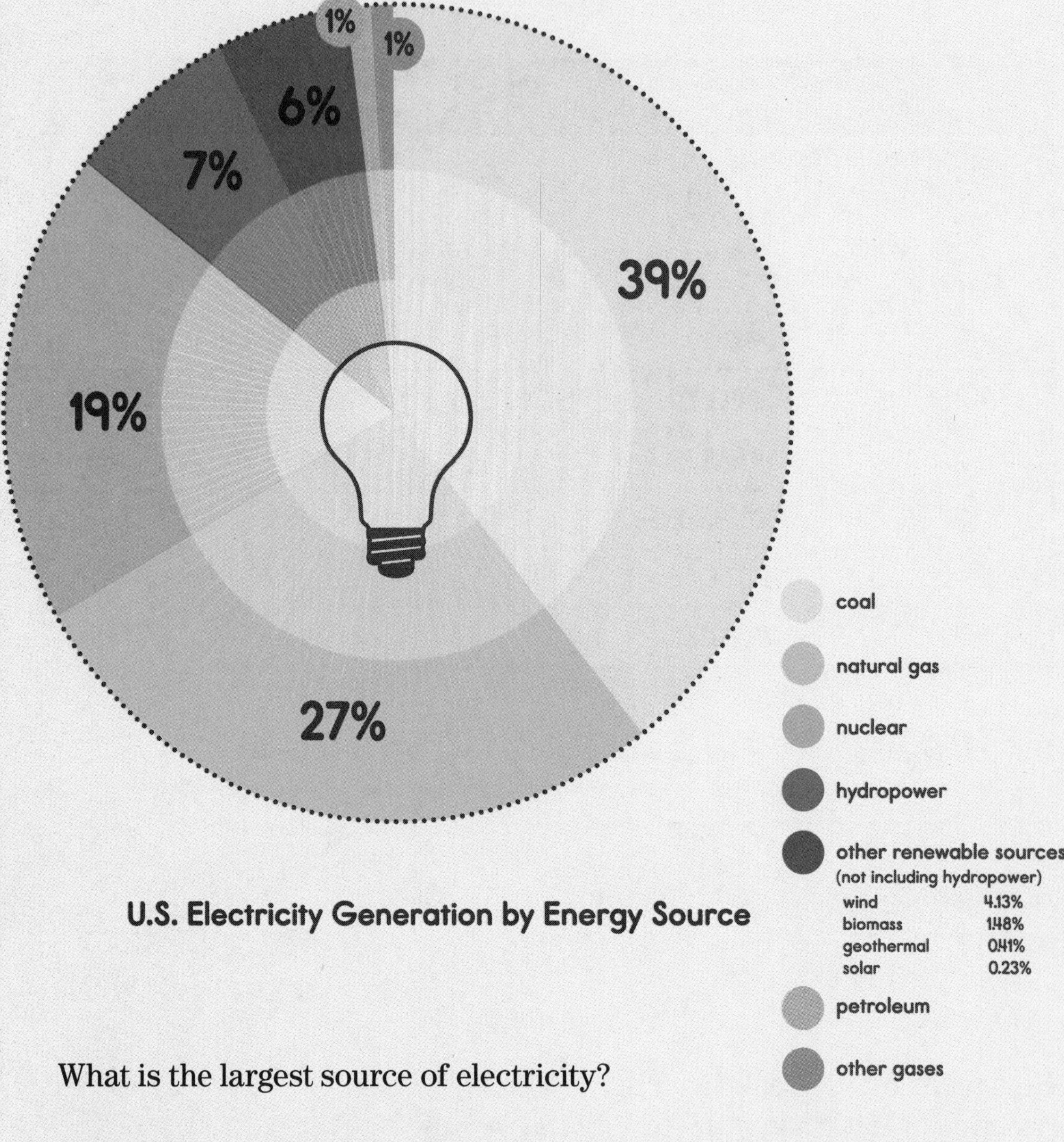

U.S. Electricity Generation by Energy Source

Reading Comprehension

Charts

What is the largest source of electricity?

____

What is the largest renewable energy source of electricity?

____

What percentage of U.S. electricity does wind generate?

____

What percentage of electricity does nuclear power provide?

____

Coal, natural gas, and petroleum are all fossil fuels. What percentage of electricity is currently generated by fossil fuels?

____

Brain Box

Pie charts show how a whole is divided into portions.

Fossil Fuels

Read the **diagram** about how coal forms. Then answer the questions.

How Coal Forms Over Millions of Years

1. In prehistoric swamps, trees and other woody plants die.

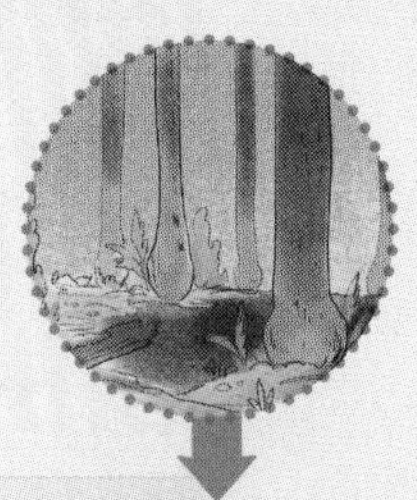

2. Through natural processes, the dead plants are buried underground.

3. As bacteria and other organisms eat the dead plants, they decompose.

4. Over time, the decomposed plants are pushed further underground.

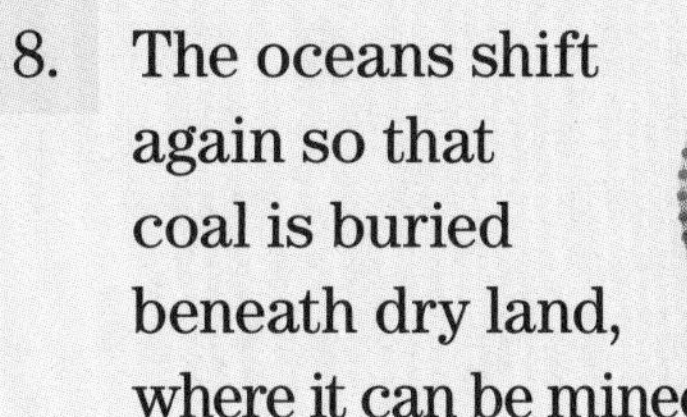

5. Oceans shift and cover the ground under which the plants are buried.

6. The decomposing plants become peat, another form of fuel.

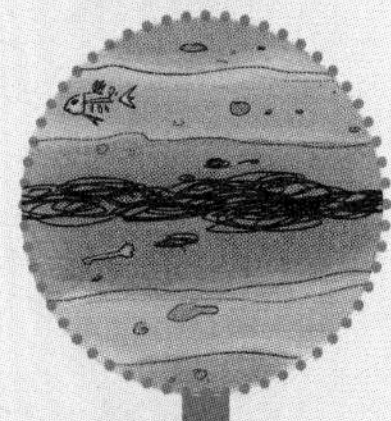

7. Finally after millions of years, they become coal.

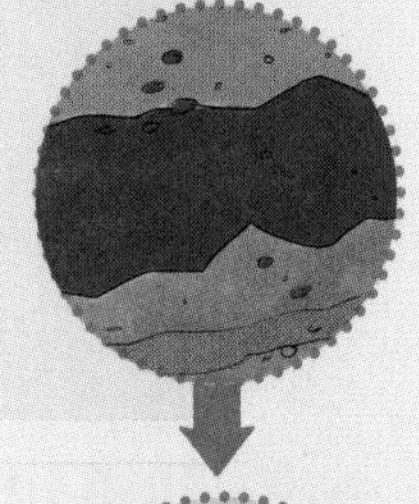

8. The oceans shift again so that coal is buried beneath dry land, where it can be mined.

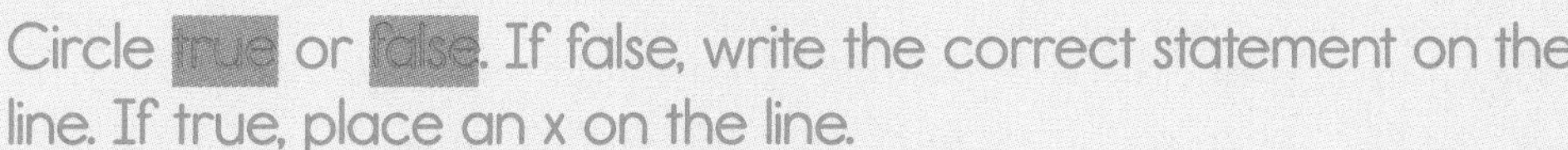

Circle true or false. If false, write the correct statement on the line. If true, place an x on the line.

Coal forms from dinosaur remains. true false

____

The plants are buried through natural processes. true false

____

Bacteria eat the dead plants. true false

____

Coal is formed by desert plants. true false

____

Reading Comprehension

Drawings and diagrams

Brain Box

Drawings and **diagrams** can show how something works.

Revolutionary Times!

Read the **timeline** about the Revolutionary War.

October 14, 1774	The First Continental Congress (twelve delegates from the thirteen colonies) opposes Britain and asserts the rights to "life, liberty, and property."
February 1, 1775	Congress prepares for war.
February 9, 1775	Britain declares Massachusetts to be in a state of rebellion.
March 23, 1775	American politician Patrick Henry gives his famous speech in Virginia, declaring, "Give me liberty or give me death!"
April 18, 1775	700 British soldiers are deployed to Concord, Massachusetts. Paul Revere warns the colonists.
April 19, 1775	The "shot heard round the world" is fired, beginning the Revolution.
April 23, 1775	Colonial soldiers place Boston under siege.
May 10, 1775	George Washington is named commander-in-chief of the revolutionary army.
June 17, 1775	The Battle of Bunker Hill is the first major battle in the war, with a loss of about 1,000 British soldiers and 400 revolutionary soldiers.
March 4–17, 1776	The British pull out of Boston, ending the nearly yearlong siege.
May 2, 1776	France promises financial support to the revolutionary war effort.
July 4, 1776	The United States declares its independence from Britain.
August 27–29, 1776	Washington's army is defeated in the Battle of Long Island. A series of defeats follows.
December 25–26, 1776	Washington leads a surprise attack on 1,500 British soldiers, who surrender, turning the tide of the war.
February 27, 1782	The British House of Commons votes to discontinue the war in America.
September 3, 1783	The United States and England sign the Treaty of Paris. The war is officially over.

Answer the questions.

When was the Battle of Long Island?

____

What happened on May 2, 1776?

____

What did Patrick Henry say on March 23, 1775?

____

When was the "shot heard round the world" fired?

____

Between what two events should the following item go?
July 10, 1778: France declares war against Britain.

____

How did France first promise to support America in the war?

____

About how many soldiers were lost in the Battle of Bunker Hill?

____

Who won the Battle of Long Island?

____

When was the Treaty of Paris signed?

____

How long did the siege of Boston last?

____

Brain Box

A **timeline** shows a sequence of events.

Roping the Wind

Read the **article.** Then answer the questions.

Greenville Students Harness the Wind

Students at Greenville Middle School have raised $20,000 to purchase a wind turbine for their school. The turbine will supply up to 20 percent of the school's energy. It will also teach students at the school about renewable energy.

Principal Ana Martin said, "This is going to save the school money on energy sources and will teach the students first-hand about renewable energy sources. And it has already taught students how to accomplish civic goals."

The effort was led by the Green Team, a club made up of 37 seventh and eighth grade members. Club president Magda Kita, 14, said, "We thought the biggest impact our club could have would be to help our school switch to clean energy."

To raise money, the Green Team held a recycling drive, collecting used carpeting, clothing, and electronics, which they sold back to various manufacturers. They also sought sponsorships from local businesses, whose names appear on plaques on the wind turbine.

Jack Ahn, who is the owner of Kokoroko Maki House, is one of the 10 gold sponsors. He said the Green Team members frequented his restaurant after school. "They are good kids," he said. "They had this big dream and I wanted to support them."

Reading Comprehension

News article

How much money have the students raised for the wind turbine?

____

What is the name of the club that raised the money?

____

How did the club raise money?

____

What are two things Principal Ana Martin likes about the turbine?

____

What is one direct quote from the article? Who said it?

____

Brain Box

News articles in print or on the web can tell you what is happening throughout the world.

Holy Guacamole!

Read the **recipe**. Then answer the questions.

Guacamole Dip

Ingredients:
4 avocados
1 tomato
1 onion (optional)
1 lime
1 teaspoon salt
Tortilla chips

Directions:

1. Cut the avocados into fourths. Peel off the skin. Discard the skin and the pits.
2. In a large bowl, mash the avocados with a fork.
3. Slice the tomato. Add to the avocados.
4. Chop up the onion if using. Add to the avocado mixture.
5. Slice the lime in half and squeeze the juice into the mixture.
6. Add the salt.
7. Stir until all the ingredients are well combined.
8. Serve with chips.

How many avocados are needed?

____

What step in the directions could you skip and why?

____

How many bowls will you need to make this dip?

____

What kitchen tools will you need?

____

Will you mash or chop the avocado?

____

How will you get the juice out of the lime?

____

Brain Box

A **recipe** tells you how to cook or bake a particular food dish.

Step by Step

Read the **instructions.**

How to Assemble Your Snow Cone Maker

Machine Base	**Motor**	**Shaver**	**Lid**	**Bowl**

1. Make sure the machine base (A) is unplugged.
2. Place the motor (B) inside the hollow area of the machine base (A). Press down until it clicks into place.
3. Align the shaver (C) with the machine base (A). Turn it until it clicks into place.
4. To make a snow cone, fill the shaver (C) with ice cubes. Put on the shaver lid (D). Put the bowl (E) under the shaver. Press Start. The machine will stop automatically when the ice is shaved.

Brain Box

Instructions teach you how to do something.

Name the parts of the snow cone machine. Write the number 1 next to the first part you need, then number the other parts in the order you need them to build your snow cone maker.

D ______________

C ______________

E ______________

B ______________

A ______________

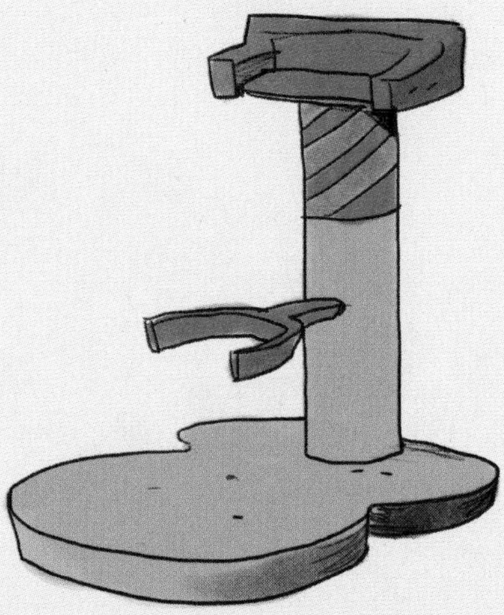

Lightbulb Moment!

Read the **persuasive essay**. Then write the **opinion** and **supporting evidence**.

Turn Them Off!

by Magda Kita, Green Team President

Our school needs to turn off lights and all electronic devices at night. If you drive by the school at night, you can see lights on in almost every window. In the morning, you can see that the beverage machines in the cafeteria and the computers in the library have been left on overnight. This wastes energy, and wasting energy wastes money. The Seattle School District saved $20,000 just by turning off beverage machine lights at night. If all American workers turned off their computers at night, they would save a total of $2.8 billion. Imagine how much our school could save by shutting off lights, computers, and beverage machine lights at night.

Opinion:

____

Supporting Evidence:

____

____

____

____

____

____

____

____

____

____

Reading Comprehension

Fact and opinion

Brain Box

A **persuasive essay** is used to try to get someone to do or agree with something. The opinions stated need **evidence** to support them.

Pink Lake

Circle Fact if the statement is a fact. Circle Opinion if it's an opinion.

Lake Hillier in Australia is bubble gum pink.	Fact	Opinion
When scooped up in a clear glass, the water still appears pink.	Fact	Opinion
Pink is a pretty color.	Fact	Opinion
Lake Hillier isn't the only pink lake in Australia.	Fact	Opinion
There is a pink lake called Pink Lake.	Fact	Opinion
Lake Hillier and Pink Lake are salt lakes.	Fact	Opinion
The water is full of salt-loving algae and bacteria.	Fact	Opinion
It is safe to swim in pink lakes.	Fact	Opinion
Salt lakes are better than freshwater lakes.	Fact	Opinion
Every lake should be pink.	Fact	Opinion

Reading Comprehension

Fact and opinion

Brain Box

A **fact** is something that can be proven to be true. An **opinion** states what someone thinks, feels, or believes.

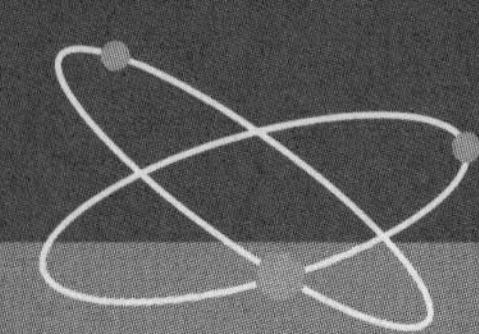

Naked Mole . . . Ants?

Read the short essays. Circle whether they are organized in **chronological order** or by **comparing and contrasting**.

Reading Comprehension

Organization

50 States in 50 Weeks

This year, my brothers and I are taking off school to visit every state in America. We started in Kansas, where we hiked in the Flint Hills. Next, we traveled through Missouri, home of the St. Louis Arch. In Illinois, we toured Chicago's museums. We'll watch a baseball game in Indiana next week. I can't wait to reach the East Coast states next month.

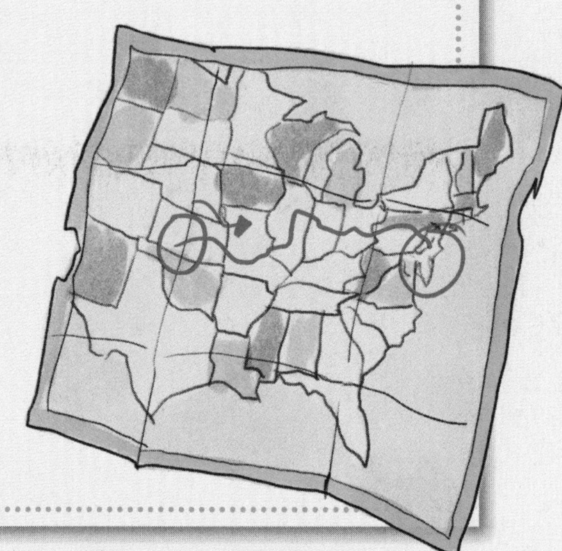

chronological order   comparing and contrasting

Swamps and Marshes

Swamps and marshes are both wetlands. However, they are different in that a swamp has trees, such as mangroves and cypresses. A marsh does not have trees but rather has grasses and sedges. Both swamps and marshes can be either saltwater, freshwater, or a mixture. Both serve as nurseries for fish and other wildlife. Whether the vegetation is woody or grassy, it provides lots of places for fish and other baby animals to hide from predators that would eat them easily in other environments.

chronological order   comparing and contrasting

Brain Box

There are different ways to **organize** an essay. For instance, it can be written in **chronological order**, which is the order in which the events occurred. Or it can **compare and contrast** two or more things by showing how they are alike and different.

Naked Mole . . . Ants?

Naked mole rats are mammals, which means they are not related to ants at all. And yet the two animals have surprisingly similar lifestyles. First, they both live in colonies. Like ant colonies, naked mole rat colonies have a single queen. She is the only one in the colony that can have babies. The other naked mole rats are workers that gather food, dig burrows, and take care of the queen. Ant workers perform the same jobs. Naked mole rats and ants also follow trails that colony members mark with their scents. Scientists have discovered other vertebrates that live similarly to ants, but none so similarly as the naked mole rat.

chronological order   comparing and contrasting

Strange Fossils

Did you know that much of today's dry land was once underwater? One example is the North American Inland Sea. In the early Cretaceous Period, tectonic plates shifted, creating lower land in the center of North America. The sea level was also much higher at the time than it is now because of a warmer climate. By 100 million years ago, the inland sea covered much of Canada and twenty U.S. states. Later in the Cretaceous Period, the land was uplifted. Over time, the seaway shrank and ultimately disappeared. Recently, fossils of giant sea reptiles have been found in states such as Kansas.

chronological order   comparing and contrasting

66

Volcano!

Read the **secondhand** and **eyewitness accounts** of the eruption of Mount Vesuvius. Then answer the questions.

Reading Comprehension

Points of view

Brain Box

An event can be described from different **points of view**. An **eyewitness account** is the point of view of a person who witnessed an event. A **secondhand account** is the point of view of a person who was not there but who learned about an event from other sources.

Secondhand Account:

Article about Mount Vesuvius

Mount Vesuvius erupted in 79 CE, sending a mushroom cloud of gas, ash, and rock into the sky. The people living nearby hadn't known that Vesuvius was an active volcano and were caught off guard. However, those who fled right away were able to survive. Some people instead chose to take cover and wait out the eruption. For people living in the towns closest to the volcano, Herculaneum and Pompeii, staying put was a disastrous choice.

Ashes and pumice rained down on their roofs, and some people died when buildings collapsed from the weight. But that wasn't the most dangerous effect of the volcano. The deadliest result of the eruption occurred when the mushroom cloud rising above the volcano collapsed several times, causing 570°F gases and ash to surge down the mountain. The gases and ash reached Herculaneum and Pompeii, killing everyone who remained in the towns.

Pliny the Younger was a scholar who lived in Misenum. Misenum was farther away from the volcano than Herculaneum and Pompeii, and the townspeople there survived the volcano. Pliny later wrote to a friend describing the events he witnessed during the eruption. His letters have been preserved for thousands of years and have helped historians understand what happened during the eruption.

Eyewitness Account:

Excerpts from the Pliny Letter

Ashes were already falling, not as yet very thickly. I looked round: a dense black cloud was coming up behind us, spreading over the earth like a flood. "Let us leave the road while we can still see," I said, "or we shall be knocked down and trampled underfoot in the dark by the crowd behind."

You could hear the shrieks of women, the wailing of infants, and the shouting of men; some were calling their parents, others their children or their wives, trying to recognize them by their voices. People bewailed their own fate or that of their relatives, and there were some who prayed for death in their terror of dying.

At last the darkness thinned and dispersed into smoke or cloud; then there was genuine daylight, and the sun actually shone out, but yellowish as it is during an eclipse. We were terrified to see everything changed, buried deep in ashes like snowdrifts. We returned to Misenum where we attended to our physical needs as best we could, and then spent an anxious night alternating between hope and fear.

In what year did Mount Vesuvius erupt? ______________________

Why were the people not prepared for the event? ______________________

What is one way that historians have learned about the volcano?

____

Why did Pliny want to get off the road while fleeing from the volcano?

____

Circle the details told in the secondhand account.

Those who fled Herculaneum and Pompeii right away survived.

The surges of gases and ash were the deadliest effect of the volcano.

The people were terrified to see their town buried in ashes.

Pliny's letters would survive for thousands of years.

Circle the details told in the eyewitness account.

Men and women were shrieking and yelling.

There was a risk of being trampled as people fled.

A dark cloud spread over the land.

In some places, the temperature during the eruption reached 570°F.

68

Meet the Neanderthals

Read the story.

Reading Comprehension

Main ideas and details

The Bison Wrestler

Jon and his uncle had walked for months in search of reliable hunting grounds, and here the bison were plentiful. As time passed, however, the days grew colder than anything Jon had experienced. Animal furs kept them warm at night, but during the day, Jon and his uncle shivered as they tracked the herd.

Then one morning, Jon woke to growling and grunting. He stepped outside the cave in which he and his uncle were camped. There, he saw a man—larger than he and his uncle—wrestling a bison. The bison violently butted heads with the man, who fell backward. Jon thought the blow would have killed the man. Incredibly, he climbed to his feet and stabbed the bison with a spear. Then the man, bleeding and limping, dragged the heavy bison behind him through the woods.

Jon followed him, ducking behind trees so that he wouldn't be seen. He was concerned about the man's injury and awestruck that he had survived the bison's attack. Jon also now realized that the man was wearing animal fur. Jon wanted to find out more about the man's people; how did they make their warm clothing?

The man reached a cave and ducked inside. Jon knew it was risky, but he emerged from the shadows and stood in the doorway of the cave. Two girls jumped to their feet and pointed spears at him. They were big, like the man, and wore the same fur blankets as clothing, but Jon thought that they must be his own age. Their brows were large and their skin was white. One girl's face was speckled, like a spotted bird's egg.

Jon smiled at them and held up his hands. Who were these strange people? What could they teach him about this strange land?

Brain Box

The **main idea** of a story is supported by **details**.

Write the **supporting details** for the **main idea**.

Main idea

Jon is observing his new environment and the people who live there.

First supporting detail

It's colder than Jon has ever experienced.

Second supporting detail

______

Third supporting detail

______

Fourth supporting detail

______

Fifth supporting detail

______

Sixth supporting detail

______

Write what happens next in the story.

______

______

______

______

______

______

______

______

Reading Comprehension

Main ideas and details

The Snow Queen

Read the excerpt from Hans Christian Andersen's fairy tale, "The Snow Queen."

The walls of the palace were formed of drifted snow, and the windows and doors of the cutting winds. There were more than a hundred rooms in it, all as if they had been formed with snow blown together. The largest of them extended for several miles; they were all lit up by the vivid light of the aurora, and they were so large and empty, so icy cold and glittering!

There were no amusements here, not even a little bear's ball, when the storm might have been the music, and the bears could have danced on their hind legs and shown their good manners. There were no pleasant games of snapdragon, or touch, or even a gossip over the tea table, for the young-lady foxes. Empty, vast, and cold were the halls of the Snow Queen. The flickering flame of the Northern Lights could be plainly seen, whether they rose high or low in the heavens, from every part of the castle.

In the midst of its empty, endless hall of snow was a frozen lake, broken on its surface into a thousand forms; each piece resembled another, from being in itself perfect as a work of art, and in the center of this lake sat the Snow Queen, when she was at home. She called the lake "The Mirror of Reason," and said that it was the best, and indeed the only one, in the world.

Reading Comprehension

Illustration

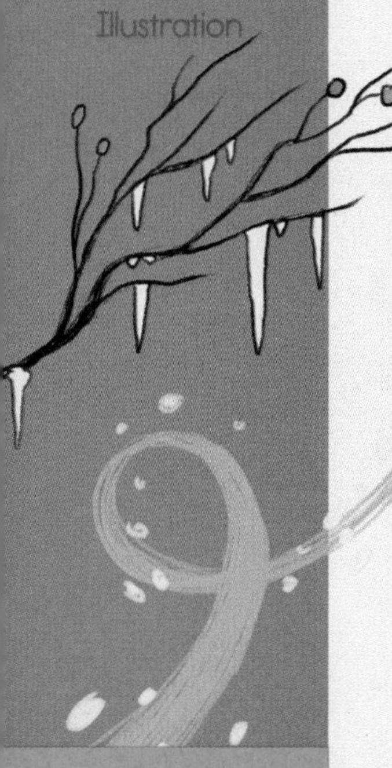

List details from the story that could be included in an **illustration**.

____

____

____

____

____

____

____

____

Brain Box

An **illustration** is a piece of artwork that is part of a book. Illustrations contribute to the meaning, tone, and beauty of the text.

What Happened?

Read each paragraph. Circle the correct **inference** or **inferences**.

Marnie wanted to make brownies and saw that her family had a box of brownie mix in the kitchen cabinet. She poured the mix, water, and oil into a bowl. Then she opened the refrigerator to get the eggs. "Oh no!" she said.

A. Marnie remembered she doesn't like chocolate.

B. Marnie's brother was going to eat all the brownies.

C. There were no eggs.

D. The oven was broken.

Austin checked his pocket for the necklace. It was still there. He rushed to his locker, which was next to Elsa's. There, Elsa was staring dreamily at her locker door.

"I have something to tell you," Austin said.

"I have something to tell you, too," she said.

"You go first," Austin said.

Elsa said, "Liam asked me to go out with him!"

Austin's stomach dropped. "Oh, that's great," he said. "Yeah, I remember you saying you liked him earlier this year. I didn't know you still did. But you do, so that's great."

"What were you going to say?" Elsa asked.

"Umm . . ." Austin said.

A. Austin was going to tell Elsa that he liked her.

B. Elsa doesn't like necklaces.

C. Austin was going to give Elsa the necklace.

D. Liam is mean to Austin.

Reading Comprehension

Inferences

Brain Box

An **inference** is a logical conclusion. You can make an **inference** by combining what you already know with what the author has told you.

Jimmy and Kate

Read the story about a family living in New York in the late 1890s.

Though the sun was not yet up, Jimmy's shirt already stuck to him with sweat. His sister Kate was still asleep on the floor. She had kicked off her thin blanket, which was for comfort—not warmth—on this sweltering summer night. Though they always had blankets and food enough to fill their bellies, they'd never owned beds. Those were for rich people!

Jimmy recounted the money in his pockets. Two dollars. Actually, he was rich! For today, anyway. He tiptoed to the door. Opening it, he winced at the creaking noise.

"Jimmy?" Kate said groggily.

Jimmy paused. "Go back to sleep, Kate," he said.

"But I'm coming with you."

He shook his head. "Not today. Mom needs your help."

Jimmy frowned as he left the apartment. He had wanted to wish his sister a happy birthday, but he was afraid it would ruin the surprise. He ran past the corner where he usually sold apples. He needed to make his way downtown.

Meanwhile, back at the apartment, Kate made porridge for her mother, who had been working late the night before, and herself. Her mother woke up to the smell.

"Happy birthday," her mother said. "I should be making breakfast for you."

"Very well, then. I'd like a nice ham. And some bread and your finest marmalade, please."

"Coming right up!" her mother said. They laughed. Ham and marmalade were only on the menu in the fancy restaurants and large mansions uptown.

"So what are we making today?" Kate asked.

"A dress," her mother said. She was a seamstress who usually sewed loads and loads of boring shirts. A dress was a bit more fun. Time flew by as Kate and her mother sewed. They didn't talk much, but sometimes one sang a few lines from a song and the other joined in. Soon it was nearly nightfall.

The sun finally sank beneath the buildings, and the heat let up. Just then Jimmy opened the door.

"How was your day?" their mother asked.

He shook his head. "I didn't sell a single apple."

"Not one?" Kate asked. No wonder he'd forgotten her birthday. He was always so worried about selling apples because of bad days like this.

Then, from behind his back, Jimmy took a doll. "I took a trip downtown instead!" he said. "Happy birthday! From Mom and me."

Kate wiped a tear from her eye. It was her first doll. She was beautiful.

Circle the character for which each statement is true.

He/She worries about work.	Kate	Jimmy
He/She likes to surprise people.	Kate	Jimmy
He/She is cheerful while working.	Kate	Jimmy
He/She is helpful.	Kate	Jimmy
He/She can keep a secret.	Kate	Jimmy

Match the statements about the **characters** with the corresponding details from the story.

Jimmy and Kate's mother is overworked.

Jimmy cares about his sister.

Jimmy often thinks about money.

Kate is used to helping her mother.

Kate has a good imagination.

Kate is grateful for gifts.

Jimmy gives his sister her first doll.

Jimmy recounts the money in his pocket.

Kate sheds a tear over how beautiful her first doll is.

Kate asks her mother for a fancy breakfast.

Kate knows that sewing dresses is more fun than sewing shirts.

Their mother was still asleep because she had worked late the night before.

74

A Different Side of the Story

Read the story. Then answer the questions.

Reading Comprehension

Point of view

The Pea and the Princess

Once upon a time, there was a beautiful pea. The pea dreamed of being left alone in its pod. In the castle beside the garden, there lived a prince. He dreamed of finding a real princess. But that should have nothing to do with the pea. Right? Am I an expert at knowing who is a real princess? No, I'm not. See, I'm the pea.

The prince had searched high and low for a real princess, and apparently all he could find were fake princesses. Then one day, a woman came to the castle claiming to be a princess.

"Really?" said the queen. "*You're* a princess?"

"Yes," said the princess.

But the queen didn't take the princess's word for it. I think a reasonable course of action would have been to send a message to the princess's alleged kingdom asking if she was a real princess there.

But the queen had a different idea. Some might say she had a *pea-brained* idea. "I know," thought the queen, "let's drag Pea into this mess and make his life miserable!"

So the queen plucked me from the vine and from my pod.

Then she covered me with ten mattresses. Ten! And on top of all of them, the princess lay down.

"We'll see if the so-called princess can feel that!" the queen said as she walked out.

Well, I don't know about the princess, but I can tell you who did feel it. Me. Pea. Pea felt it!

The next morning, the queen knocked on the door. "Good morning, princess," the queen said. "How did you sleep?"

"Terrible!" I blurted out. "I am bruised and in a great deal of pain."

"Wonderful!" the queen said, thinking it was the princess who had spoken.

When the queen burst in the door, the princess, who had been dozing away, woke up.

"You passed the test," the queen said. "You're a real princess!"

But was she really a real princess? Don't ask me. As I said, I'm not an expert on princesses. I'm just a pea. A smashed pea.

Brain Box

In a story, **point of view** refers to who is telling the story. Point of view can affect how a story is told.

What does Pea want?

____

What does the prince want?

____

From whose point of view is this story told?

____

How does Pea think the queen should determine whether or not the princess is a real princess?

____

What does Pea say the queen is thinking when she decides to pick Pea?

____

What mix-up occurs in this story that leads the queen to believe the princess passed the test?

____

Draw an illustration to go with the story, perhaps from the Pea's point of view.

Reading Comprehension

Genre

What Kind of Story?

Read the description of the different **genres** and then circle the correct genre.

Realistic Fiction

Setting: the present

Plot: events that could happen in real life

Historical Fiction

Setting: the past

Plot: the way events in real life could have happend

Mystery

Setting: usually the past or present

Plot: the solving of a puzzle, usually a crime

Fantasy

Setting: usually a world that is full of magic

Plot: often involves a quest or a battle between forces of good and evil

Science Fiction

Setting: usually the future or an outer space world

Plot: often involves a quest or battle with elements based on scientific theories

As soon as the teacher turned her back, Lily stared out the window again. There were the usual flowering trees, the dog that was always left outside, and the squirrels raiding the compost pile. But now Lily also saw a man carrying a large duffel bag. And now she saw that there was a hole dug in his yard. He lowered the bag into the hole. Then he disappeared for a moment and came back with a tree for planting. He placed that in the hole, too. Lily thought that he must be pretending that the hole was for the tree when really it was for the bag. But what was in the bag? "Lily!" the teacher said.

realistic fiction | historical fiction | mystery | fantasy | science fiction

Brain Box

A **genre** is a category or type of artistic work with a particular style, form, or content.

Blake stared straight ahead as he made his way down the hall. He wondered if the other students could tell he was different. He hadn't been different at his old school. But this school was in Verona Hills, and that meant the students were rich, which meant their parents had designed them to be genetically perfect or as perfect as possible. (Scientists were still learning about genes that made people tall, good looking, smart, and athletic.)

realistic fiction | historical fiction | mystery | fantasy | science fiction

Where Liana was from, the mermaids had tails in every color, just like the other creatures that lived in the coral reef. But here, the ocean colors were icy blue and white. The mermaids' tails were all white, too. They wore coats that made them look like polar bears.

realistic fiction | historical fiction | mystery | fantasy | science fiction

Lottie awoke choking on dirt. The sod ceiling had partially collapsed again. Well, better dirt than mud, which is what they slept in when it rained. She had heard that along riversides, people were building big log cabins. But here in the sea of grass, there wasn't a single tree to be chopped down for shelter.

realistic fiction | historical fiction | mystery | fantasy | science fiction

Miguel had studied all night for the math test. He'd hardly slept a wink. As he walked to school that morning, past the suburban homes and falling autumn leaves, an idea popped into his head. What if he simply pretended to be sick today? Then he'd have the entire day to study for the test. He'd take the exam tomorrow and ace it, but would he feel guilty about lying?

realistic fiction | historical fiction | mystery | fantasy | science fiction

Brain Box

Fiction genres can include: **realistic fiction**, **historical fiction**, **mystery**, **fantasy**, and **science fiction**. Books within each genre share characteristics. Some books overlap genres.

78

What a Character!

Read the paragraphs. Then circle the highlighted word or words that complete each sentence correctly.

Reading Comprehension

Characters

Makayla took a deep breath. Then she belted out the last word of the song. The auditorium erupted in cheers. She smiled. Then she caught a glimpse of Lia in the back of the room. Her arms were folded against her chest. She was scowling. Lia was Makayla's best friend, but she was the only one not clapping.

Makayla shows that she is happy about her performance through her **words** **actions**.

Lia shows that she is not happy for Makayla through her **words** **actions**.

Lia may have wished **she was chosen to sing the solo** **she had brought Makayla flowers**.

There was a commotion on the playground, and Deeandra ran over to see what was happening. Deeandra couldn't believe her eyes. Her brother Dale was wrestling another boy. She had seen him stand up for himself, but never like this. He was always smiling and joking around. Now, his face was beet red and he had the other boy pinned. She rushed over and pulled Dale off the boy. Dale's arms thrashed, and she could now hear that he was sobbing. She hugged him close until he finally stood still.

The other boy stood up and laughed.

"It's okay, Dale," Deeandra said, glaring at the other boy. "Just tell me what happened."

Deeandra shows that she cares about her brother through her **words** **actions** **words and actions**.

Dale shows that he is upset through his **words** **actions** **words and actions**.

Deeandra can't believe that her brother is fighting because he is usually **scared** **mild-mannered**.

Coach Daniels signaled for Joshua to come over. "You're going in," Coach said. "You throw harder than anyone on this team. You just need to throw strikes."

Joshua's heart pounded as he took the pitcher's mound. His hands shook. He wound up and threw. The batter fell to the ground to avoid being hit in the head. Joshua fought back a lump in his throat.

"Relax," Coach said. "Throw strikes."

But Joshua knew those were two things he could never do. He closed his eyes, wound up again, and prepared for doom.

Coach Daniels shows that he has faith in Joshua through his **words** **actions** **words and actions**.

Joshua is someone who **is confident but lacks talent** **is talented but lacks confidence**.

Reading Comprehension

Characters

Brain Box

The people in a work of fiction are called **characters**. You can learn about the characters through their actions, thoughts, and speech.

80

Summer Crush

Read the **poem** by William Shakespeare. Then answer the questions.

Sonnet 18

Shall I compare thee to a summer's day? — Quatrain 1
Thou art more lovely and more temperate.
Rough winds do shake the darling buds of May,
And summer's lease hath all too short a date.

Sometime too hot the eye of heaven shines, — Quatrain 2
And often is his gold complexion dimm'd;
And every fair from fair sometime declines,
By chance, or nature's changing course, untrimm'd;

But thy eternal summer shall not fade — Quatrain 3
Nor lose possession of that fair thou ow'st;
Nor shall Death brag thou wander'st in his shade,
When in eternal lines to time thou grow'st;

So long as men can breathe or eyes can see, — Couplet
So long lives this, and this gives life to thee.

Reading Comprehension

Poetry

Brain Box

Stanzas, **meter**, and **rhyme** provide the structure of poems.

A **stanza** consists of lines in a poem that are grouped together. In an English sonnet, there are always three 4-line **stanzas** called **quatrains** followed by a 2-line **couplet**.

Meter is the rhythm of the poem. A **sonnet** is written in **iambic pentameter**, meaning that each line has 10 syllables. Syllables 2, 4, 6, 8, and 10 are stressed.

Rhyme is the repetition of the ending sounds of words, often occurring at the end of a line. Rhymed words commonly share all sounds following the word's last stressed syllable.

What is the first quatrain about?

a. Comparing the loved one to a summer's day

b. The fun of summer

c. The windiness of May

In the first quatrain, which two pairs of syllables rhyme?

a. "day" and "-rate," "May" and "date"

b. "shall" and "rough," "thou" and "and"

c. "day" and "May," "-rate" and "date"

How could the second quatrain be paraphrased?

a. Gold is a valuable metal.

b. The beauty of some things fades with time.

c. It can get extremely hot during summer.

What is the theme of this poem?

a. Nature isn't as beautiful as most people think.

b. Beauty in nature fades, but the beauty of the loved one never will.

c. Everything is beautiful in its own way.

Reading Comprehension

Poetry

No! Vember

Read the poem. Then complete the sentences.

"November" by Thomas Hood

No sun—no moon!
No morn—no noon—
No dawn—no dusk—no proper time of day.
No warmth, no cheerfulness, no healthful ease,
No comfortable feel in any member—
No shade, no shine, no butterflies, no bees,
No fruits, no flowers, no leaves, no birds!
November!

"Moon" rhymes with ________________.

"Ease" rhymes with ________________.

"Member" rhymes with ________________.

"Dawn" and "dusk," "shade" and "shine," and "fruits" and "flowers" are examples of ________________.

Write three more lines for this poem, using at least one **sound effect**.

No ____

No ____

No ____

____

____

Brain Box

Poets use **sound effects** to reinforce meaning.

Alliteration: words that start with the same letter or sound close together.

Internal rhyme: rhyme that occurs within one line of a poem.

Onomatopoeia: words that mimic sounds.

Rhyme scheme: the pattern of rhyming the last sounds of the lines.

Crossword Puzzle

Across

1 A _________ consists of lines in a poem that are grouped together.

4 An _________ is a piece of artwork that is part of a book.

6 A _________ presents organized data.

9 Persuasive arguments need _________ to support them.

10 _________ refers to words that mimic sounds.

12 An _________ expresses what someone thinks, feels, or believes.

13 _________ is the rhythm of the poem.

Down

2 The use of groups of words beginning with the same letter or sound is called _________.

3 A _________ is something that can be proven to be true.

5 One main purpose of _________ is to teach new information.

7 An _________ is a logical conclusion.

8 A main idea is supported by _________.

11 _________ of view refers to who is telling the story.

Writing

What's Your Point?

Circle the main **purpose** of each summary of a piece of writing or speech.

A defense attorney gives a closing argument stating that his client is not guilty.

informs   entertains

persuades   connects to the human experience

A comedian tells jokes.

informs   entertains

persuades   connects to the human experience

Writing

Purpose

A travel writer details the smells and sights of the foods that street vendors are selling.

informs   entertains

persuades   connects to the human experience

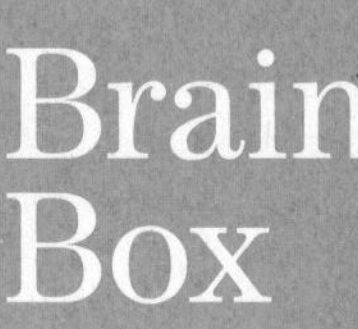

Brain Box

The **purpose** of a piece of writing can be to inform, entertain, persuade, or connect people to the human experience. The human experience includes feelings such as love, loss, longing, anger, fear, compassion, and courage.

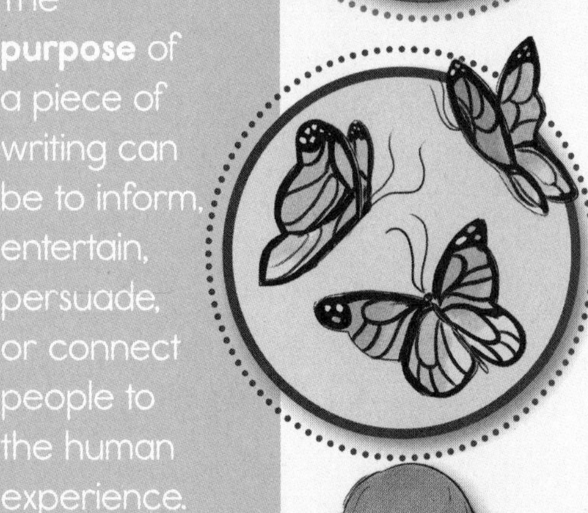

A science writer gives a report on the migration of monarch butterflies.

informs   entertains

persuades   connects to the human experience

A novelist writes about a character who loses a friend.

informs   entertains

persuades   connects to the human experience

Step by Step

Fill in the blanks with the correct step in the **writing process**.

brainstorm	research	plan	write	revise	proofread

Joey is trying to write a story, but he feels disorganized. He should ______________ how the story will go.

Julie needs to write a story about her life, but she doesn't know what to write about. She should ______________ .

Saskia has a story in mind and a plan for telling it. She should ______________ the story.

Lena wants to write a story set in a bakery. But she doesn't know what bakers do all day. She should ______________ .

Darcy has written a rough draft of her story. She should ______________ it.

There may be some spelling and grammar mistakes in Dwight's second draft. He should ______________ it.

Brain Box

The **writing process** is the series of steps that allow you to transform an idea into a piece of writing to share. The process includes the following steps: **brainstorming**, **researching**, **planning**, **writing**, **revising**, and **proofreading**.

Did I Ever Tell You About the Time . . .

Fill in the blanks, and use these writing prompts to think of a topic for a **personal essay**.

A problem I have had to overcome is . . .

____

____

Nothing went as planned the day I . . .

____

____

A big misunderstanding occurred when I . . .

____

____

A long time ago, my friend and I got in trouble when we . . .

____

____

I got to know ____________________ much better when . . .

____

____

I've never been so surprised as when . . .

____

____

I knew I had a true friend when . . .

____

____

I've never been so scared as when . . .

____

____

Writing

Personal essay

Brain Box

A **personal essay** tells a true story from the author's point of view. Funny or serious, it often has a universal theme that allows people to relate to the story even if they have never experienced the exact same thing.

I Remember Like It Was Yesterday

Choose one of the writing prompts from page 86. Write down as many details as you can remember about the memory using the prompts from the cards below.

Where were you?

Who was with you?

What did the place look like?

Do you recall any distinct sounds or smells?

How did you feel?

How old were you?

What were some of the things you and other people said?

Why do you think you remember this event?

Brain Box

Brainstorming is thinking of ideas. While brainstorming, you should write down everything that comes to mind. Don't worry if it is important.

Planning Your Story

Fill in the **story map** to plan how you will write your personal essay.

Paragraph 1: Introduction
(State the situation or problem. Try to "hook," or interest, the reader right away.)

___

___

___

Paragraph 2: Important Event Number 1

___

___

___

Paragraph 3: Important Event Number 2

___

___

___

Paragraph 4: Important Event Number 3

___

___

___

Paragraph 5: Summary/Conclusion
(Reflect on what this event meant to you or how it changed you.)

___

___

___

___

Writing

Planning

Brain Box

A **story map** can help you organize your writing. It should include the most important events that happen in the story.

BEGINNING
MIDDLE
END

Writing . . . and Rewriting

Using your story map from page 88 and the details you brainstormed on page 87, write your personal essay. It should be five paragraphs long. Each paragraph should have a topic sentence and two to four supporting sentences.

Have someone read your personal essay. Ask the person to tell you two things he or she likes about the essay, two things that could be better, and if the person has any questions. Use this feedback to make changes in your personal essay.

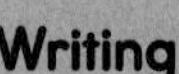

Feedback

Brain Box

Feedback is input that people provide in response to something you have done. You can use feedback to make the next draft better.

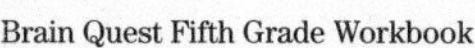

Choose Your Own Adventure

Read the story prompts below.

A middle school basketball player is talented, but his nerves are causing him to mess up during big games. A necklace a teammate sells him is supposed to give him better balance. He finds that it does much more than that. It gives him nerves of steel. But it also changes him into a person he doesn't want to be.

Lily goes on a cruise with her family. When passengers begin disappearing, she suspects a supernatural force is to blame.

Rose wouldn't talk to Jacob if they were the last two people on Earth. Then one day, she wakes up to find that they are the last two people on Earth. Or, at least, there are no other humans as far as Rose can see. They have all been turned into monsters.

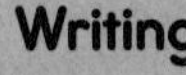

Writing

Narrative writing

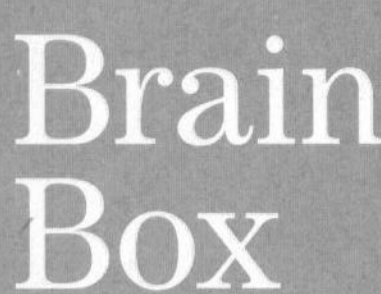

Brain Box

Most stories feature a **main character** trying to overcome a problem and growing from that experience.

At the end of the Ice Age, rapid warming leads to the melting of the glaciers that loom over Yugo's homeland. Yugo dreams that an icy megaflood is on its way. Can Yugo and his people escape the pending disaster?

During a block party, a neighbor is found dead. Neighbors and police suspect the neighborhood troublemaker, a man who doesn't keep up his yard, has loud parties, and is known for angry outbursts. But Jake begins to suspect that the neighbor is a scapegoat for the real culprit who's on the loose.

Create your own story starter by giving a fictional character a problem to overcome.

Interview with the Protagonist

Get to know the **main character** in your story by pretending that you are the **protagonist** and you are being interviewed. Answer the questions using "I," "me," and "my."

Writing

Character development

Where do you live?

____

What is your home like?

____

Is your world like our own—that is, present-day Earth? If not, what is it like?

____

____

What do you do all day?

____

____

What is your daily mode of transportation? (car, bike, horse, etc.)

____

Who are your friends?

____

Do you have any enemies? If so, who?

____

What do others think about you?

____

____

What is your biggest flaw or weakness?

____

____

What do you want more than anything else?

____

What is happening right now that will change your life?

____

____

What do you eat for dinner? Whom do you eat with?

____

What worries keep you up at night?

____

What else should we know about you?

____

____

Your story should begin on an important day in your main character's life. Draw a picture of what happens on the day your story begins.

Writing

Character development

Brain Box

A **protagonist** is the **main character** in a story. He or she must overcome an important problem by taking action.

World Building

Draw a map of the **setting** for your story. Label at least five important places on the map.

Writing

Setting

Brain Box

The **setting** of a story is the time and place in which it occurs. Drawing a map of your story's setting can help you to get to know your character's world. It can be a map of a small area, like a school or neighborhood, or of a larger area, like a group of planets on which a science fiction story takes place.

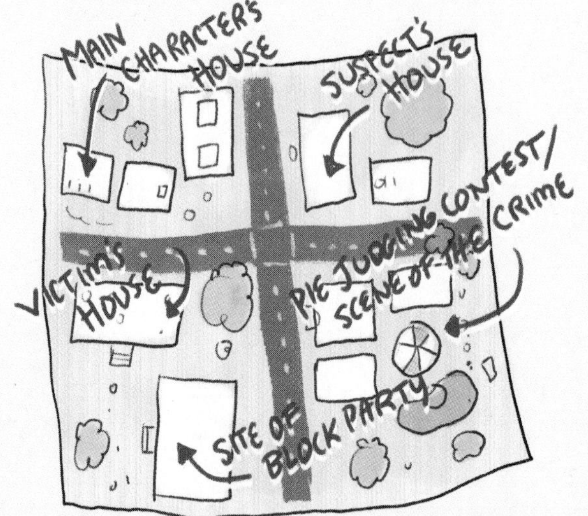

The Five Senses

Imagine you are in the setting shown in the picture. Complete the statements about the setting by using your senses.

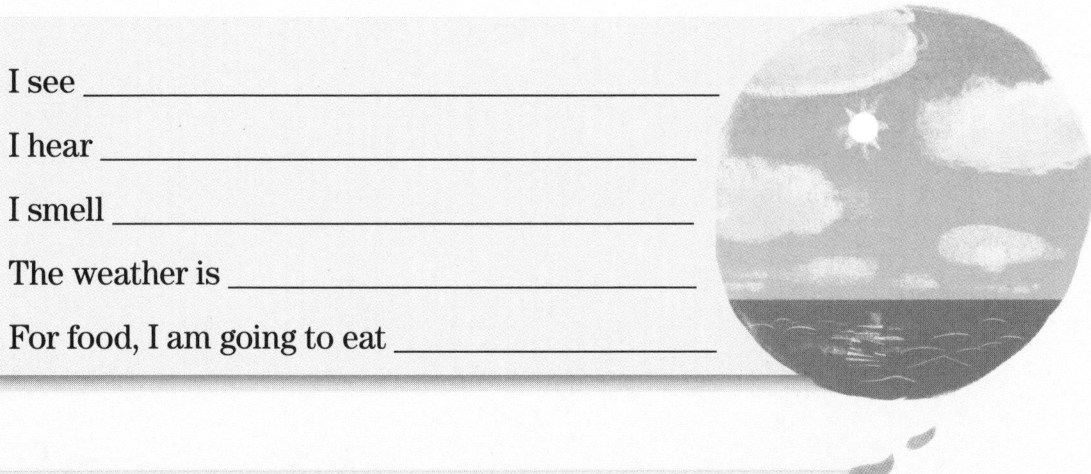

I see ______________________________

I hear ______________________________

I smell ______________________________

The weather is ______________________________

For food, I am going to eat ______________________________

I see ______________________________

I hear ______________________________

I smell ______________________________

The weather is ______________________________

For food, I am going to eat ______________________________

I see ______________________________

I hear ______________________________

I smell ______________________________

The weather is ______________________________

For food, I am going to eat ______________________________

I see ______________________________

I hear ______________________________

I smell ______________________________

The weather is ______________________________

For food, I am going to eat ______________________________

Writing

Setting

Brain Box

Every setting has distinct sights, sounds, smells, weather, wildlife, people, and foods. For instance, a forest may be shadowy and cool whereas a meadow may be warm and bright.

Starting at the Beginning

Write the first page of your story. Use the **first person** point of view. In other words, write as if you are the main character.

Writing

First person point of view

Brain Box

Stories are usually told from the **first person** or **third person** point of view. The first person uses "I" and "we." If you write in the first person, your main character is usually the "I" in the story.

Say What?

Write three lines of **dialogue** for each set of characters in the illustrations. Remember to use quotation marks and to write who said what.

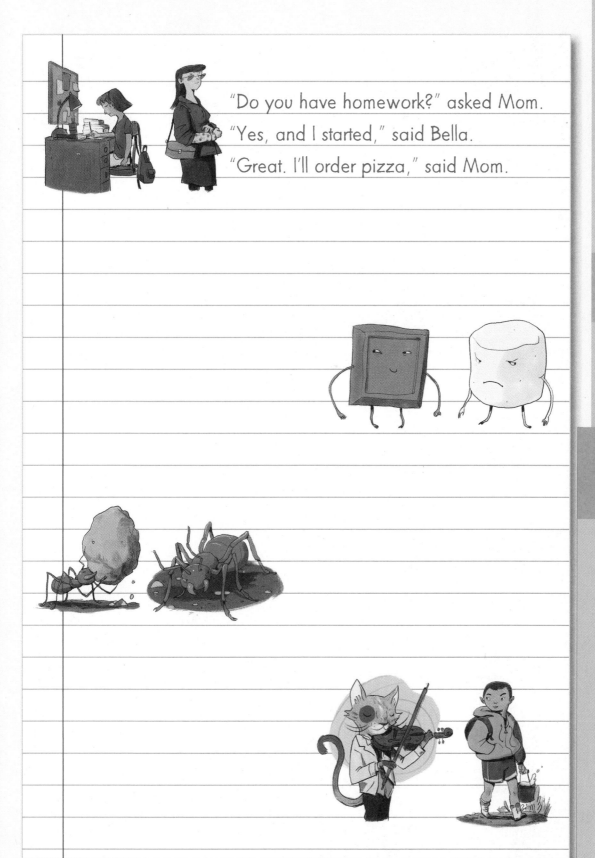

"Do you have homework?" asked Mom.

"Yes, and I started," said Bella.

"Great. I'll order pizza," said Mom.

Brain Box

Dialogue is what characters say. It can be used to show what characters are like. Do they speak kindly? Do they speak with an accent? It can also be used to show how characters relate to one another. Do they get along well? Do they argue? Do they know each other very well?

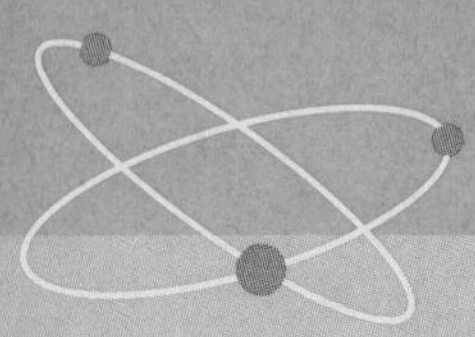

Day in the Life

Circle one character. Write a diary entry about the day from that character's **point of view**. Include an illustration.

Dear Diary,

Signed,

Writing

Point of view

Brain Box

Different characters have different **points of view**. That means they see the world differently from one another.

Fractured Fairy Tale

Choose one of the fairy tale characters from the cards.
Write the fairy tale from that character's point of view.

An evil stepsister in "Cinderella"

The wolf in "Red Riding Hood"

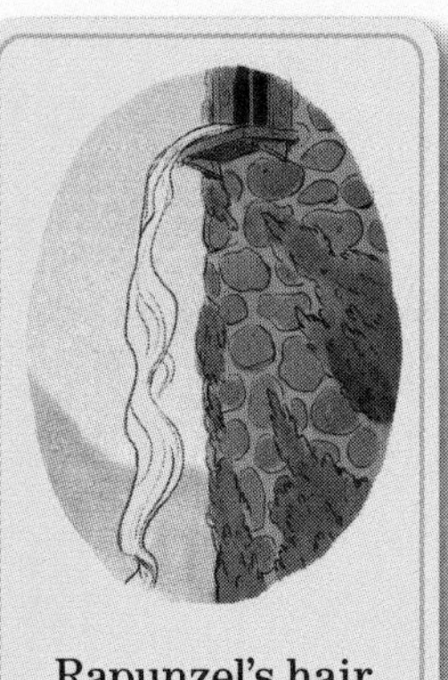

Rapunzel's hair in "Rapunzel"

One of the seven dwarfs in "Snow White"

Once upon a time . . .

Writing

Point of view

Brain Box

A **fractured fairy tale** is a traditional fairy tale told in an unexpected way. For instance, the setting, plot, or point of view can be different from the original.

100

Fly on the Wall

Write three sentences about what each of the four characters below is thinking, saying, or doing.

Paul

____

____

____

Dante

____

____

____

Mila

____

____

____

Farrah

____

____

____

Writing

Third person point of view

Brain Box

The third person point of view uses he, she, and they. In the third person, a narrator tells the story.

What's Their Story?

Imagine what the characters in the illustrations are like.
Then fill in the blanks in the character maps, following the example.

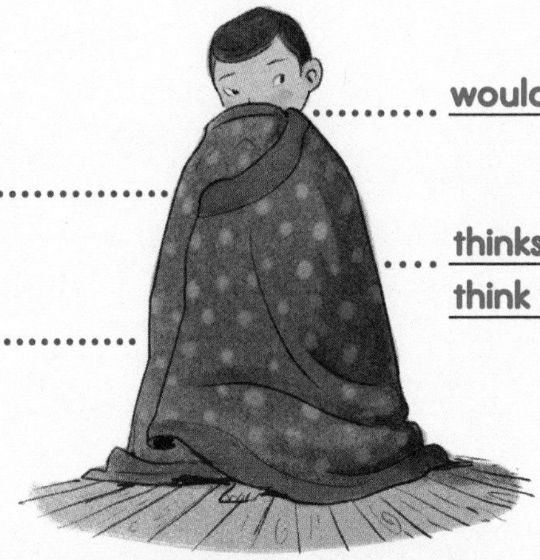

would like to make a friend

shy

thinks that a friend would think the blanket is babyish

attached to blanket

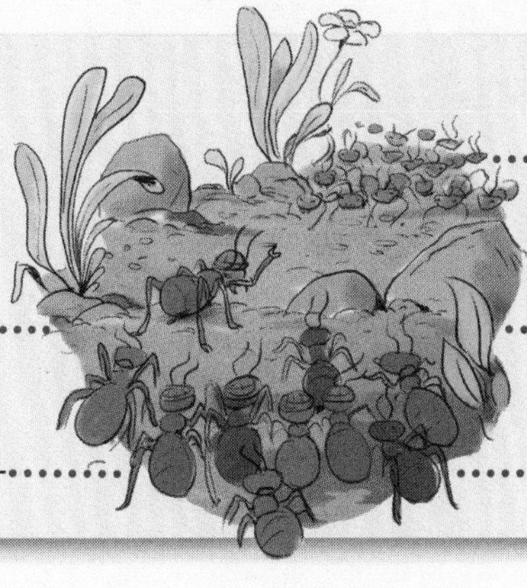

Writing

Character map

Brain Box

A **character map** lists traits that a character has. Examples: immature, wise, funny, vain.

Who, What, Why?

Write the **focus** of each well-known story in three sentences or fewer.

Cinderella

Cinderella works hard but is treated cruelly by her stepmother and stepsisters. Then a fairy godmother helps her get ready for a ball, where she meets Prince Charming.

The Three Little Pigs

____

____

____

Jack and the Beanstalk

____

____

____

Sleeping Beauty

____

____

____

Writing

Focus

Brain Box

Every story needs a **focus**. The focus is what happens on the most basic level. It answers the questions who did what and why.

Fortunately, Unfortunately

Finish the "Fortunately, Unfortunately" story. Then write your own by using the given starter sentence. The "Fortunately" lines should tell something good that happens to the character. The "Unfortunately" lines should tell something bad that happens.

Evie went swimming in a pond.

Unfortunately, a snapping turtle bit her toe.

Fortunately, the turtle only clipped Evie's toenail.

Unfortunately, that made the turtle mad and he ______________________

Fortunately, ______________________

Unfortunately, ______________________

Fortunately, ______________________

____

____

Christopher built a snowman in the woods.

Unfortunately, ______________________

Fortunately, ______________________

Unfortunately, ______________________

Fortunately, ______________________

Unfortunately, ______________________

Fortunately, ______________________

____

____

____

____

Brain Box

The **plot** consists of the main events of a story. The ups and downs that the characters experience contribute to the plot.

What Next?

Complete each story prompt. Then write what happens next.

While on a field trip to a science lab, you accidently drink a scientific formula instead of your water and turn into a ________________________.

What happens next?

____

____

In New York City, a skyscraper comes to life as a robot.

What happens next?

____

____

____

Writing

Plot

You discover a tiny village made of acorn houses and groves of dandelions. ________________________ live there.

What happens next?

____

____

You awake to a crash against your window. You go outside and see that a __________________ has fallen from the sky.

What happens next?

____

____

____

New to a small town, you meet your next-door neighbor George, who is your age. But when you start asking around, no one has ever heard of George. What happens next?

____

____

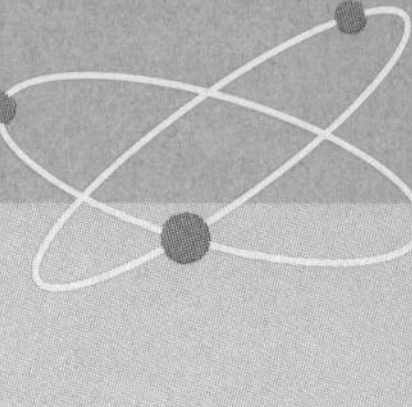

Judging a Book by Its Cover

Look at **book covers** in your home or local library. Think about which covers you like. Then design a cover for your book. Include the title, the author's name, and an illustration.

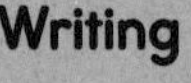

Writing

Visual elements

Brain Box

A **book cover** should show the reader what kind of book it is and make the reader want to read it.

This I Love

Brainstorm people, places, and things you love.

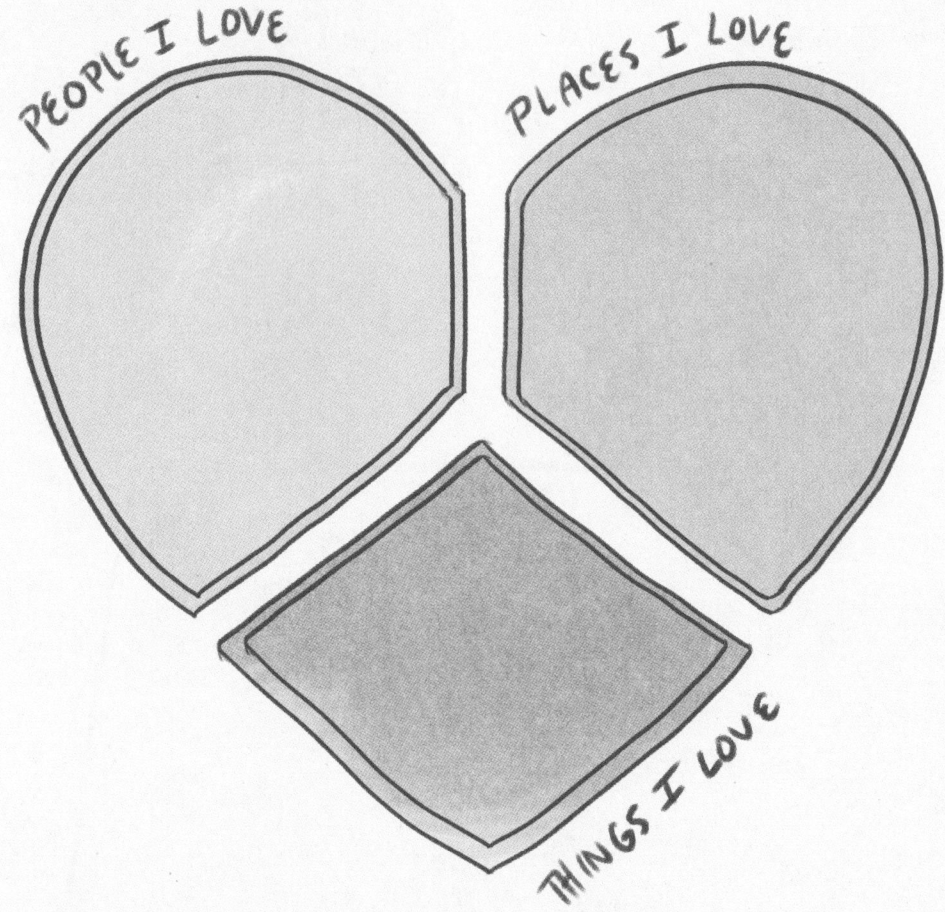

Read the sonnet on page 80. Then write a sonnet of your own by writing 14 lines with 10 syllables in each line.

Title: ______________________________

1. ______________________________
2. ______________________________
3. ______________________________
4. ______________________________
5. ______________________________
6. ______________________________
7. ______________________________
8. ______________________________
9. ______________________________
10. ______________________________
11. ______________________________
12. ______________________________
13. ______________________________
14. ______________________________

Shall I Compare Thee to a Piece of Cheese?

Write three possible opening lines to **parody** Shakespeare's Sonnet 18.

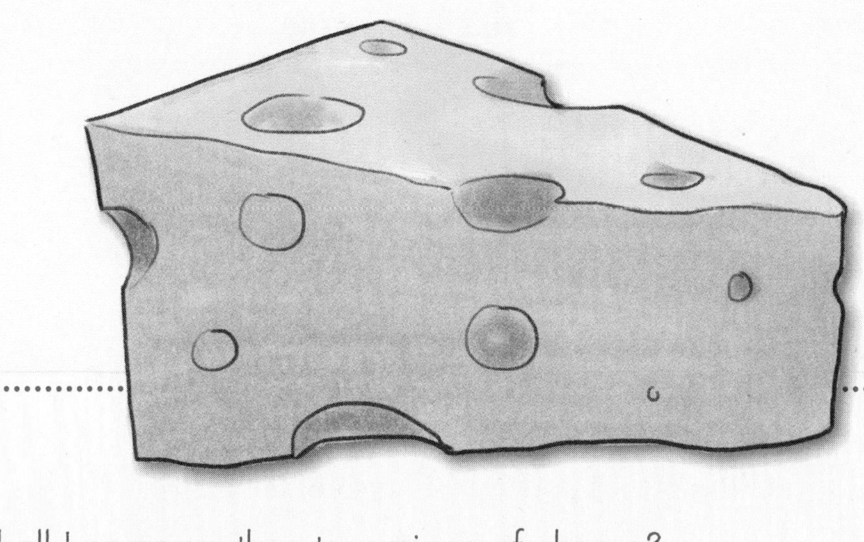

Shall I compare thee to a piece of cheese?

Thou art more square, more smelly, and more cheesy.

Shall I compare thee to a ______________________________?

Thou art more ______________________________.

Shall I compare thee to a ______________________________?

Thou art more ______________________________.

Shall I compare thee to a ______________________________?

Thou art more ______________________________.

Writing

Parody

Brain Box

A **parody** imitates a poem, story, or other work in a funny way.

A Day at the Beach

Write 2 to 3 lines about each picture using one of the **sound effects** from the cards below. Write the sound effect you used.

alliteration
a series of words that start with the same sound

internal rhyme
rhyming that occurs within one line of a poem

onomatopoeia
words that mimic sounds, such as drip and drop

rhyme scheme
the pattern of rhyming that occurs between the last words of each line

Writing

Sound effects

Crunch drip drip
Nothing beats a
Chip after a dip

Sound effects used: onomatopoeia

Brain Box

You can use **sound effects** to add meaning, beauty, or humor to a poem or other composition.

____

____

____

Sound effect used: ______________

____

____

____

Sound effect used: ______________

____

____

____

Sound effect used: ______________

____

____

____

Sound effect used: ______________

To Whom It May Concern

Read the **formal letter** below.

Writing

Letter writing

Johnny Maatha
10 East Winthrope Street
Fairway, Kansas 66205

May 4, 2015

Principal May
Fairway Middle School
33 East Valley Road
Fairway, Kansas 66205

Dear Principal May:

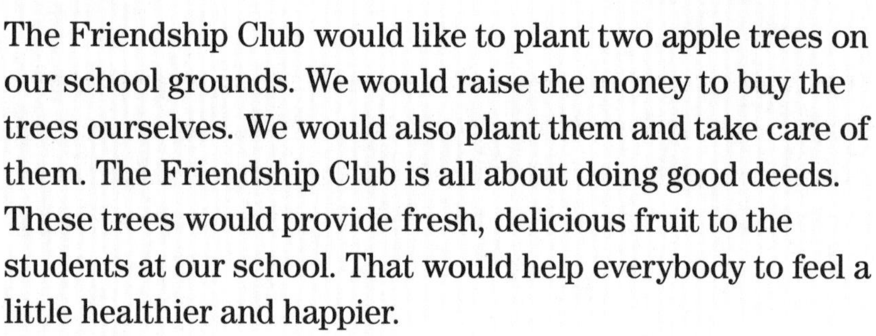

The Friendship Club would like to plant two apple trees on our school grounds. We would raise the money to buy the trees ourselves. We would also plant them and take care of them. The Friendship Club is all about doing good deeds. These trees would provide fresh, delicious fruit to the students at our school. That would help everybody to feel a little healthier and happier.

Sincerely,
Johnny Maatha
5th grade

Choose a topic from the cards. Then write a formal letter. Label the letter with the following: your address, the date, the address of the person or company you are writing to, one or two paragraphs, and your signature.

Purrfect Pets
1009 W. Mission Road
San Diego, California 92106
Ask your local animal shelter for the opportunity to volunteer there.

Renata Movie Theater
10 South Mill Street
Woburn, Massachusetts 01801
Tell your local movie theater that the sound was not working when you saw a movie.

New York Culinary Academy
135 Broadway
New York, NY 10013

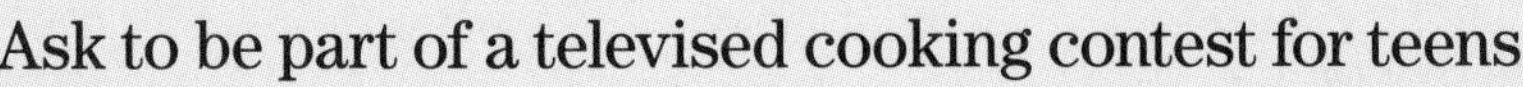

Ask to be part of a televised cooking contest for teens.

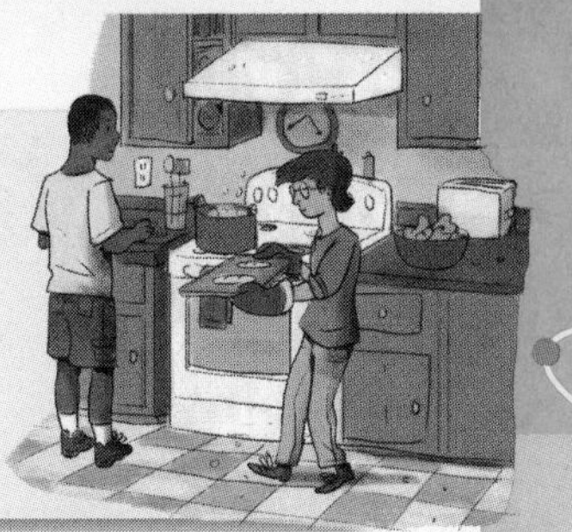

An Author You Like
103 Sleepy Hollow Drive
Tarrytown, New York 10591

Tell an author why you like his or her book.

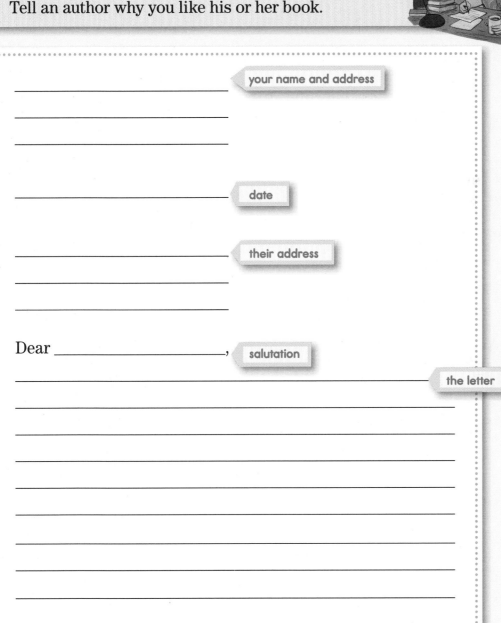

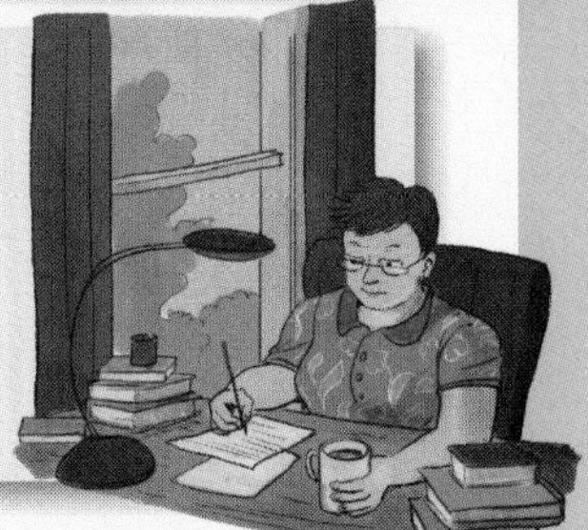

______________________ your name and address
____
____

______________________ date

______________________ their address
____
____

Dear ____________________, salutation

____ the letter
____
____
____
____
____
____
____
____

Sincerely,

______________________ your signature

Writing

Letter writing

Brain Box

You write a **formal letter** to someone you don't know well. The letter should be short and to the point. Formal letters are written for a variety of reasons, including: to state concerns, to ask to be accepted into a school, to contact a person you admire, to ask for a job or support, or to gather information.

What Should I Write About?

Brainstorm topics for an **informal email** to a grandparent or other older relative. Then write the email and send it.

Something funny that has happened in the last few weeks is ________
____.

Something interesting that happened is________________________
____.

Something exciting that happened is __________________________
____.

Something new I've tried is _________________________________
____.

Lately I've been enjoying ___________________________________
____.

A challenge I've had lately is _______________________________
____.

I thought of you recently when ______________________________
____.

I remember when you ______________________________________
____
____
____.

A question I have is ______________________
____
____
____.

Writing

Letter writing

Brain Box

An **informal letter** or an **email** is written to someone you know well. Both can include thoughts, stories, and questions.

One Prickly Pet

Read the **opinion piece**. Then answer the questions.

A hedgehog makes a good pet. Hedgehogs are quiet, so they don't bother you when you are trying to sleep. They don't take up much space, so they can fit in even a small apartment. Hedgehogs won't wear you out with hyperactivity—they mostly relax all day! While you may have heard that hedgehogs are prickly, their spines only stick up when they are scared. Once your hedgehog is used to you, its spines no longer stick up when you pick it up.

What is the opinion?

____

List the four facts that support the opinion.

1. ______________________________
2. ______________________________
3. ______________________________
4. ______________________________

Brain Box

An **opinion piece** states an opinion and supports the opinion, or backs it up, with logical arguments and facts.

True or False

Read the information on the web pages below. Circle whether the web page is a **reliable** or **unreliable** source for information.

Getanswers.com

How did the dinosaurs go extinct?

Answer 1: It was a meteor.

Answer 2: It was a meat eater.

Answer 3: Not sure. Guessing it was their small brain size. LOL

reliable **unreliable**

The National Museum of Natural History, NMNH.org

The Extinction of the Dinosaurs

Non-avian dinosaurs went extinct 65 million years ago. Scientists are not sure why, but there are two prevailing theories. One is that a large asteroid or comet struck Earth. The other is that volcanoes erupted on a large scale. Either event would have sent debris into the atmosphere, thus blocking the sun, which is essential to life.

reliable **unreliable**

paleontolo-guy.blogspot.com

About me: I have been a professor of paleontology at the University of Utah for 20 years.

January 11, 2014

Whatever happened to the dinosaurs?

When I tell people that I'm a paleontologist, the first question I get is, "What killed the dinosaurs?" Of course, some dinosaurs are still living today—birds. Aside from that, there are two schools of thought regarding the extinction—that a large comet or asteroid did them in, or that an extreme volcano event did so. I believe that both occurred, and here's why . . .

reliable **unreliable**

coolstuff.blogspot.com

About me: I just love cool stuff. I mean, who doesn't? I do, and I post about it all the time. Enjoy!

Whatever happened to the dinosaurs?

Here's something I've been thinking about: what if the dinosaurs were so big that they fell through the surface of the earth into the lava at the core? Could that be why they are extinct? Has anyone researched this?

reliable **unreliable**

Brain Box

It's important to use **reliable sources** when doing Internet research. Reliable sources include: websites of museums, universities, and professional associations; articles published in major newspapers, magazines, or professional journals, blogs, or web pages.

Unreliable sources may include: sites that allow anyone to answer questions or web pages that have a biased point of view.

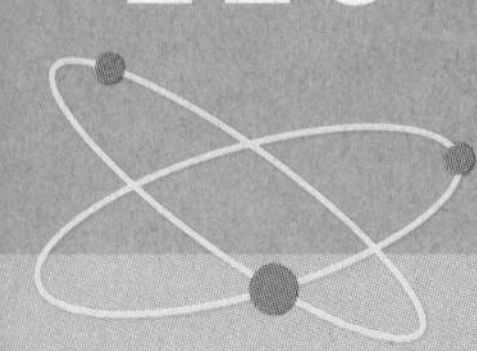

Do Your Research

Find three different sources about a topic you're interested in. List them as shown in the examples below. (Hint: You can underline words that are italicized.)

Book

Author's last name, author's first name. *Title of book.*
Place of publication: Name of publisher, date of publication.

Nguyen, Tom. *Eruption! Countdown to Extinction.*
New York: Graham & Bosch, 2014.

Article

Author's last name, author's first name. "Title of article."
Name of publication. Date.

Bartkowski, Frank. "New Timeline for the Extinction of Dinosaurs." *The New York Times.* May 4, 2014.

Website

Author's last name, author's first name. "Title of article."
Name of website. Date of posting (if provided). Website URL.

Dean, Emma. "The Extinction of the Dinosaurs."
The National Museum of Natural History. NMNH.org.

Interview

Last name of person interviewed, first name of person interviewed. The word "Interview." Date of interview.

Jorisch, Stefan. Interview. February 14, 2014.

____

____

____

____

____

____

____

Brain Box

To build knowledge, you must research several different sources. These can include books, magazines, newspapers, websites, and interviews with people knowledgeable about the topic.

You must list these sources in a **bibliography**.

Take Note

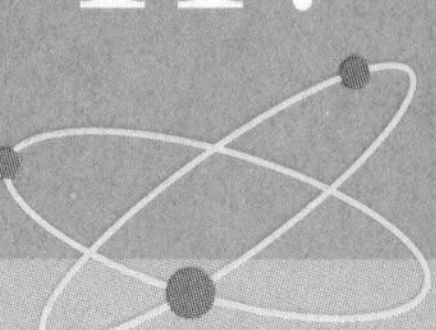

Use one of the three sources you found. Write the name of the source on the first note card. On each card, **paraphrase** one fact that you found in your source.

Writing

Taking notes

Brain Box

When taking notes, it's important to **paraphrase** so you don't accidentally copy the exact wording but instead get only the info you need. When you paraphrase, you put the author's words into your own words.

Piggy, Please?

Circle one of the animals from the cards. Research the animal online.

rabbit

Writing

Opinion

Brain Box

You can do research online at home, school, or a public library.

Write a letter to your parents or guardians asking if you can have one of on the animals on page 118 for a pet. Include facts and logical arguments to support your request.

Dear ____________________,

Love,

____

What Do You Want to Know?

List **topics** that interest you in each category.

People	Places	Things
Wangri Maathai	The Andaman Islands	Volcanoes

Plants/Animals	Books/Movies	Historical Times
Capybaras	Star Wars: The Complete Saga	The Revolutionary War

Circle the topics that interest you the most.

Writing

Choosing a topic

Be More Specific

Research your topic by using either a book or a website. Then jot down possible narrower topics.

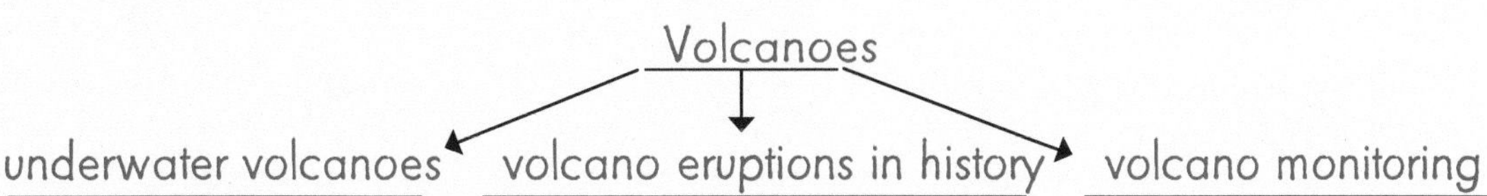

Topic: ______________________

Narrower Topics

- ______________________
- ______________________
- ______________________
- ______________________
- ______________________
- ______________________
- ______________________
- ______________________
- ______________________
- ______________________
- ______________________
- ______________________
- ______________________
- ______________________
- ______________________

Circle the narrower topic that you want to write about.

Writing

Narrowing the topic

Brain Box

When writing about a topic, you can widen or narrow the scope. **Widening the scope** means enlarging the area or subject matter that you write about. **Narrowing the scope** means shrinking the subject matter. When widening the scope of a story on capybaras, you might include other large rodents. When narrowing the scope, you might write about a specific clan of capybaras.

Get Organized!

Read the **notes** about honeybees.

The queen's only job is to lay eggs.

When the bee stings someone, the venom sac detaches from the bee, and kills the bee.

Honeybees live in a hive.

Female bees known as workers find food, build the hive, clean, care for the baby bees, and make honey.

Drones (male bees) mate with the queen.

Bees drink nectar from flowers.

Back in the hive, the bees regurgitate the nectar into the honeycomb.

The water in the nectar evaporates. Honey is left behind.

Hives are usually in hollow trees.

Eighty thousand bees can live in a hive.

Bees sting to defend themselves or the hive.

Their stingers are barbed.

The stinger is attached to a venom sac inside the bee.

Bees eat honey in the winter when there are no flowers.

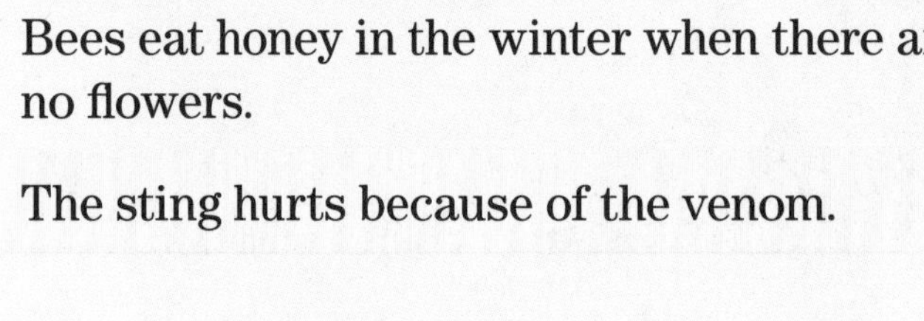

The sting hurts because of the venom.

Writing

Organizing notes

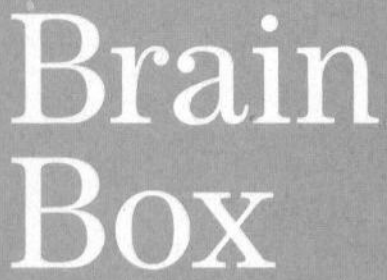

Brain Box

An **outline** can help you organize your **notes** in the order in which they will appear in your report.

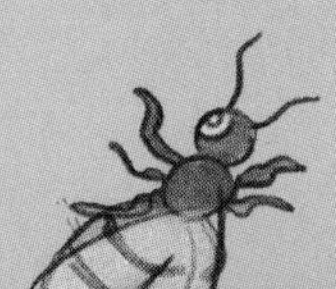

Fill in the **outline** with the facts from the notes.

A The hive

1. ______________________________
2. ______________________________
3. ______________________________

B Workers, queens, and drones

1. ______________________________
2. ______________________________
3. ______________________________

C How and why bees make honey

1. ______________________________
2. ______________________________
3. ______________________________
4. ______________________________

Writing

Organizing notes

D Bee stings

1. ______________________________
2. ______________________________
3. ______________________________
4. ______________________________
5. ______________________________

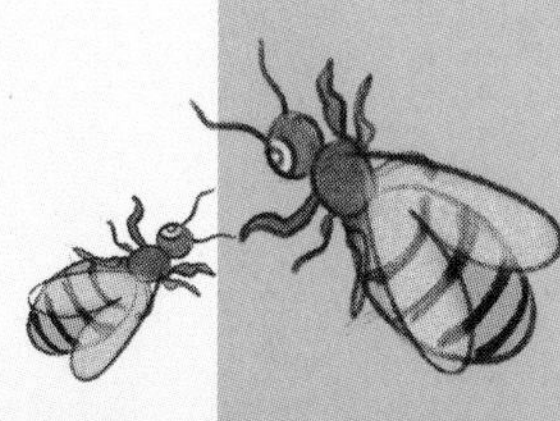

You Be the Editor

Proofreading Marks	Examples
Capitalize ≡	The white House
Lowercase /	The Library is closed
Insert word or letter ∧	The zoo ∧(is) open
Delete	Call me me after the party.
Change order	Today Thursday is.
Spell out (SP)	There are (7) days a week. (SP)
Add comma	You look great Tom.
Add period ⊙	The end ⊙
New paragraph ¶	"Are you done with your sandwich?" he asked. ¶ "No, I'm still eating," I said.

Writing

Proofreading

Correct the article using the proofreading marks.

Capybaras

Capybaras are the world's largest Rodents. They live in the rainforests and savannas of central america and south america. Weighing 75 to 100 pounds, they are the size of a large dog. The giant rodents are are semi-aquatic. They cool off in the water, graze on aquatic plants, and also use water for protection predators include jaguars anacondas and caimans. If a predator threatens a, it dives underwater. A capybara can hold its breath underwater for 5 minutes!

Capybarras live in groups of 3 to 30. Together, they their defend territory. Capybaras communicate through scent and sound. They bark to warn each other of trouble A male's scent indicates his social status and whether whether he is ready to mate.

The closest rellatives to capybaras are guinea pigs. Like guinea pigs, capybaras are easily domesticated. In some places, they are now raised on ranches. Some people even keep them as pets

Brain Box

Proofreading marks show mistakes in writing and how to correct them.

Math Skills

Number Machine

Write the words as numbers.

three thousand two hundred and seventy-five ____________________

nine hundred ninety-nine billion nine hundred ninety-nine million nine hundred ninety-nine thousand nine hundred and ninety-nine

____

seventy-seven thousand seven hundred and seventy-seven

____

five hundred thousand two hundred and twenty-three

____

eight hundred million four hundred thousand and two hundred

____

forty-five million four hundred fifty-three thousand eight hundred and ninety-two

____

seven hundred and three ____________________

nine hundred twenty-two thousand and three ____________________

two hundred two million and two ____________________

thirty-three thousand ____________________

Put the numbers in order from smallest to largest.

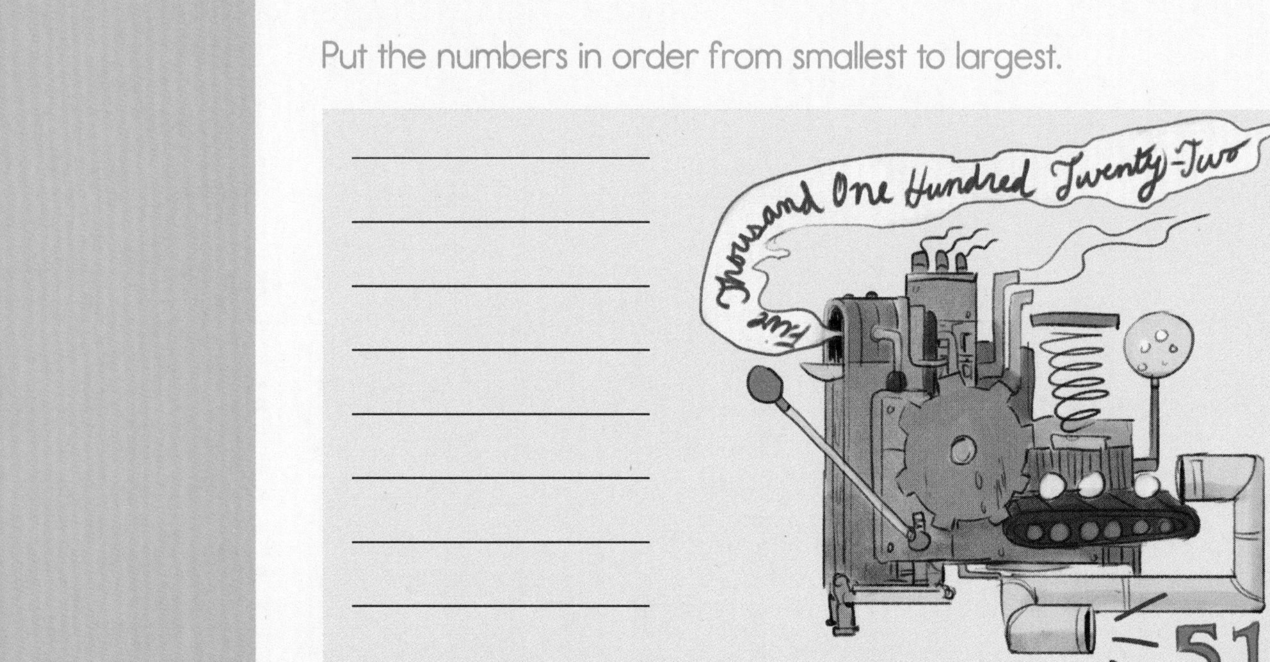

Math Skills

Spelled-out numbers

Blank Check

Write out the amount of money in words on the blank lines of the checks.

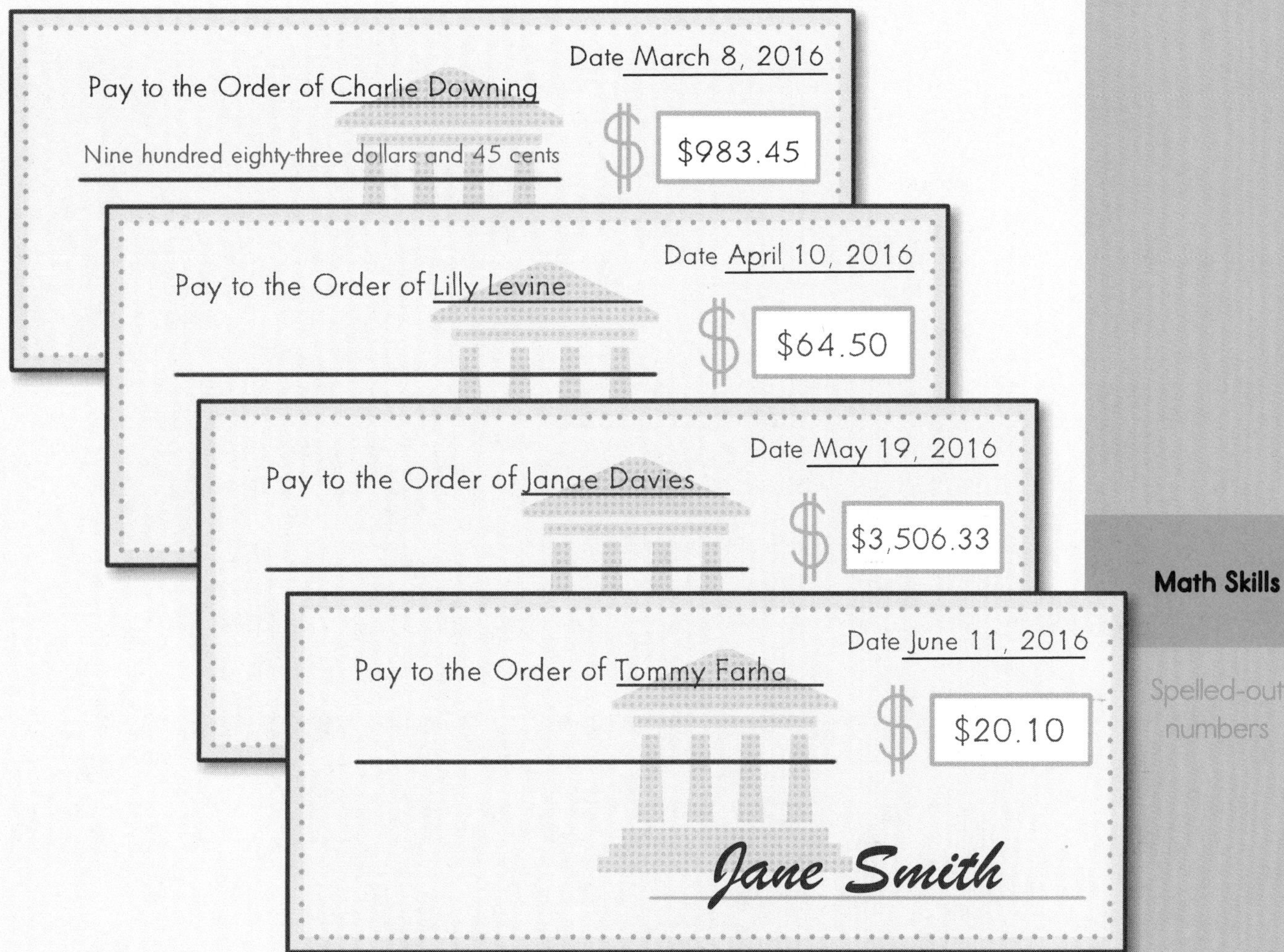

Date March 8, 2016
Pay to the Order of Charlie Downing
Nine hundred eighty-three dollars and 45 cents
$983.45
Date April 10, 2016
Pay to the Order of Lilly Levine
$64.50
Date May 19, 2016
Pay to the Order of Janae Davies
$3,506.33
Date June 11, 2016
Pay to the Order of Tommy Farha
$20.10
Jane Smith

Sarah's paycheck amounts to $983 for two weeks. Add up the bills in the Needs column. With the money remaining, circle the items she can afford in the Wants column.

Needs		Wants	
Groceries	$ 100	Dinner out with friends	$ 40
Rent	$ 480	Second dinner out	$ 40
Electricity bill	$ 70	Coffee every morning	$ 30
Heating bill	$ 100	Lunch out every day	$ 70
Transportation	$ 50	Gym membership	$ 30
Savings	$ 100		
TOTAL	$_____	Money left over for wants	$_____

Math Skills

Spelled-out numbers

Brain Box

Checks are written in **number form** and **word form**. For the word form, the dollar amount is written out followed by the cents.

Crazy Eights

Circle the **8** in each number. Write its **place value**.

8,432 ________________

468 ________________

585 ________________

832 ________________

1,278 ________________

489 ________________

873,322 ________________

5,810 ________________

80,100 ____________

Write a number with an 8 in the given place value.

Ones _____

Tens ______

Hundreds ____________

Thousands ________________

Ten thousands ________________

Hundred thousands ________________

Brain Box

The **place value** of a digit in a number is determined by where it appears in the number.

Example: **643,987**

Hundred thousands	Ten thousands	Thousands	Hundreds	Tens	Ones
6	4	3	9	8	7

All Aboard

Draw the number of people or items represented by each digit based on the place value.

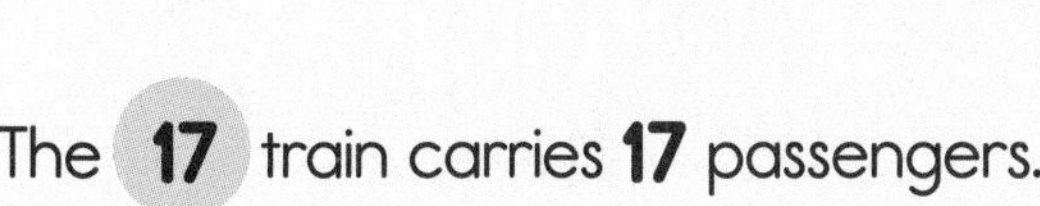

The **17** train carries **17** passengers.

Tens

Ones

The **22** train carries **22** apples.

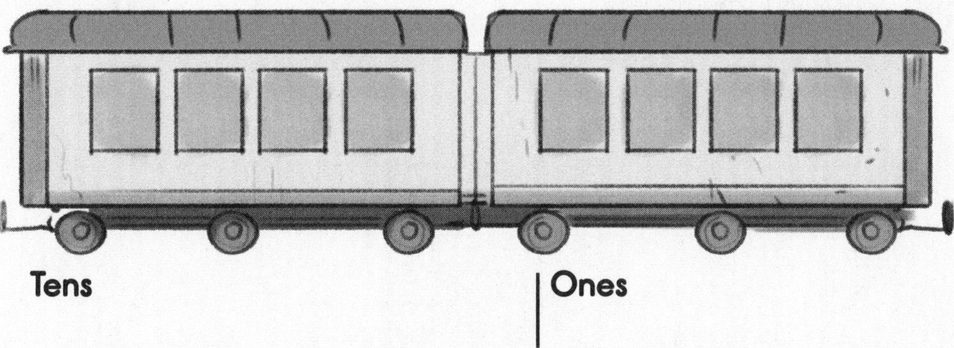

Tens

Ones

The **12** train carries **12** beach balls.

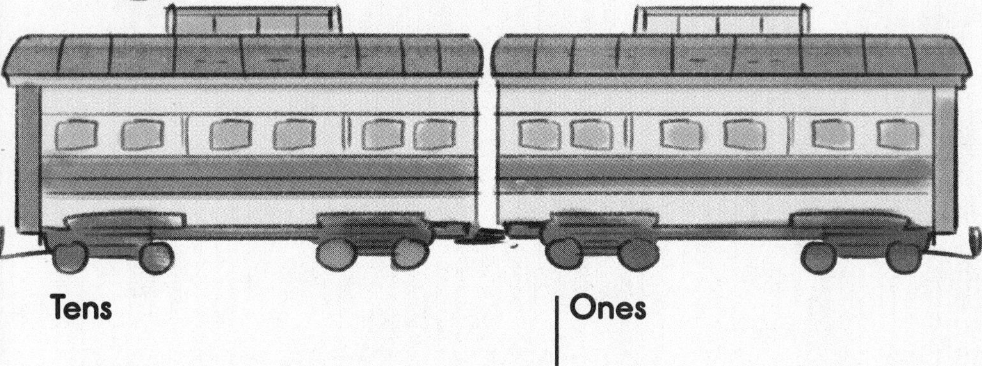

Tens

Ones

The **24** train carries **24** cupcakes.

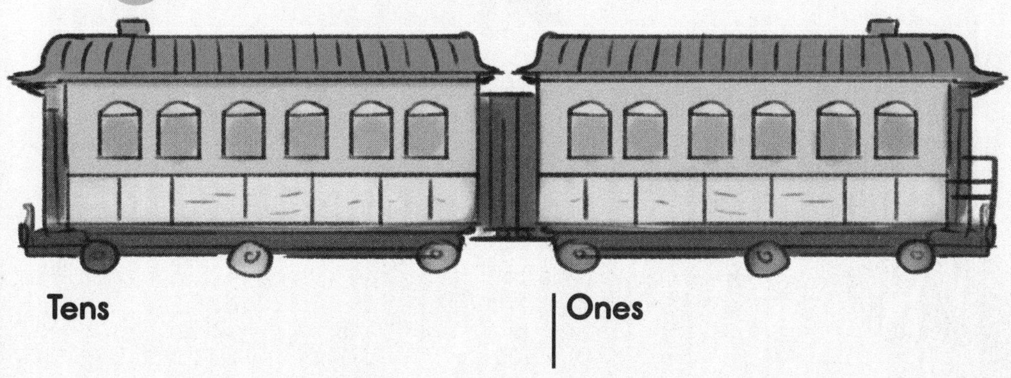

Tens

Ones

Math Skills

Expanded and standard notation

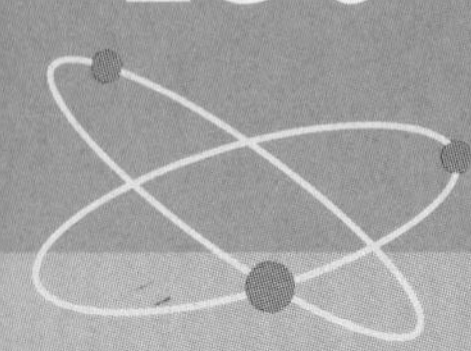

Expand on That

Math Skills

Expanded notation

Write out the **expanded notation** for each number.

		Thousands		Hundreds		Tens		Ones
1,246	=	________	+	________	+	________	+	________
2,357	=	________	+	________	+	________	+	________
3,467	=	________	+	________	+	________	+	________
4,578	=	________	+	________	+	________	+	________
5,689	=	________	+	________	+	________	+	________
6,790	=	________	+	________	+	________	+	________
4,219	=	________	+	________	+	________	+	________
3,652	=	________	+	________	+	________	+	________
5,342	=	________	+	________	+	________	+	________
9,243	=	________	+	________	+	________	+	________

Brain Box

The **standard notation** for a number is the way it is typically written.

Example: 3,579

The **expanded notation** shows how much each digit in the number is worth based on its place value.

3,579 = 3,000 + 500 + 70 + 9

The 3 is worth 3,000, the 5 is worth 500, the 7 is worth 70, and the 9 is worth 9.

Write the **standard notation** for each expanded notation below.

Ten Thousands		Thousands		Hundreds		Tens		Ones		
90,000	+	1,000	+	800	+	30	+	7	=	________
40,000	+	6,000	+	500	+	40	+	6	=	________
70,000	+	4,000	+	300	+	50	+	9	=	________
80,000	+	8,000	+	200	+	00	+	1	=	________
20,000	+	9,000	+	800	+	10	+	2	=	________
30,000	+	2,000	+	700	+	80	+	4	=	________
20,000	+	3,000	+	100	+	90	+	5	=	________
50,000	+	5,000	+	300	+	80	+	8	=	________
10,000	+	9,000	+	200	+	30	+	4	=	________

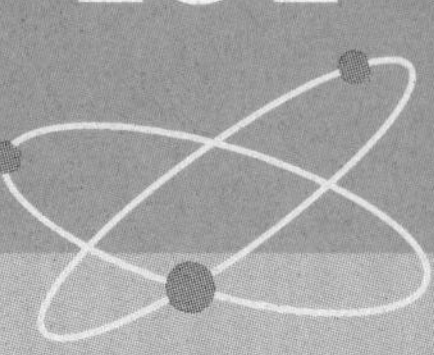

Balloon Math

Write the missing number that makes the balloon bigger.

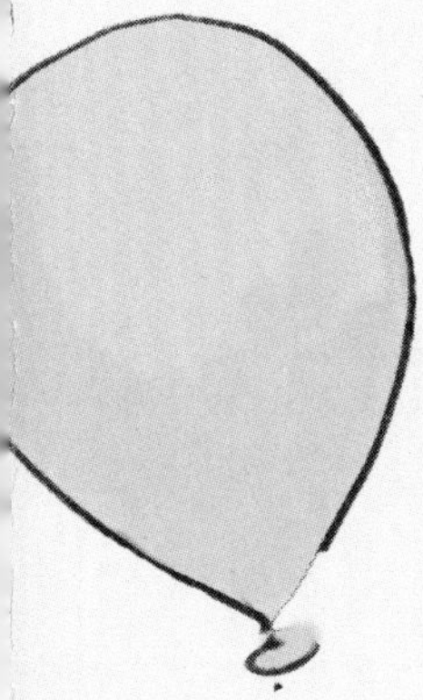

4 × ____ = 40

5 × ____ = 500

9 × ____ = 9,000

7 × ____ = 700,000

30 × ____ = 30,000

67 × ____ = 67,000

422 × ____ = 4,220

5,500 × ____ = 55,000

65,700 × ____ = 6,570,000

320,000 × ____ = 32,000,000

Math Skills

Place value

Brain Box

When **multiplying** a whole number by 10, put a zero at the end. When multiplying by 100, put two zeroes. When multiplying by 1,000, put three zeroes, and so on.

76 × 10 = 760
76 × 100 = 7,600
76 × 1,000 = 76,000

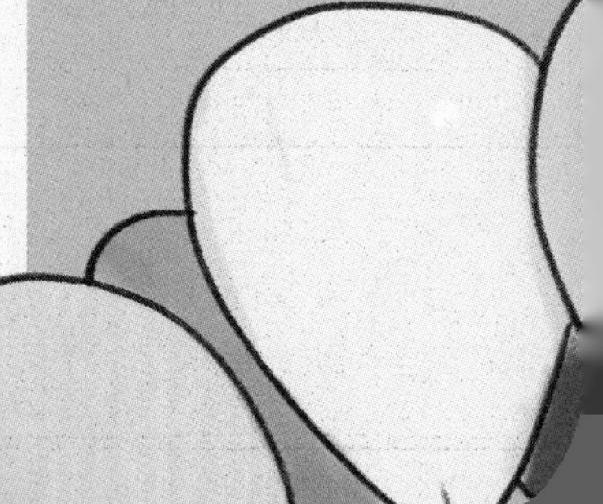

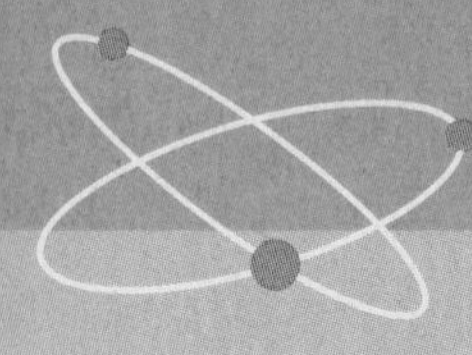

Balloon Math II

Write the missing number that makes the balloon smaller.

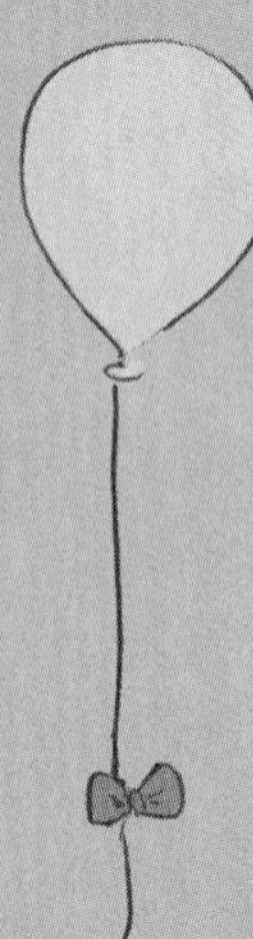

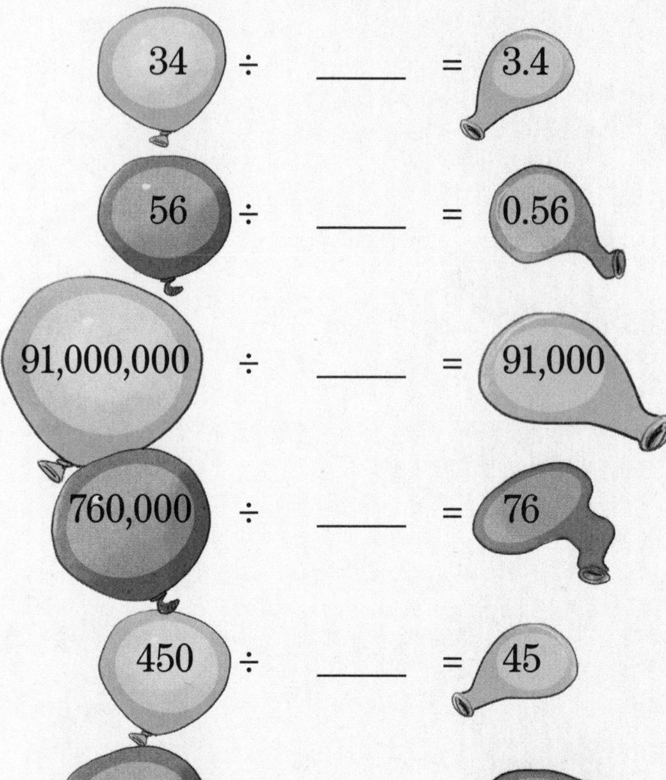

34 ÷ ____ = 3.4

56 ÷ ____ = 0.56

91,000,000 ÷ ____ = 91,000

760,000 ÷ ____ = 76

450 ÷ ____ = 45

789,000 ÷ ____ = 7,890

8,263,591 ÷ ____ = 826,359.1

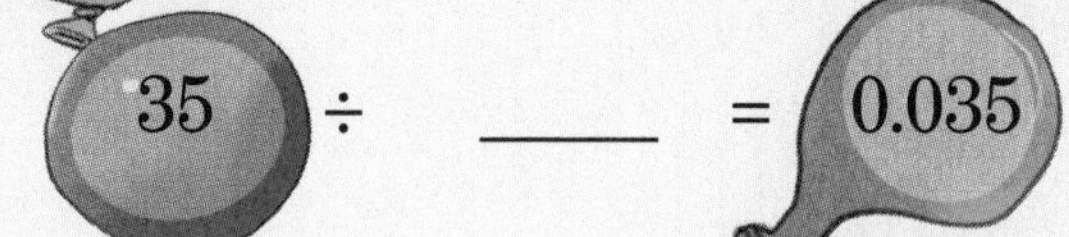

35 ÷ ____ = 0.035

46,243 ÷ ____ = 462.43

3.14 ÷ ____ = 0.314

Math Skills

Place value

Brain Box

When **dividing** a number by a multiple of 10, first put a decimal at the end of the number if it does not already have one.

76 = 76.0

Then move the decimal one place to the left. When dividing by 100, move the decimal two places to the left. When dividing by 1,000, move it three places to the left, and so on. Insert zeroes as you move the decimal farther to the left.

76 ÷ 10 = 7.6
76 ÷ 100 = 0.76
76 ÷ 1,000 = 0.076

The 25

Place an X over the **non-prime numbers** with help from the clues. Remember, the number 1 isn't prime! Then color the 25 boxes that contain **prime numbers**.

1	2	3	4	5	6	7	8	9	10
11	12	13	14	15	16	17	18	19	20
21	22	23	24	25	26	27	28	29	30
31	32	33	34	35	36	37	38	39	40
41	42	43	44	45	46	47	48	49	50
51	52	53	54	55	56	57	58	59	60
61	62	63	64	65	66	67	68	69	70
71	72	73	74	75	76	77	78	79	80
81	82	83	84	85	86	87	88	89	90
91	92	93	94	95	96	97	98	99	100

All even numbers have the **factor** 2. There is only one even prime number, which is 2. The number 2 can only be divided evenly by itself and 1. Place an X over all other even numbers.

Numbers ending with 5 and 0 have 5 as a factor. (The exception is 5, which is a prime number for the same reason that 2 is a prime number.) Cross out those numbers.

Cross out numbers that have 3 as a factor (other than 3, which is a prime number).

(Hint: When the digits in a multi-digit number add up to a number divisible by 3, such as 6, 9, 12, 15, or 18, that multi-digit number is divisible by 3. Example: 69 is divisible by 3 because 6 + 9 = 15.)

Place an X over the 3 remaining numbers with 7 as a factor: 49, 77, 91 (7 itself is a prime number.)

Math Skills

Prime numbers

Brain Box

The two numbers in a multiplication problem are called **factors.** A **prime number** is a number greater than 1 that can be divided evenly only by 1 or itself. For instance, the number 7 is a prime number because its only factors are 7 and 1. The number 6 is not a prime number because it has 4 factors: 6 and 1, 3 and 2. There are 25 prime numbers from 1 to 100.

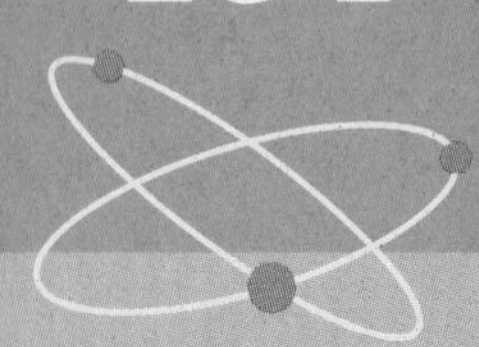

Break It Down

Fill in the circles to make a factor tree for each number. Circle the prime numbers. Then multiply the prime numbers to get the original number.

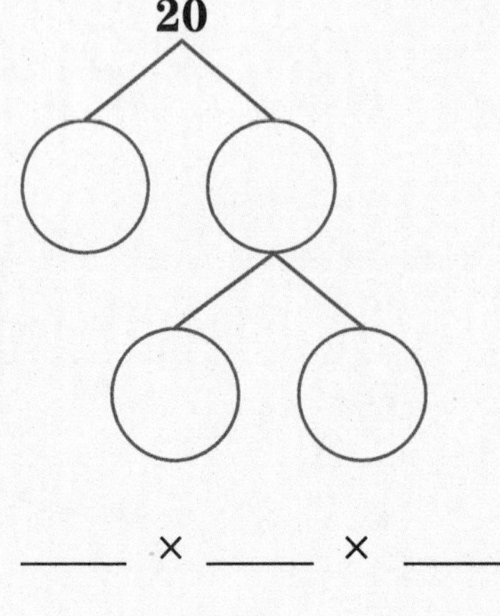

____ × ____ × ____ = 20

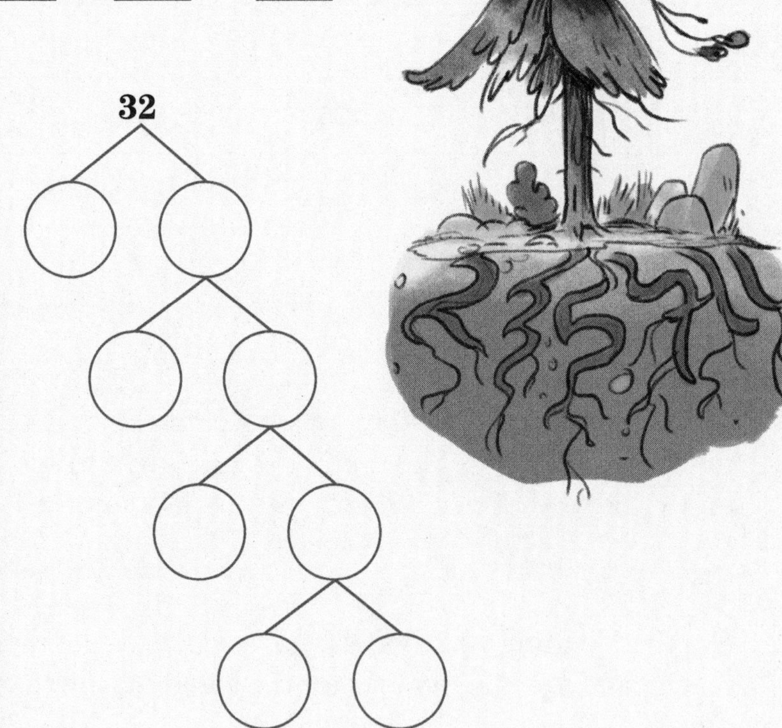

____ × ____ × ____ × ____ × ____ = 32

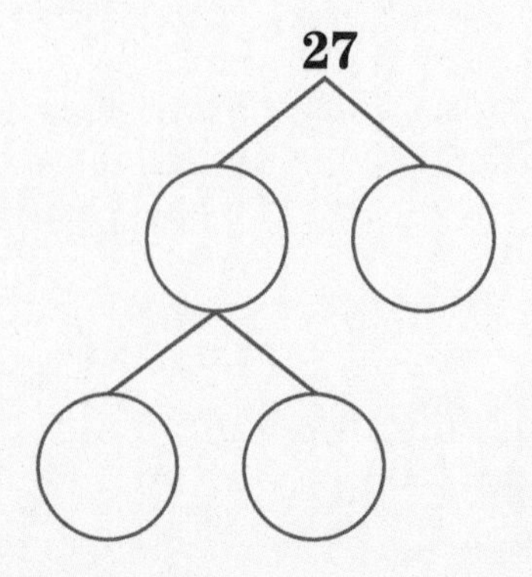

____ × ____ × ____ = 27

Math Skills

Factors

Brain Box

A **factor tree** is a diagram used to break down a number into its prime number factors. To make a factor tree, start by writing the largest factor and its counterpart underneath the number.

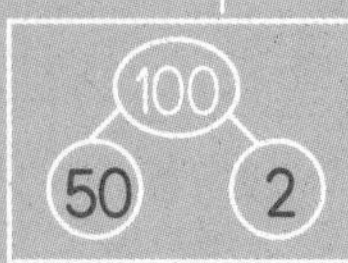

Do the same thing with any factors that are not yet prime numbers.

If you multiply the prime number factors, the **product** is the original number:

5 × 2 × 5 × 2 = 100

The answer to a multiplication problem is the **product.**

Multiplication and Division

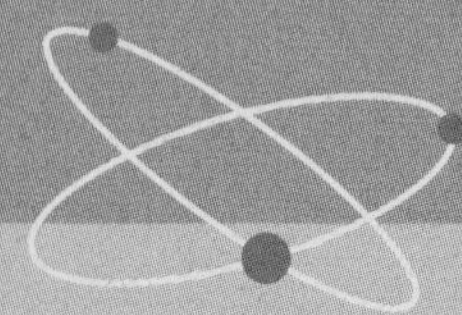

Ocean Life

Fill in the missing numbers to **multiply** each set.

4 + 4 + 4 = 12
4 × 3 =

____ + ____ + ____ + ____ =
____ × ____ =

____ + ____ + ____ =
____ × ____ =

____ + ____ + ____ + ____ =
____ × ____ =

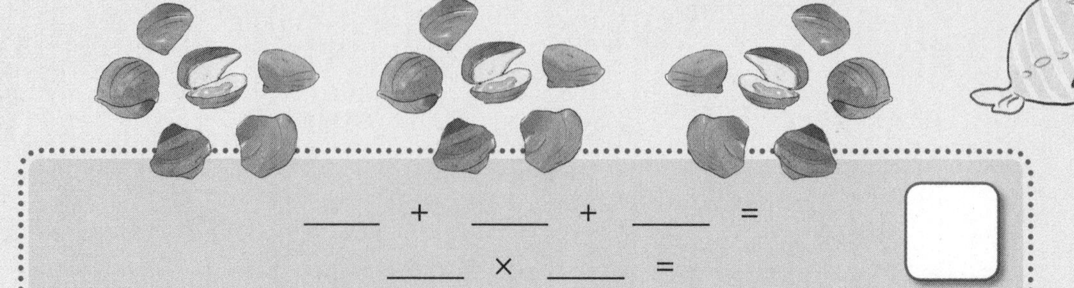

____ + ____ + ____ =
____ × ____ =

Multiplication and Division

Multiplication

Brain Box

Multiplication is adding groups of the same number.

2 + 2 + 2 = 6

2 × 3 = 6

Break It Down

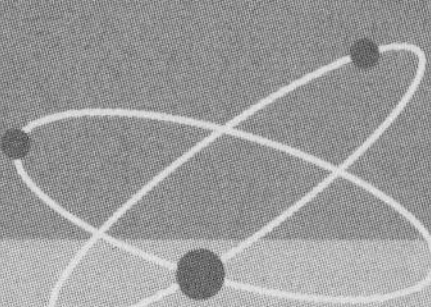

Write all the possible sets of **factors** for each **number**.

10

1 × 10 = 10 2 × 5 = 10

12

14

15

16

18

Multiplication and Division

Factors and products

Brain Box

A number can have multiple sets of **factors**.

4

1 × 4 = 4

2 × 2 = 4

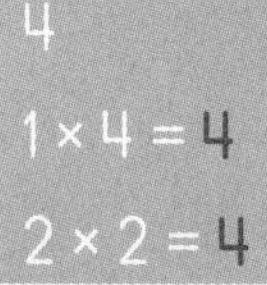

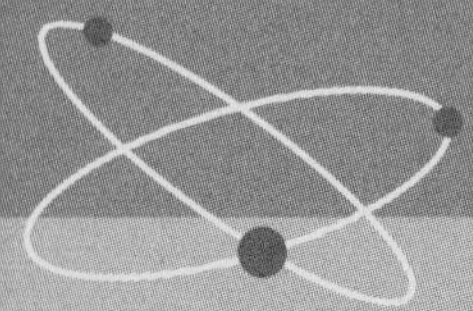

More Cheese, Please

Write out the multiplication problems needed to find the amount of cheese at each table. Solve the problems. Circle the table that has the most cheese.

Multiplication and Division

Multiplication

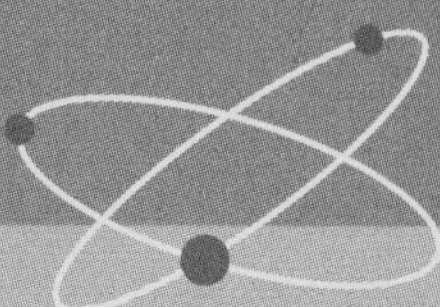

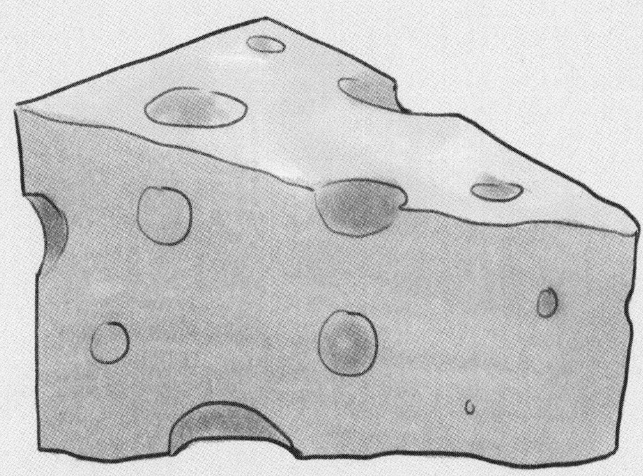

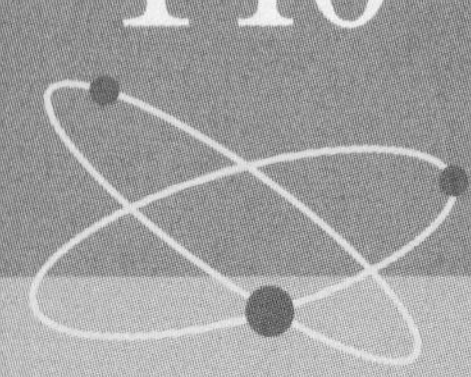

Fruitilicious

Write out the multiplication problems needed to find the number of seeds in each bowl of fruit. Solve the problems. Circle the bowl that has the most seeds.

5 × 5 = 25

Multiplication and Division

Multiplication

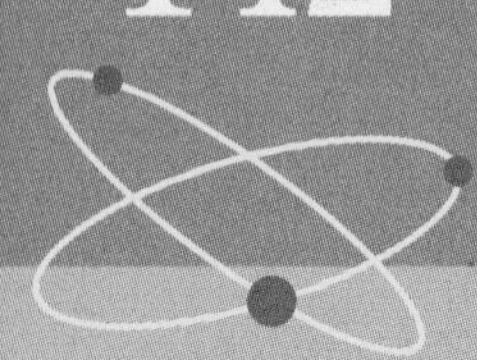

Remember, No Carrying Over

Multiply using **partial product multiplication**. Show your work.

258 × 3	582 × 6	814 × 9
147 × 2	693 × 7	936 × 2
369 × 4	701 × 8	347 × 8
		479 × 5

Brain Box

Another method of multiplying is called **partial product multiplication**. There is no carrying, and all of the adding happens below the line.

132 × 9 18 270 900 1,188

Step 1: Multiply the numbers in the ones columns. 9 times 2 equals 18.
Write that product below the line.

Step 2: Multiply the product in the ones and tens columns. Remember that the 3 is really worth 30. 9 times 30 equals 270. Write that number below the line.

Step 3: Multiply the numbers in the ones and hundreds columns. Remember that the 1 is really worth 100. 9 times 100 equals 900. Write that product below the line.

Step 4: Add up all the products.

Carry On

Multiply. Regroup as needed. Show your work.

$$\begin{array}{r} 192 \\ \times\ 3 \\ \hline 576 \end{array}$$

$$\begin{array}{r} 384 \\ \times\ 5 \\ \hline \end{array} \qquad \begin{array}{r} 594 \\ \times\ 3 \\ \hline \end{array} \qquad \begin{array}{r} 892 \\ \times\ 7 \\ \hline \end{array}$$

$$\begin{array}{r} 475 \\ \times\ 6 \\ \hline \end{array} \qquad \begin{array}{r} 387 \\ \times\ 2 \\ \hline \end{array} \qquad \begin{array}{r} 768 \\ \times\ 9 \\ \hline \end{array}$$

$$\begin{array}{r} 675 \\ \times\ 8 \\ \hline \end{array} \qquad \begin{array}{r} 241 \\ \times\ 3 \\ \hline \end{array} \qquad \begin{array}{r} 352 \\ \times\ 6 \\ \hline \end{array}$$

Brain Box

There are two ways to multiply multi-digit numbers. One way is shown below.

$$\begin{array}{r} {\scriptstyle 21} \\ 132 \\ \times\ 9 \\ \hline 1{,}188 \end{array}$$

Step 1: Multiply the numbers in the ones column and regroup. 9 times 2 is 18, so you write the 8 in the ones place and carry the 1 into the tens column.

Step 2: Multiply the numbers in the ones and tens columns. Add the number carried over. 9 times 3 is 27 plus 1 is 28. Write the 8 in the tens place. Carry the 2 to the hundreds column.

Step 3: Multiply the numbers in the ones and hundreds column. Add the number carried over. 9 times 1 is 9 plus 2 is 11. Write those numbers in the hundreds and thousands places.

$$\begin{array}{r} {\scriptstyle 2\ 1} \\ 132 \\ \times\ 9 \\ \hline 1{,}188 \end{array}$$

Big Numbers

Multiply. Show your work.

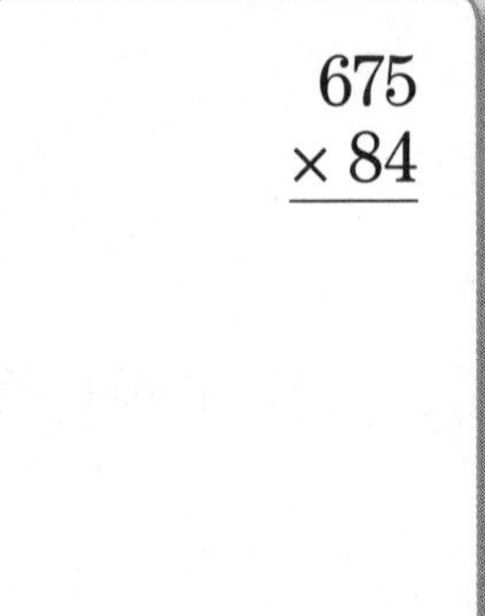

$$\begin{array}{r} 675 \\ \times\ 84 \\ \hline \end{array}$$

$$\begin{array}{r} 392 \\ \times\ 57 \\ \hline \end{array}$$

$$\begin{array}{r} 584 \\ \times\ 39 \\ \hline \end{array}$$

$$\begin{array}{r} 294 \\ \times\ 45 \\ \hline \end{array}$$

$$\begin{array}{r} 386 \\ \times\ 63 \\ \hline \end{array}$$

Multiplication and Division

Multiplying multi-digit numbers

Brain Box

Here's another way to multiply multi-digit numbers.

Step 1: Multiply as usual for the ones place (8 times 332).

Step 2: Put a 0 in the ones column. Cross out the numbers you carried because you will have new numbers to carry.

Step 3: Multiply the tens place number (4 times 332).

Step 4: Add the products.

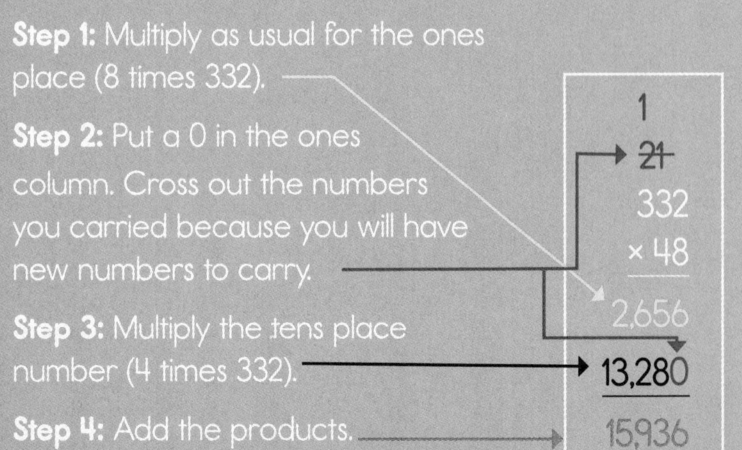

$$\begin{array}{r} 985 \\ \times\ 74 \\ \hline \end{array}$$

$$\begin{array}{r} 736 \\ \times\ 28 \\ \hline \end{array}$$

$$\begin{array}{r} 293 \\ \times\ 89 \\ \hline \end{array}$$

$$\begin{array}{r} 851 \\ \times\ 62 \\ \hline \end{array}$$

$$\begin{array}{r} 375 \\ \times\ 26 \\ \hline \end{array}$$

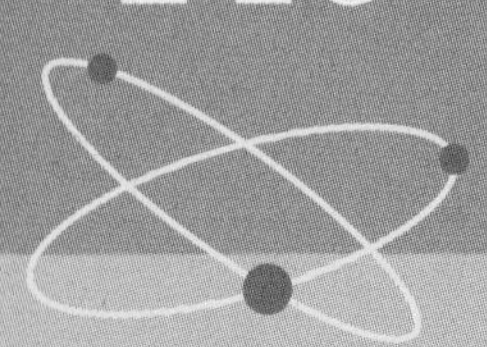

Big Numbers II

Multiply using partial product multiplication. Show your work.

589 × 29	485 × 19	936 × 87	873 × 39

854
× 67

Multiplication and Division

Multiplying multi-digit numbers

Brain Box

Here's how to multiply multi-digit numbers using partial product multiplication.

Step 1:
Multiply as usual for the ones place (8 times 332).

```
  332
 × 48
   16
  240
2,400
```

Step 2:
Multiply the tens place number (4 times 332). But remember, the 4 is really worth 40. So multiply 40 times 2 (80), 40 times 30 (1,200), and 40 times 300 (12,000).

```
  332
 × 48
   16
  240
2,400
   80
1,200
```

Step 3: Add the products.

```
   332
  × 48
    16
   240
 2,400
    80
 1,200
12,000
15,936
```

648 × 56	346 × 92	783 × 47	242 × 99

978
× 43

Multiplication and Division

Multiplying multi-digit numbers

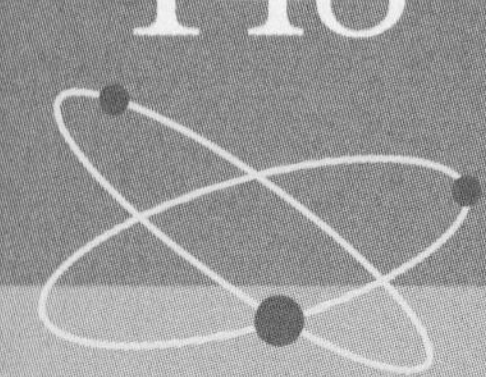

Teamwork

Divide the players into even teams. Circle the groups. Write the equation underneath.

Divide 12 soccer players into 3 teams of 4.

$12 \div 3 = 4$

Divide 20 basketball players into 4 teams of 5.

Divide 9 lacrosse players into 3 teams of 3.

Divide 24 wrestlers into 6 teams of 4.

Divide 28 gymnasts into 7 teams of 4.

Divide 32 football players into 4 teams of 8.

Divide 18 soccer players into 6 teams of 3.

Multiplication and Division

Division

Brain Box

Division is the process of dividing a number into even groups.

$12 \div 3 = 4$

12 divided by 3 equals three groups of 4.

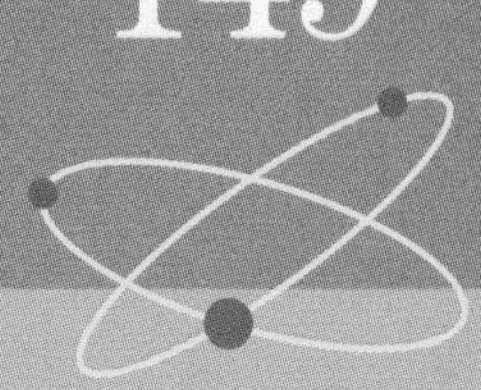

Divide and Conquer

Write out the problem. Then solve it. Circle the **quotient**.

The divisor is 8. The dividend is 57.

57 ÷ 8 = 7 r1

The dividend is 121. The divisor is 11.

The dividend is 56. The divisor is 7.

The dividend is 43. The divisor is 6.

The divisor is 9. The dividend is 63.

The dividend is 66. The divisor is 8.

The dividend is 81. The divisor is 9.

The dividend is 49. The divisor is 7.

Multiplication and Division

Divisor and dividend

Brain Box

The number being divided is called the **dividend**. The number being divided into it is called the **divisor**. The answer to a division problem is called the **quotient**. The quotient may include a **remainder**.

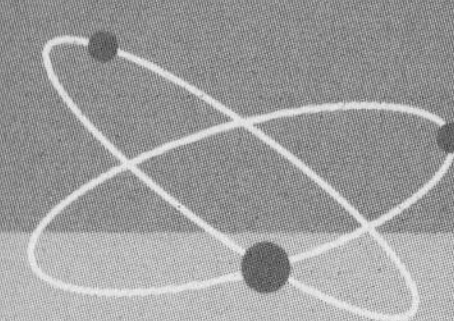

Step by Step

Divide. The answer may or may not include a remainder.

$8\overline{)589}$	$9\overline{)477}$	$7\overline{)639}$
$4\overline{)326}$	$6\overline{)282}$	$3\overline{)741}$

Multiplication and Division

Long division

Brain Box

One way to divide a large number by a smaller number is like this:

Step 1: Divide into the hundreds.

Step 2: Multiply and subtract.

Step 3: Bring down the tens and then divide into the tens.

Step 4: Multiply and subtract again.

Step 5: Bring down the ones and divide into the ones.

Step 6: Multiply and subtract. If there is a remainder, write it at the end of the quotient.

```
   128 r1
7) 897
  -7
   19
  -14
    57
   -56
     1
```

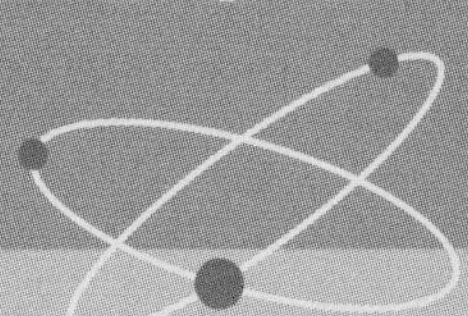

Two Are Better Than One

Divide.

$36\overline{)7{,}884}$	$22\overline{)4{,}686}$	$84\overline{)2{,}352}$
$48\overline{)8{,}064}$	$52\overline{)9{,}568}$	$32\overline{)6{,}784}$

Multiplication and Division

Dividing multi-digit numbers

Brain Box

You can divide a two-digit number into a larger number like this:

Step 1: Divide into the hundreds. If that's not possible, divide into the tens.

Step 2: Multiply and subtract.

Step 3: Bring down the ones. Then divide into the ones.

Step 4: Multiply and subtract again.

Step 5: If there is a remainder, write it at the end of the quotient.

$$\begin{array}{r} 48 \\ 26\overline{)1{,}248} \\ -104\downarrow \\ \hline 208 \\ -208 \\ \hline 0 \end{array}$$

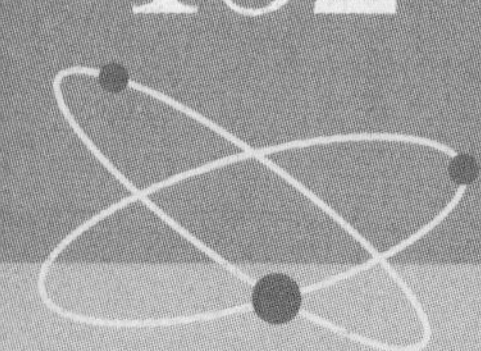

Rectangular Math

Divide using the **area model.**

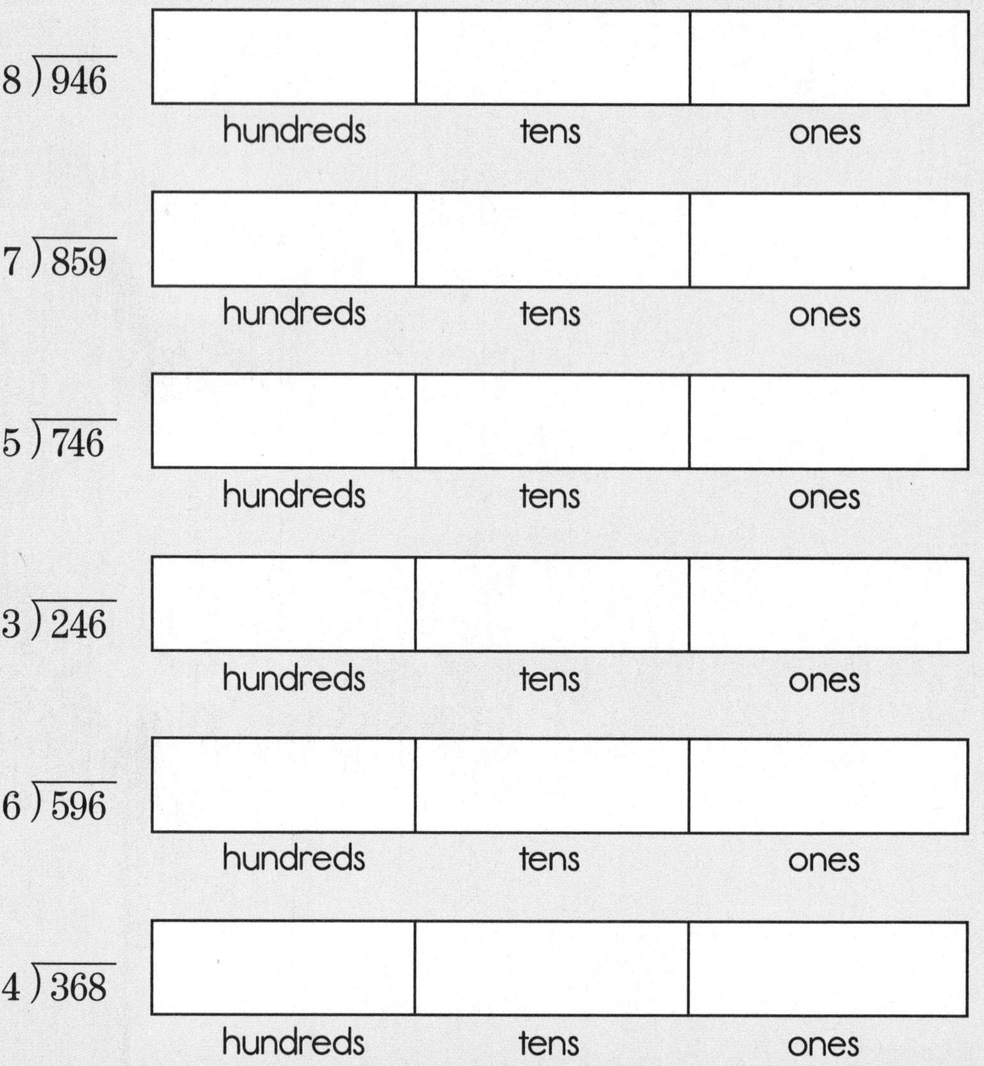

Brain Box

To divide using the **area model**, picture the dividend, 897, as the area of a rectangle. One side is the divisor, 7. The other side is the quotient.

	?
7	897

Step 1: Draw a rectangle that is divided into three columns.

hundreds	tens	ones

Step 2: Find how many hundreds (times 7) go into 897. 100 × 7 (700) goes into 897. Write 100 above the hundreds column. Subtract 700 from 897 and write the remaining amount in the tens column.

Step 3: Find how many tens (times 7) go into 197. 20 × 7 (140) goes into 197. Write 20 above the tens column. Subtract 140. Write the remaining amount in the ones column.

Step 4: Find how many ones (times 7) go into 57. 8 × 7 (56) goes into 57. Write 8 above the ones column. Subtract 56. The remaining amount is the **remainder**.

Step 5: The quotient is written in expanded notation. Write it in standard notation. (100 + 20 + 8 r1 = 128 r1)

	100	20	8 r1 = 128 r1
7	897 -700 197	197 -140 57	57 -56 1
	hundreds	tens	ones

Rectangular Math II

Divide using the area model.

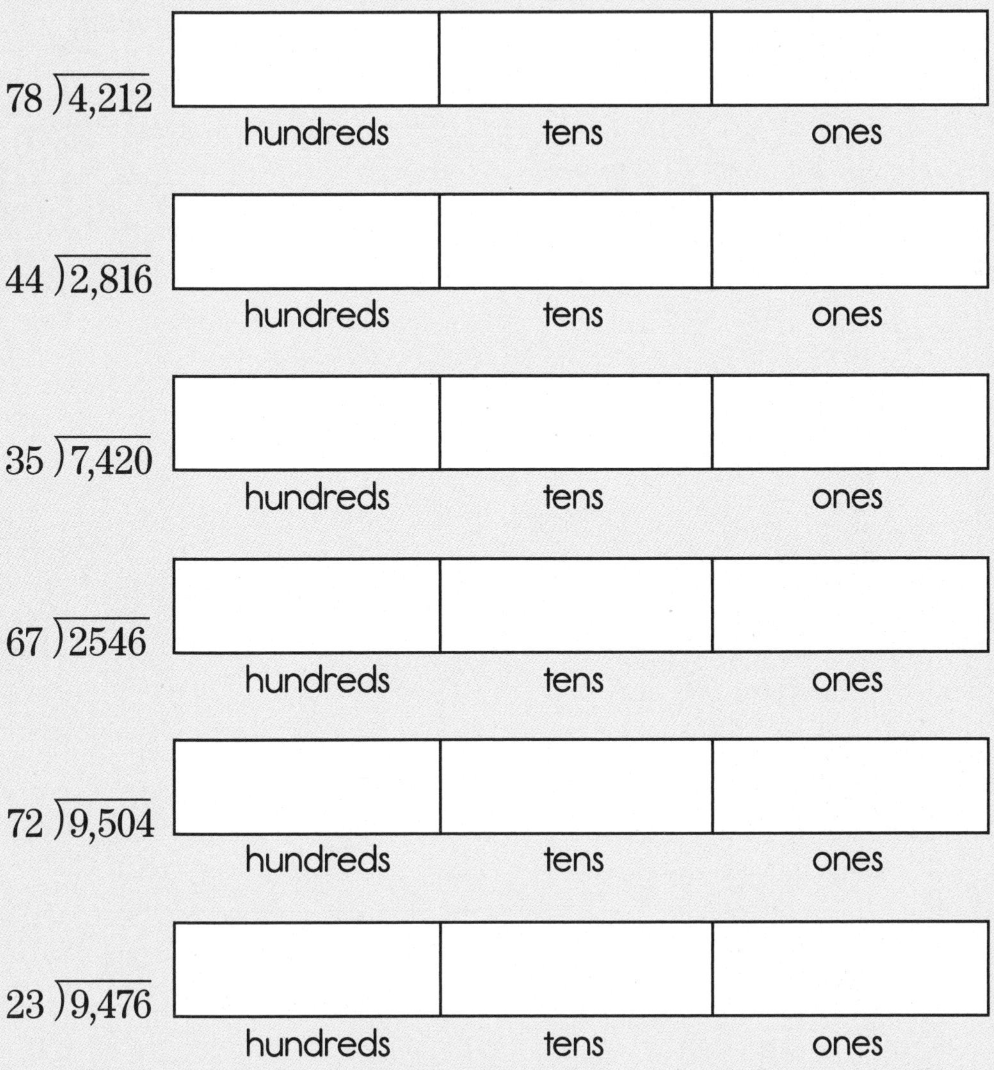

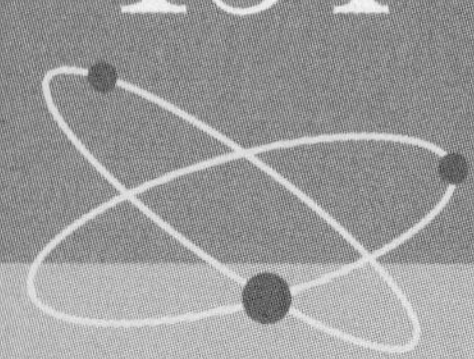

Check It

Divide. Then check your answer by multiplying.

$$\begin{array}{r} 32 \text{ r1} \\ 23\overline{)737} \\ -69\downarrow \\ \hline 47 \\ 46 \\ \hline 1 \end{array} \qquad \begin{array}{r} 32 \\ \times\ 23 \\ \hline 96 \\ +\ 640 \\ \hline 736 \\ +\ 1 \\ \hline 737 \end{array}$$

$24\overline{)1,536}$

$35\overline{)1,580}$

$64\overline{)3,584}$

$53\overline{)4,613}$

$21\overline{)546}$

$47\overline{)3,861}$

$24\overline{)6,024}$

Multiplication and Division

Checking your answer

Brain Box

You can check the answer to a division problem by multiplying the quotient by the divisor. Then add the remainder if there is one. The answer should be the same as the dividend.

Practice Makes Perfect

Divide. Show your work.

$18\overline{)8{,}442}$

$13\overline{)4{,}953}$

$47\overline{)7{,}191}$

$28\overline{)4{,}116}$

$36\overline{)7{,}596}$

$42\overline{)6{,}972}$

$56\overline{)7{,}392}$

$66\overline{)7{,}128}$

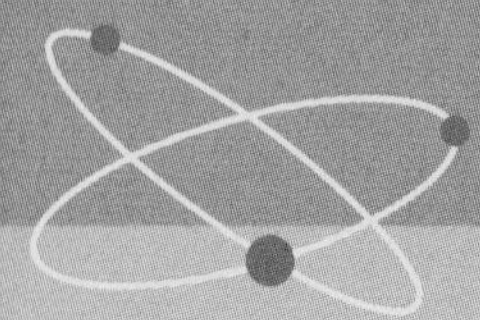

Best Guess

Estimate the product by rounding each factor to the nearest ten and multiplying.

57 × 46	rounds off to	× ___	=	
42 × 39	rounds off to	× ___	=	
44 × 81	rounds off to	× ___	=	
39 × 78	rounds off to	× ___	=	
76 × 34	rounds off to	× ___	=	
92 × 28	rounds off to	× ___	=	
48 × 99	rounds off to	× ___	=	

Multiplication and Division

Estimating

Brain Box

An **estimate** is an approximation. To estimate a product, round the factors up or down as necessary.

43 x 28 rounds off to 40 x 30 = 1,200

To estimate a quotient, round the dividend and the divisor as necessary.

1,204 ÷ 43 rounds off to 1,200 ÷ 40 = 30

Estimate the quotient by rounding the divisor to the nearest hundred and the dividend to the nearest ten and then dividing.

6,784 ÷ 23	8,756 ÷ 42	3,476 ÷ 67
7,843 ÷ 29	9,857 ÷ 33	8,124 ÷ 94

Fractions and Decimals

Pizza Party

Write the **numerator** and **denominator** that show how much of a whole pizza is left.

Numerator $\frac{3}{8}$ Denominator

Numerator ___ Denominator

Numerator ___ Denominator

Numerator ___ Denominator

Numerator ___ Denominator

Numerator ___ Denominator

Numerator and denominator

Fractions and Decimals

Brain Box

A **fraction** represents a part of a whole. The **denominator** tells how many equal parts are in the whole. The **numerator** tells how many of those parts are being counted. For instance, if a pizza starts out having 8 pieces, and now has 5 pieces left, the fraction that describes how much pizza is left is $\frac{5}{8}$. 8 is the denominator, and 5 is the numerator.

An 8-piece pizza arrives for you and your friends. When you're done eating, 2 slices remain. Write a fraction that describes how much of the whole pizza is left.

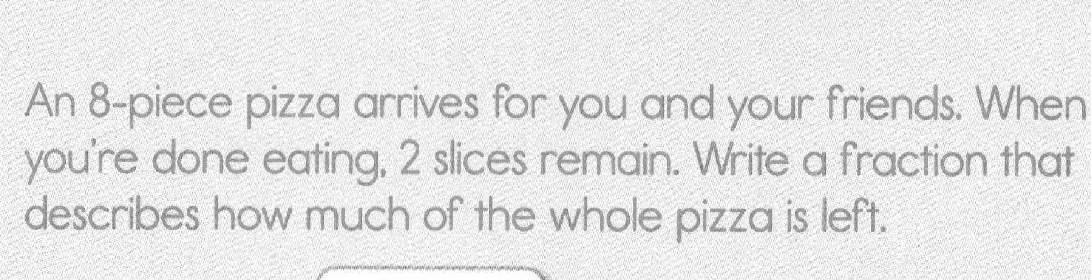

Nice and Simple

Simplify the **fraction**. Shade in the correct amount.

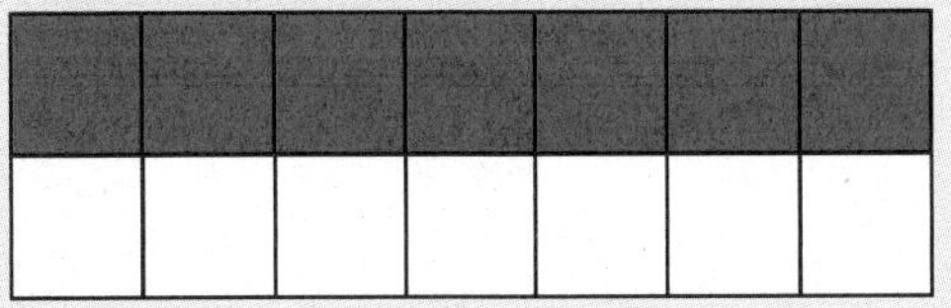

$\frac{7}{14}$

$\frac{1}{2}$

$\frac{2}{10}$

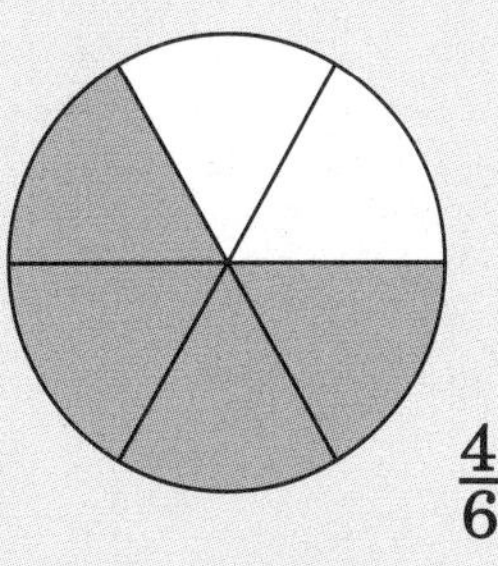

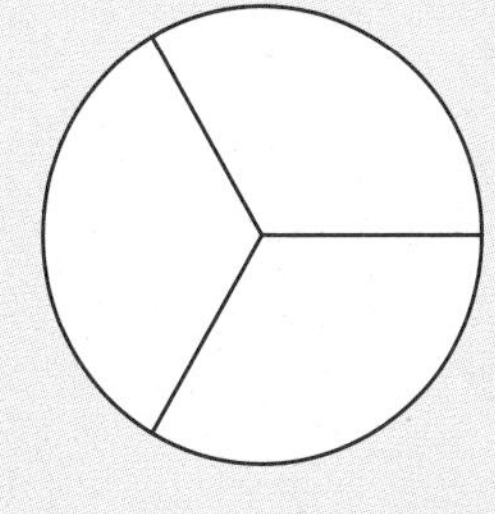

$\frac{4}{6}$

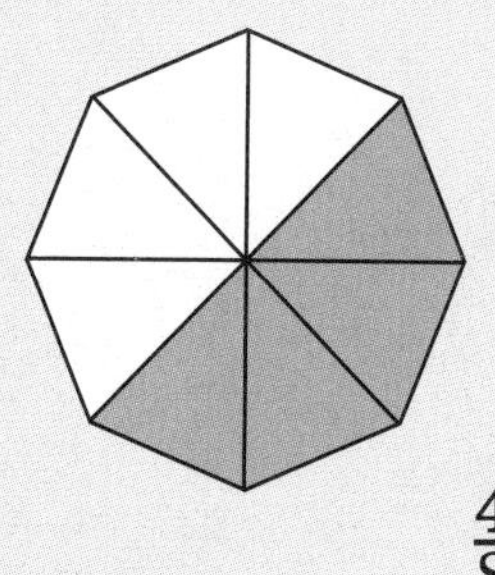

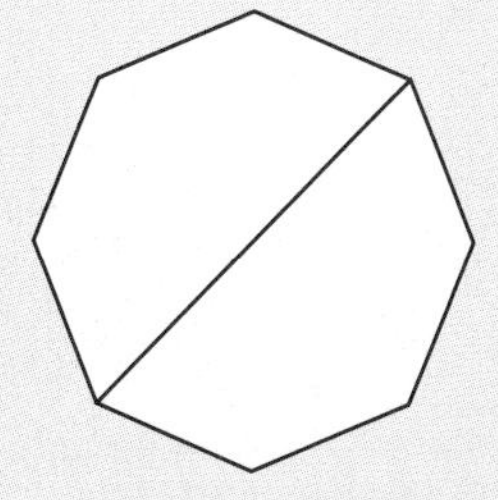

$\frac{4}{8}$

Brain Box

When the numerator and denominator share a common factor, the fraction can be simplified. Example:

$\frac{6}{8}$ =

The 6 and 8 can both be divided by 2.

$6 \div 2 = 3$

$8 \div 2 = 4$

The simplified fraction is $\frac{3}{4}$.

As you can see, the two fractions represent equal amounts.

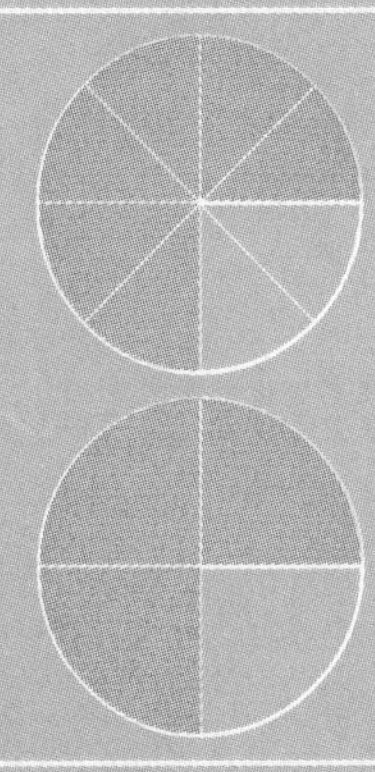

Sharing Is Caring

Fill in the blank with a fraction to solve the word problem.
Simplify the fractions.

6 sisters share 2 calzones.
Each sister gets $\frac{2}{6}$ or $\frac{1}{3}$ of a calzone.

64 band members share 8 pizzas.
Each band member gets _____ or _____ of a pizza.

81 villagers share 9 pounds of sugar.
Each villager gets _____ or _____ pound of sugar.

36 students share 4 packs of paper.
Each student gets _____ or _____ pack of paper.

12 soccer players share 6 oranges.
Each player gets _____ or _____ of an orange.

45 teachers share 9 gallons of glue.
Each teacher gets _____ or _____ of a gallon.

Draw a picture to help solve the problem.

24 chefs share 6 sticks of butter.
Each chef gets _________ or _________ stick of butter.

Simplifying fractions

Fractions and Decimals

Brain Box

A division problem can be written as a fraction.

3 divided by 4 can be written as $\frac{3}{4}$.

This means that if 4 people share 3 chocolate bars equally, they should each get $\frac{3}{4}$ of a bar.

Mixed Results

Find the correct **mixed number** for each word problem. Simplify fractions if necessary.

9 cooks share 50 pounds of butter.
How many pounds of butter does each cook get? _______

7 mice share 68 pieces of popcorn.
How many pieces of popcorn does each mouse get? _______

12 kids share 40 pieces of paper.
How many pieces of paper does each kid get? _______

11 crafters share 115 glue sticks.
How many glue sticks does each crafter get? _______

8 ants share 62 crumbs.
How many crumbs does each ant get? _______

22 students share 46 packs of crayons.
How many packs does each student get? _______

Draw a picture to help solve the problem.

4 smoothie stands share 26 pounds of bananas.
How many pounds of bananas does each smoothie stand receive?

Brain Box

When a quotient has a remainder, the quotient can be written as a **mixed number**, which is a whole number plus a fraction.

If you evenly divide 13 cookies among 4 people, each person would get $3\frac{1}{4}$ cookies.

3 r1

$4\overline{)13}$

Turn the remainder into a fraction by placing it over the divisor.

$3\frac{1}{4}$

The Pluses and Minuses of Fractions

Add or subtract the **fractions**. Simplify if needed.

$\frac{5}{8} + \frac{1}{8}$

$\frac{3}{4} - \frac{1}{4}$

$\frac{4}{5} + \frac{3}{5}$

$\frac{6}{7} - \frac{3}{7}$

$\frac{8}{9} + \frac{7}{9}$

$\frac{8}{11} + \frac{7}{11}$

$\frac{7}{10} - \frac{3}{10}$

$\frac{11}{14} + \frac{13}{14}$

$\frac{13}{15} - \frac{8}{15}$

Brain Box

Adding **fractions** is adding more parts to the whole. Subtracting fractions is subtracting parts from the whole. Fractions with the same denominator can be added or subtracted by adding or subtracting their numerators. The denominator stays the same.

$\frac{4}{5} + \frac{3}{5} = \frac{7}{5}$ $\frac{4}{5} - \frac{3}{5} = \frac{1}{5}$

Matchy, Matchy

Draw a line between the matching equations.

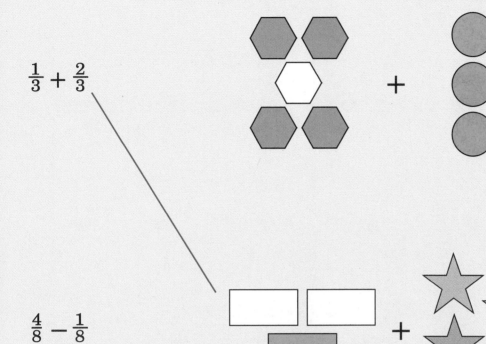

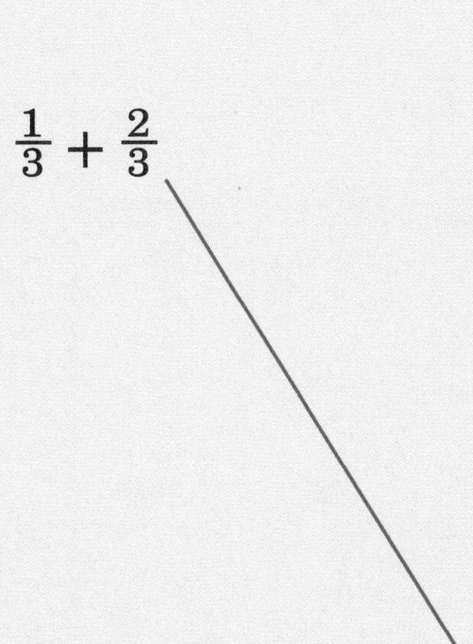

$\frac{1}{3} + \frac{2}{3}$

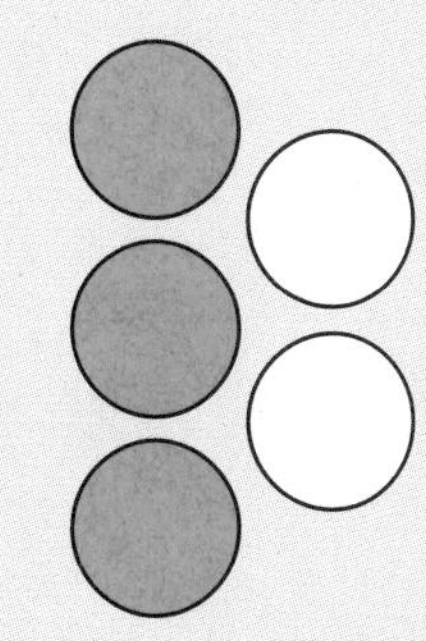

$\frac{4}{8} - \frac{1}{8}$

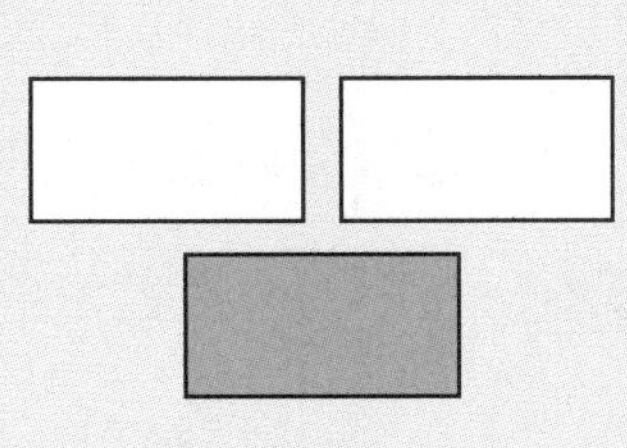

$\frac{4}{5} + \frac{3}{5}$

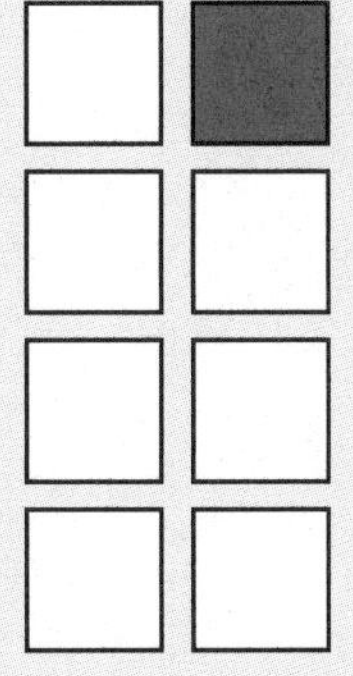

$\frac{3}{4} + \frac{1}{4}$

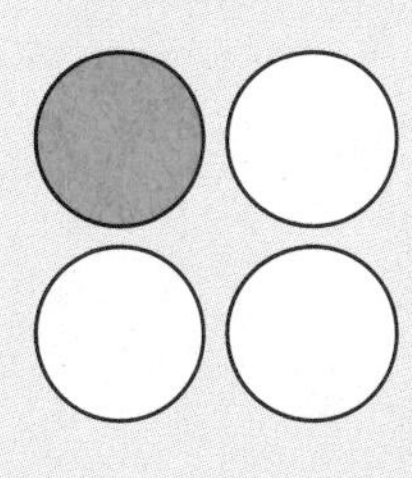

Fractions and Decimals

Adding and subtracting fractions

Bigger Products

Convert the mixed number into an improper fraction.

$2\frac{1}{4}$	$4\frac{7}{8}$ ....
$3\frac{1}{8}$	$2\frac{5}{6}$ ....
$8\frac{1}{3}$	$1\frac{7}{8}$ ....
$3\frac{2}{5}$	$6\frac{1}{2}$ ....

Brain Box

To convert a mixed number into an **improper fraction**, follow these steps:

$2\frac{1}{4}$

Step 1: Multiply the whole number by the denominator. → $2 \times 4 = 8$

Step 2: Add that product to the numerator. → $8 + 1 = 9$

Step 3: Write that sum above the denominator. $\frac{9}{4}$

Less and Less

Multiply. Show your work. Simplify all fractions.

$\frac{3}{8} \times \frac{7}{10}$	$\frac{7}{8} \times \frac{4}{5}$
$\frac{1}{2} \times \frac{3}{5}$	$\frac{1}{3} \times \frac{3}{4}$
$\frac{4}{5} \times \frac{2}{3}$	$\frac{5}{8} \times \frac{2}{3}$
$\frac{9}{10} \times \frac{3}{4}$	$\frac{3}{8} \times \frac{7}{8}$
$\frac{6}{7} \times \frac{1}{2}$	$\frac{1}{2} \times \frac{2}{3}$

Brain Box

When multiplying fractions, multiply the numerators. Then multiply the denominators.

Let's compare those fractions.

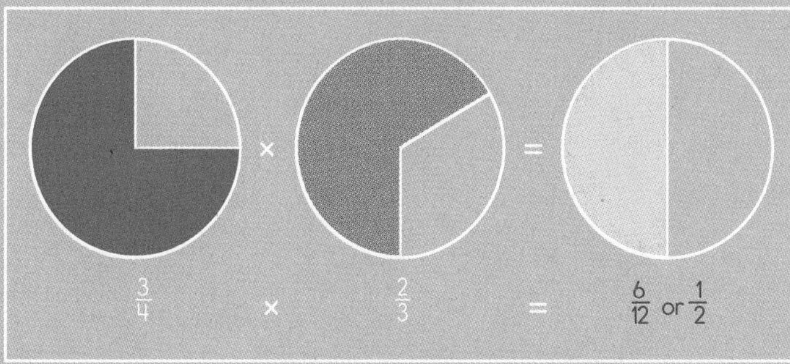

As you can see, the product is less than the factors. That's because you are multiplying two fractions that are less than 1. That means you are finding a part of a part. In this case, you are finding $\frac{2}{3}$ of $\frac{3}{4}$.

Shortcut

Multiply. Simplify as you solve by **cross-canceling.**

$\frac{3}{5} \times \frac{5}{6}$

$\frac{2}{5} \times \frac{3}{4}$

$\frac{5}{8} \times \frac{4}{5}$

$\frac{2}{3} \times \frac{1}{2}$

$\frac{2}{3} \times \frac{6}{11}$

$\frac{3}{7} \times \frac{14}{15}$

$\frac{3}{11} \times \frac{5}{12}$

$\frac{7}{10} \times \frac{5}{8}$

$\frac{4}{5} \times \frac{5}{16}$

$\frac{3}{4} \times \frac{4}{5}$

Brain Box

You can multiply fractions more easily by first **cross-canceling** the numerators and denominators.

$\frac{3}{4} \times \frac{4}{5}$

You can cross-cancel the 4s. This won't change the answer because you are dividing the equation by $\frac{4}{4}$, which is equivalent to 1, and anything divided by 1 is itself.

The new equation is

$\frac{3}{1} \times \frac{1}{5} = \frac{3}{5}$

When a numerator and denominator being multiplied share a common factor (in this case 4), they can also be cross-canceled.

$\frac{3}{8} \times \frac{4}{5}$

$\frac{4}{8}$ can be removed. The 8 becomes 2 and the 4 becomes 1.

$\frac{3}{2} \times \frac{1}{5} = \frac{3}{10}$

Flip It

Divide. Simplify as you solve.

$\frac{3}{8} \div \frac{6}{7}$

$\frac{1}{4} \div \frac{1}{2}$

$\frac{1}{2} \div \frac{3}{5}$

$\frac{6}{7} \div \frac{1}{2}$

$\frac{4}{5} \div \frac{2}{3}$

$\frac{3}{8} \div \frac{7}{10}$

$\frac{2}{5} \div \frac{4}{9}$

$\frac{9}{10} \div \frac{3}{4}$

$\frac{1}{3} \div \frac{5}{8}$

$\frac{7}{8} \div \frac{4}{5}$

Brain Box

$\frac{4}{5} \div \frac{3}{4}$

$\frac{4}{5} \times \frac{4}{3} = \frac{16}{15}$

To divide **fractions**, flip the numerator and denominator of the second fraction and multiply. A **reciprocal** is a pair of numbers that when multiplied together equal 1.

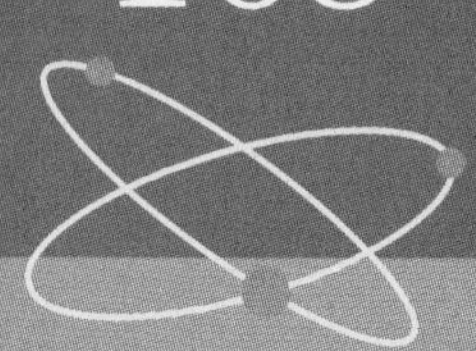

High Divide

Divide. Simplify.

$4 \div \frac{6}{7}$

$6 \div \frac{5}{8}$

$\frac{1}{2} \div 3$

$\frac{1}{4} \div 8$

$7 \div \frac{2}{3}$

$\frac{6}{7} \div 5$

$12 \div \frac{4}{9}$

$9 \div \frac{7}{10}$

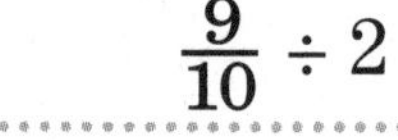

$\frac{9}{10} \div 2$

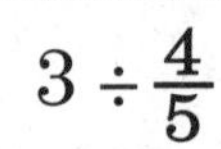

$3 \div \frac{4}{5}$

Dividing fractions

Fractions and Decimals

Brain Box

When dividing a **fraction** by a whole number (or vice versa), first insert 1 as the denominator for the whole number (this doesn't change the number because any number divided by 1 is itself). Then flip the second fraction and multiply the fractions.

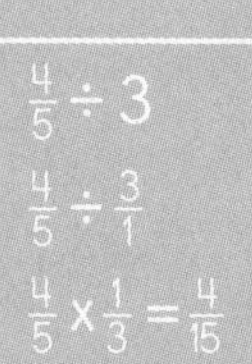

$\frac{4}{5} \div 3$

$\frac{4}{5} \div \frac{3}{1}$

$\frac{4}{5} \times \frac{1}{3} = \frac{4}{15}$

$3 \div \frac{4}{5}$

$\frac{3}{1} \div \frac{4}{5}$

$\frac{3}{1} \times \frac{5}{4} = \frac{15}{4}$

The Great Divide

Divide the shape into smaller parts based on the equation.
Solve the problem.

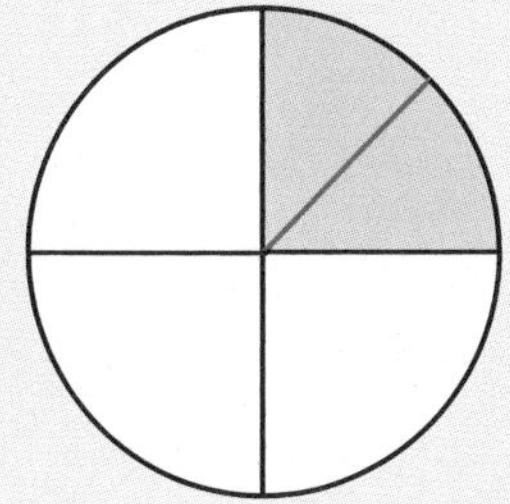

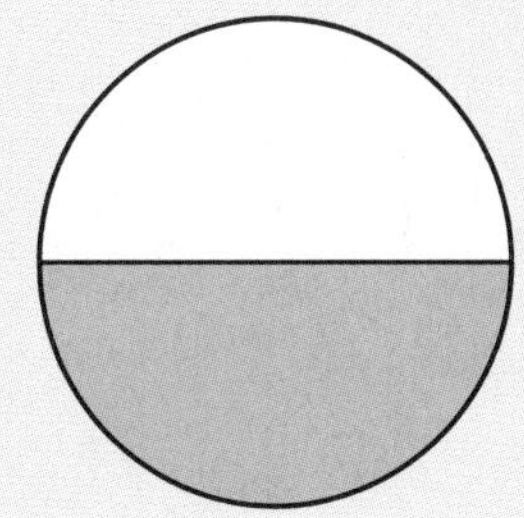

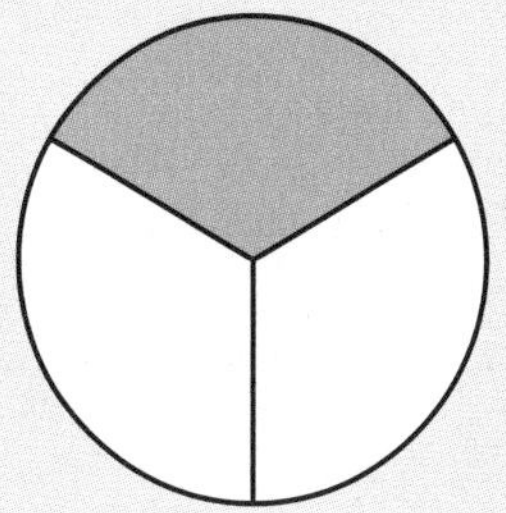

$\frac{1}{4} \div 2 = \frac{1}{8}$

$\frac{1}{2} \div 5 =$

$\frac{1}{3} \div 3 =$

Divide the shapes into more parts based on the equation.
Solve the problem.

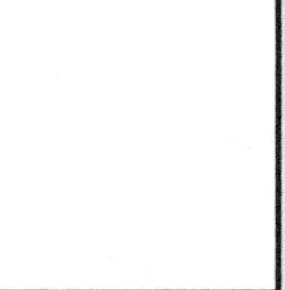

$4 \div \frac{1}{2} =$

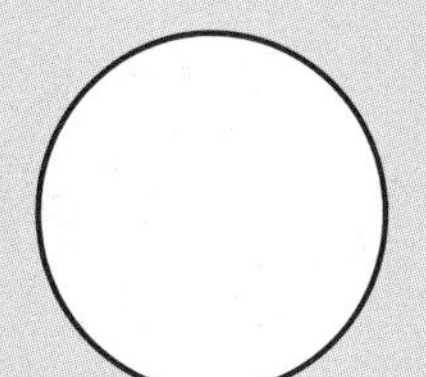

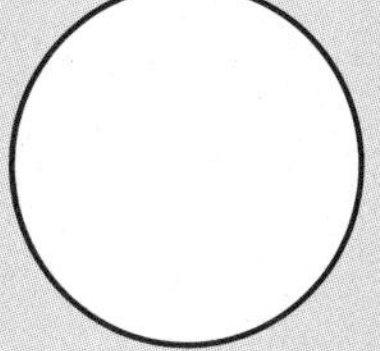

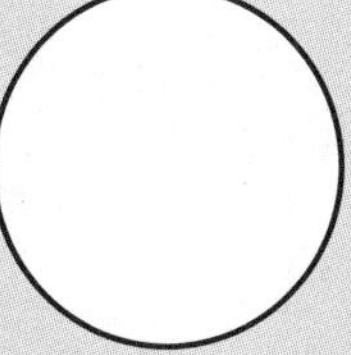

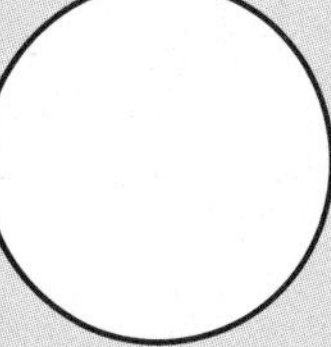

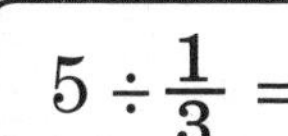

$5 \div \frac{1}{3} =$

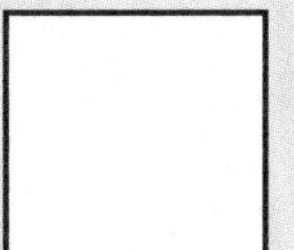

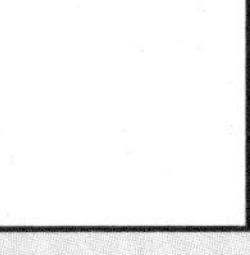

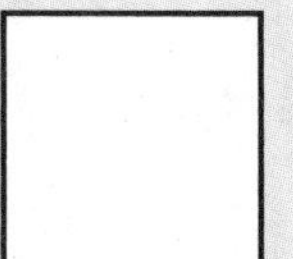

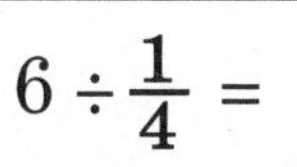

$6 \div \frac{1}{4} =$

Dividing fractions

Fractions and Decimals

Brain Box

When you are dividing a fraction by a whole number, you are dividing a part of a whole into smaller parts. So the fraction gets smaller.

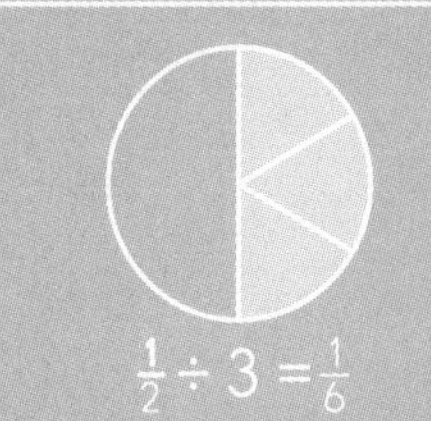

$\frac{1}{2} \div 3 = \frac{1}{6}$

When dividing a whole number by a fraction, you are dividing a whole number by a part of a whole. So the number gets bigger.

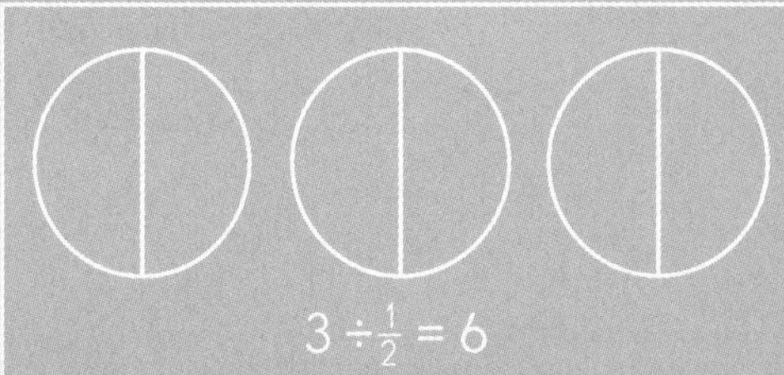

$3 \div \frac{1}{2} = 6$

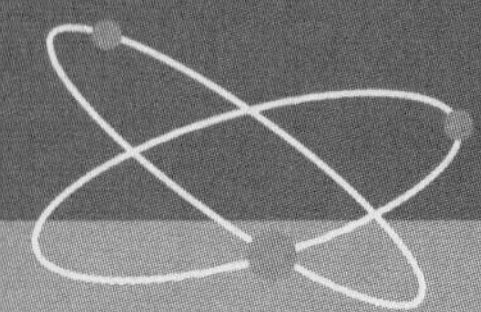

Something in Common

Add by finding the **lowest common denominator**. Simplify if necessary.

$\frac{5}{6} + \frac{1}{3} =$

$\frac{5}{6} + \frac{2}{3} =$

$\frac{5}{8} + \frac{1}{4} =$

$\frac{3}{7} + \frac{1}{2} =$

$\frac{1}{2} + \frac{2}{5} =$

$\frac{2}{3} + \frac{8}{9} =$

$\frac{3}{16} + \frac{1}{4} =$

$\frac{5}{12} + \frac{5}{6} =$

$\frac{9}{10} + \frac{1}{5} =$

$\frac{7}{12} + \frac{3}{4} =$

Brain Box

To add or subtract fractions with different denominators, find the **lowest common denominator**, or **least common multiple** of the denominators, to make the denominators equal:

$\frac{1}{6} + \frac{2}{3}$

Step 1: What is the least common multiple of both denominators? The 3 can be changed to a 6 by multiplying it by 2.

Step 2: What is done to the denominator also must be done to the numerator.

$\frac{2}{3} \times \frac{2}{2}$

Step 3: Add the new fractions.

$\frac{1}{6} + \frac{4}{6} = \frac{5}{6}$

Sometimes both denominators must be changed. Follow the same steps.

$\frac{2}{3} + \frac{3}{4}$

The least common multiple of both denominators is 12.
So multiply both fractions to get the denominator.

$\frac{2}{3} \times \frac{4}{4} = \frac{8}{12}$ $\frac{3}{4} \times \frac{3}{3} = \frac{9}{12}$ $\frac{8}{12} + \frac{9}{12} = \frac{17}{12} = 1\frac{5}{12}$

Long-Lost Twins

Change the **fraction** to a **decimal**.

$\frac{3}{10}$ = ____

$\frac{11}{100}$ = ____

$\frac{7}{10}$ = ____

$\frac{461}{1000}$ = ____

$\frac{57}{100}$ = ____

Change the **decimal** to a **fraction**.

0.9 ____

0.063 ____

0.777 ____

0.323 ____

0.17 ____

Brain Box

Like a fraction, a **decimal** represents a part of a whole: a part of 10, 100, 1,000, and so on.

$\frac{1}{10}$ = 0.1 $\frac{1}{100}$ = 0.01

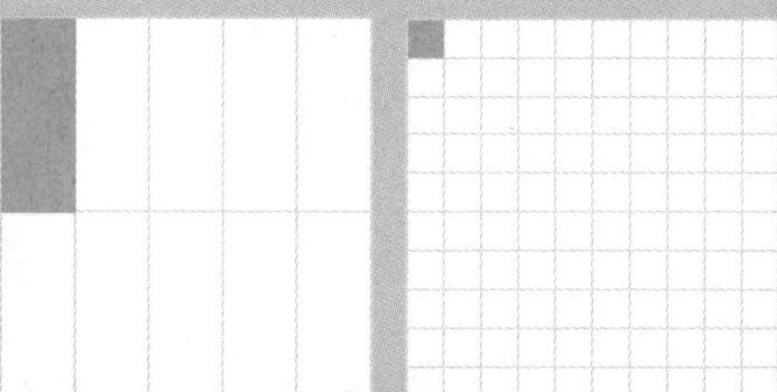

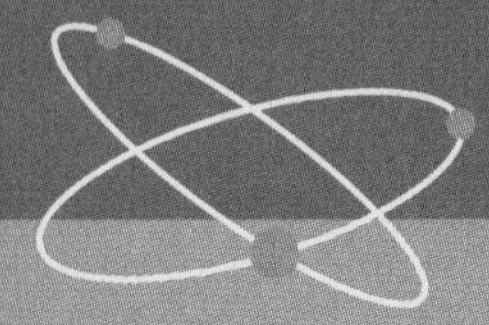

Change Is in the Air

Change the **fractions** to **decimals** by changing the denominators to 10, 100, or 1,000.

$\frac{3}{4}$ ______

$\frac{7}{25}$ ______

$\frac{1}{2}$ ______

$\frac{29}{50}$ ______

$\frac{13}{20}$ ______

$\frac{4}{5}$ ______

$\frac{3}{25}$ ______

$\frac{17}{50}$ ______

$\frac{3}{5}$ ______

Fractions and Decimals

Fractions and decimals

Brain Box

To convert a fraction to a decimal, you may need to first change the fraction's denominator to 10, 100, or 1,000.

Find a number you can multiply by the denominator to make it 10, 100, 1,000. Then multiply both the denominator and the numerator by that number.

$\frac{2}{5} \times \frac{20}{20} = \frac{40}{100} = 0.4$

Smallest to Biggest

Order the decimals from smallest to largest.

0.42, 0.04, 0.7 0.04, 0.42, 0.7 ______

0.78, 0.312, 0.1 ______

0.095, 0.856, 0.006 ______

0.613, 0.5, 0.32 ______

0.18, 0.54, 0.454 ______

0.62, 0.41, 0.19 ______

0.37, 0.4, 0.13 ______

0.11, 0.42, 0.014 ______

0.867, 0.53, 0.09 ______

0.523, 0.02, 0.29 ______

Brain Box

In **decimals**, the tenths place is worth ten times more than the hundredths place.

0.2 is worth $\frac{2}{10}$

0.02 is worth $\frac{2}{100}$

If there is no number in the hundredths or thousandths place, then the value is 0.

0.7 = 0.70

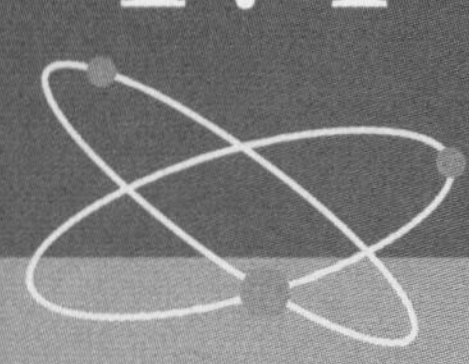

The Greatest

Compare the fractions and decimals below, using >, <, or =.

$\frac{3}{4}$ ______ 0.85

$\frac{7}{10}$ ______ 0.7

$\frac{1}{25}$ ______ 0.25

$\frac{7}{50}$ ______ 0.89

$\frac{3}{20}$ ______ 0.15

$\frac{3}{5}$ ______ 0.49

$\frac{17}{25}$ ______ 0.36

$\frac{41}{50}$ ______ 0.41

$\frac{2}{5}$ ______ 0.25

$\frac{1}{2}$ ______ 0.30

Fractions and Decimals

Comparing decimals and fractions

Brain Box

To compare decimals and fractions, change all the decimals to fractions and find a common denominator.

$\frac{1}{5}$, 0.25

$0.25 = \frac{25}{100}$

$\frac{1}{5} \times \frac{20}{20} = \frac{20}{100}$

$\frac{20}{100} < \frac{25}{100}$

Dot to Dot

Add the decimals.

0.18 + 0.051 0.231		
3.28 + 37.451	747.02 + 73.1888	10.75 + 2.25
17.014 + 129.54	0.0022 + 0.8896	3.74 + 11.4
152.3 + 31.96	7.139 + 6.264	85.45 + 90.53

Brain Box

To add decimals, make sure the decimal points are lined up. Then add the decimals just like any other number. Carry down the decimal point.

100.47
+ 2.4
102.87

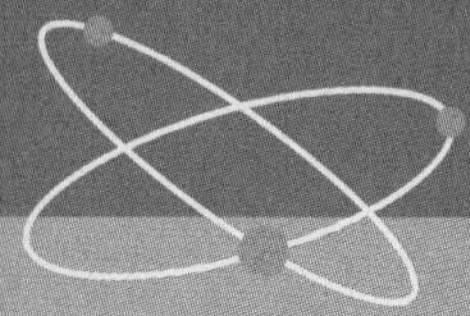

Ch-ching Ch-change

Add the U.S. coins and write the sum as a decimal.
Be sure to include the dollar sign, $.

$ 0.25
$ 0.25
$ 0.05
+$ 0.01
$ 0.56

A candy bar costs $1. Circle the collections of coins that would be enough to buy the candy bar.

Brain Box

Money can be written as a decimal. One penny is 0.01, or $\frac{1}{100}$ of a dollar. A nickel is 0.05, or $\frac{5}{100}$ of a dollar. A dime is 0.10, or $\frac{10}{100}$. A quarter is 0.25, or $\frac{25}{100}$.

Fractions and Decimals

Decimals and money

Move It

Multiply.

$$\begin{array}{r} 5.61 \\ \times\ 0.78 \\ \hline 8 \\ 480 \\ 4000 \\ 70 \\ 4200 \\ 35000 \\ \hline 4.3758 \end{array}$$

(2 decimal places)
(2 decimal places)

$\begin{array}{r} 0.328 \\ \times 0.79 \\ \hline \end{array}$

$\begin{array}{r} 1.25 \\ \times 0.81 \\ \hline \end{array}$

$\begin{array}{r} 32.4 \\ \times 0.76 \\ \hline \end{array}$

$\begin{array}{r} 44.12 \\ \times\ 0.312 \\ \hline \end{array}$

$\begin{array}{r} 98.1 \\ \times\ 7.2 \\ \hline \end{array}$

$\begin{array}{r} 88.32 \\ \times\ 67.1 \\ \hline \end{array}$

$\begin{array}{r} 4.48 \\ \times\ 0.03 \\ \hline \end{array}$

$\begin{array}{r} 82.97 \\ \times\ 0.456 \\ \hline \end{array}$

$\begin{array}{r} 5.8 \\ \times 0.3 \\ \hline \end{array}$

$\begin{array}{r} 32.48 \\ \times\ 3.77 \\ \hline \end{array}$

Multiplying decimals

Fractions and Decimals

Brain Box

Multiply decimals like any other numbers. Then count the number of digits to the right of all the decimals points. Move the decimal point that many places to the left.

Mixed Bag

Solve the fraction and decimal problems.

$\frac{1}{4} + \frac{3}{5} =$

$$\begin{array}{r} 45.2 \\ +\ \ 1.99 \\ \hline \end{array}$$

$2\frac{2}{3} \times 8\frac{1}{8} =$

$$\begin{array}{r} 0.291 \\ \times\ 0.34 \\ \hline \end{array}$$

$\frac{7}{8} \times \frac{11}{12} =$

$\frac{5}{8} \div \frac{1}{2} =$

$\frac{3}{5} \div \frac{2}{3} =$

$1\frac{1}{4} + \frac{5}{6} =$

$18 \times \frac{1}{3} =$

Geometry and Measurement

Perfect 10

Circle which unit should be used to measure the length of the following:

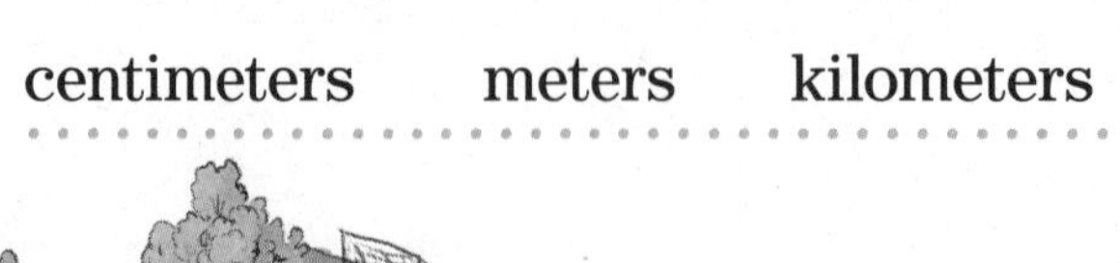

centimeters meters kilometers

centimeters meters kilometers

centimeters meters kilometers

centimeters meters kilometers

centimeters meters kilometers

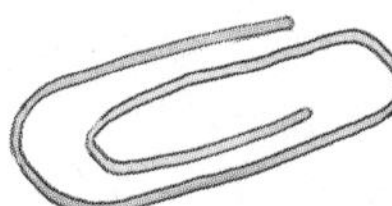

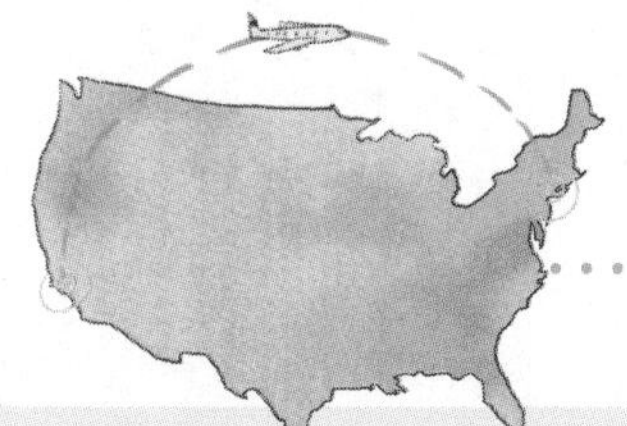

centimeters meters kilometers

Fill in the blanks.

300 cm = ______ m 5000 m = _____ km 5 m = _______ cm

4 km = ________ m 0.5 m = ________ cm

Brain Box

The **metric system** is the sole system of measurement in many countries. In the United States, it is used in science, medicine, and other fields. The metric system is based on the number 10.

There are 100 **centimeters (cm)** in a **meter (m)**, and 1,000 **meters** in a **kilometer (km)**.

100 cm = 1 m

1,000 m = 1 km

To measure something small, like a garter snake, use centimeters.

To measure something bigger, like the length of a tree, use meters.

To measure something even bigger, like the distance across an ocean, use kilometers.

Inch by Inch

Circle which unit should be used to measure the length of the following:

inches feet/yards miles

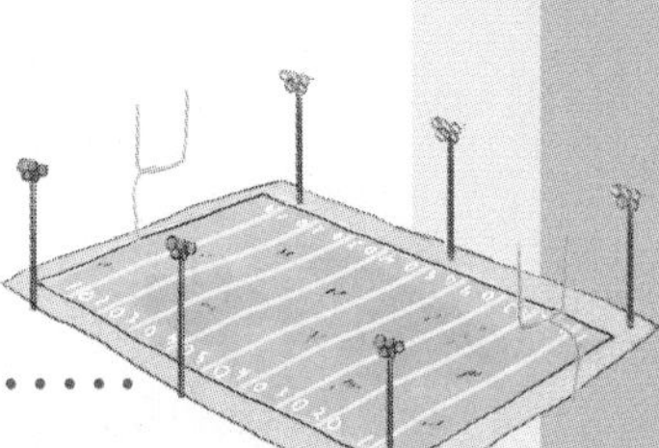

inches feet/yards miles

inches feet/yards miles

inches feet/yards miles

inches feet/yards miles

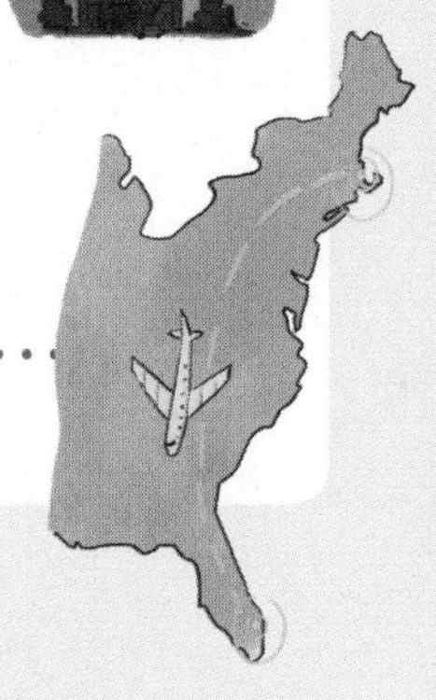

inches feet/yards miles

The U.S. customary system

Geometry and Measurement

Fill in the blanks.

2 ft. = _________ in.   2 mi. = ______ yd.   48 in. = ______ ft.

3,520 yd. = _____ mi.   100 yd. = ______ ft.

Brain Box

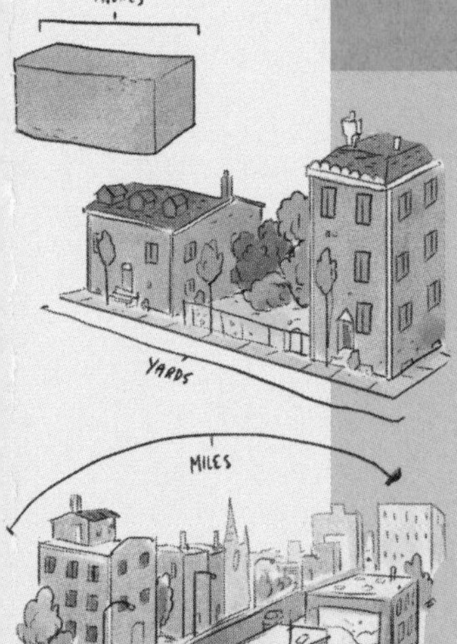

The **U.S. customary system** of measurement is also used in the United States. This system is based on everyday objects that people used long ago to measure things. For instance, people measured short distances with their own feet.

There are 12 **inches (in.)** in a **foot (ft.)**, 3 **feet** in a **yard (yd.)**, and 1,760 **yards** in a **mile (mi.)**.

12 in. = 1 ft.
3 ft. = 1 yd.
1,760 yd. = 1 mi.

To measure something small, like a brick, use inches. To measure something bigger, like the length of a city block, use feet or yards. To measure something even bigger, like the distance across a city, use miles.

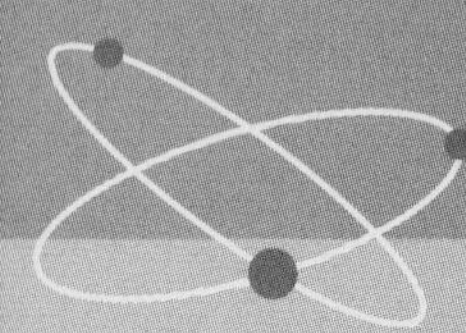

Liter-ally Liters

Write the amount in each beaker. Then answer the questions.

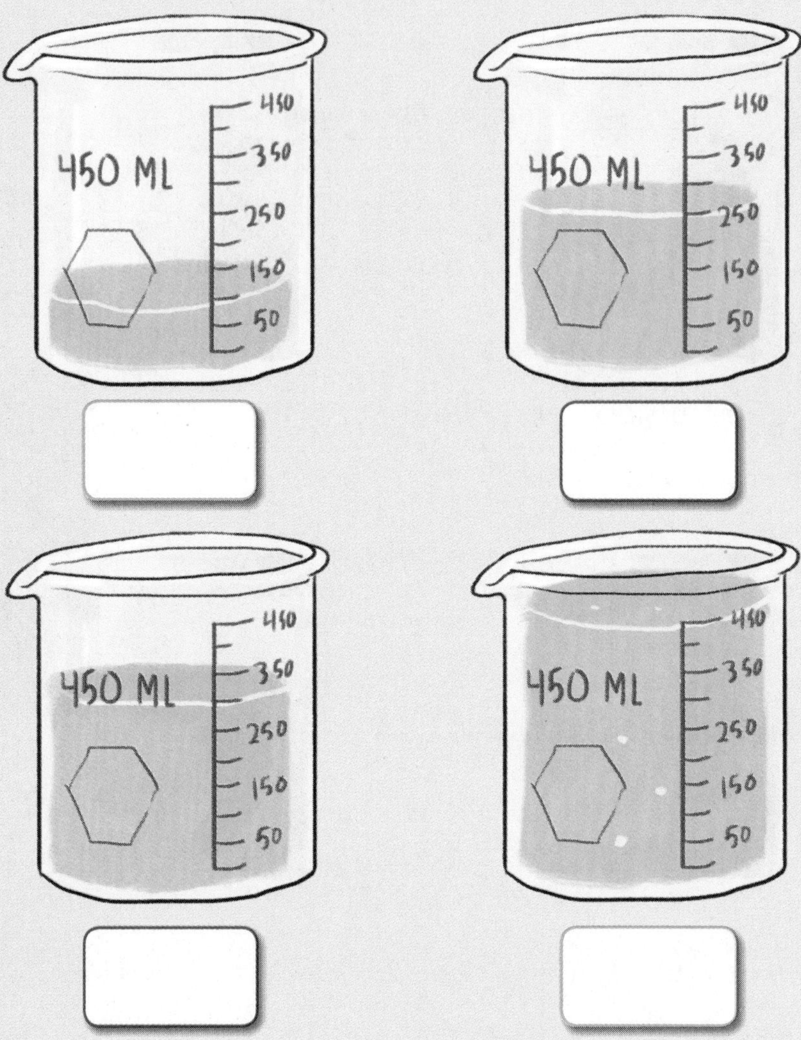

Liquid volume

How many 450 milliliter beakers do you need for 4.5 liters? ___________

How many milliliters are in a 45-kiloliter beaker? ___________

Geometry and Measurement

Brain Box

The metric unit for measuring liquids and pourable solids (such as rice or sugar) is the **liter**.

There are 1,000 **milliliters (mL)** in a **liter (L)**, and 1,000 **liters** in a **kiloliter (kL)**.

1,000 mL = 1 L

1,000 L = 1 kL

Use milliliters to measure small amounts, such as medicine.

Use liters to measure larger amounts, such as a bottle of soda.

Use kiloliters to measure even larger amounts, such as the water in a swimming pool.

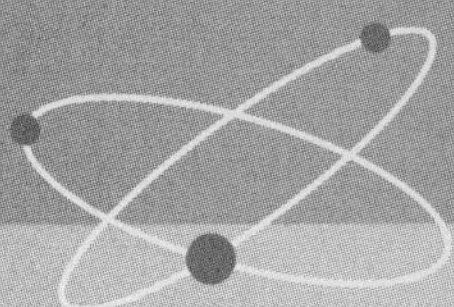

Care for a Cup?

Solve the word problems.

The oatmeal recipe calls for 4 cups of milk.
How many pints is that? ....

How many quarts is that? ....

You have 1 quart of buttermilk. You need 2 cups of buttermilk to make 1 loaf of soda bread. How many loaves of soda bread can you make? ....

There are 8 students and 2 gallons of chocolate milk. How many cups should each student get? ....

You need 1 cup of orange juice. What fraction of a quart do you need? ....

The recipe calls for ¼ cup of cream. What fraction of a pint do you need? ....

Brain Box

The U.S. customary unit for measuring liquid and pourable solids is the **cup**.

There are 2 cups in a pint (pt.), 4 cups in a quart (qt.), and 16 cups in a gallon (gal.).

2 cups = 1 pt.

2 pt. = 1 qt.

4 qts. = 1 gal.

Geometry and Measurement

Liquid volume

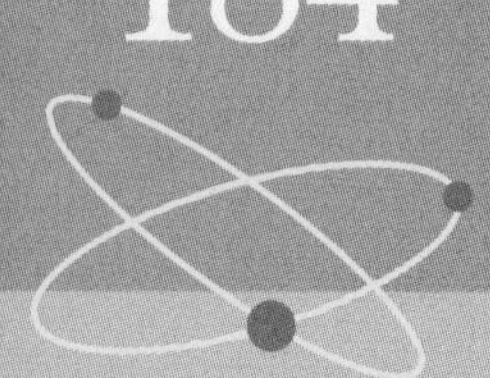

Such a Perfect Day

Fill in the blanks.

Water freezes at 0 degrees C, or ________ degrees F.

Water boils at 100 degrees C, or ________ degrees F.

Hot chocolate tastes hot but not scalding at 140°F, or ________ °C.

Cheddar cheese melts at about 65°C, or ________ °F.

A patient should call the doctor if a fever reaches 104°F, or about ________ °C.

If it were 20°C outside, or ________ °F, most people would say it was a perfect day.

41°F, or ________ °C, would be a chilly day.

95°F, or ________ °C, would be a hot day.

Geometry and Measurement

Temperature

Brain Box

The metric unit for temperature is **degrees Celsius (°C)**. The U.S. customary unit for temperature is **degrees Fahrenheit (°F)**.
0°C = 32°F

Passing the Time

Answer the questions.

The alarm buzzed from 6:00 a.m. to 6:14 a.m. How much time passed?

____

Jennica began babysitting at 6:00 p.m. She finished at 10:30 p.m. How much time passed?

____

Finn's soccer game started at 8:00 a.m. and ended at 9:15 a.m. How much time passed?

____

The school day starts at 8:00 a.m. and ends at 3:30 p.m. How much time passes each day?

____

The Daysons drove from 4:30 a.m. to 11:30 p.m. How much time passed?

____

Elise fell asleep at 9:30 p.m. She awoke at 6:30 a.m. How much time passed?

____

It rained from 10:15 p.m. to 5:00 a.m. How much time passed?

____

The forest fire burned from 6:00 a.m. Monday to 5:00 p.m. Thursday. How much time passed?

____

Brain Box

There is only one system for measuring time. There are 24 **hours (h.)** in a **day (d.)**, 60 **minutes (min.)** in an **hour (h.)**, and 60 **seconds (sec.)** in a minute. Seconds are divided into tenths of a second. In many countries, from 12:00 noon to 12:00 midnight, the time is designated **p.m.** From 12:00 midnight to 12:00 noon, the time is designated **a.m.**

To determine how much time has passed, first count the hours, then the minutes.

Hudson did his homework from 4:00 p.m. to 5:30 p.m. 4:00 p.m. to 5:00 p.m. is 1 hour. 5:00 p.m. to 5:30 is 30 minutes. A total of 1 hour and 30 minutes passed.

Totally Triangular!

Draw 3 **isosceles triangles**. Turn the triangles into colorful beach umbrellas.

Triangles

Geometry and Measurement

Brain Box

A **triangle** is a closed figure with three sides.

In a **scalene triangle**, none of the three sides is the same length as the others.

In an **isosceles triangle**, two of the three sides are the same length.

In an **equilateral triangle**, all three sides are the same length.

Draw 3 **scalene triangles**. Turn them into race cars.

Draw 3 **equilateral triangles**. Turn them into the roofs of houses.

Finding the Perfect Angle

Circle the **right angles.**

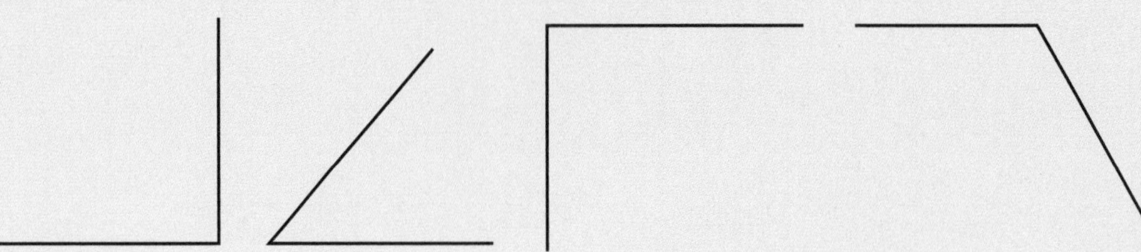

Circle the **acute angles.**

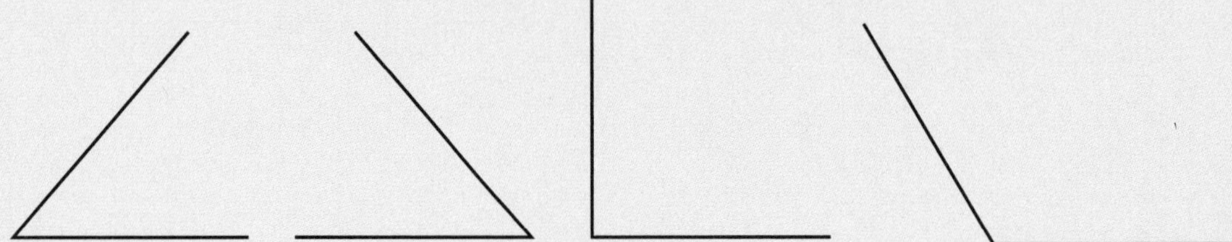

Circle the **obtuse angle.**

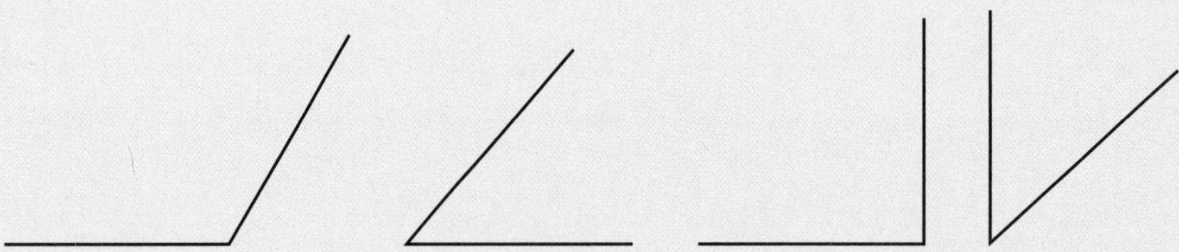

Brain Box

An **angle** is formed where two line segments meet.

A **right angle** is 90°.

An **acute angle** is less than 90°.

An **obtuse angle** is greater than 90°.

Every triangle has three angles.

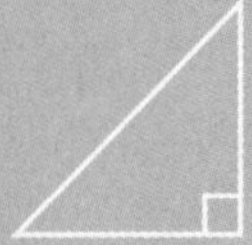

When a triangle has one right angle, it is a **right triangle**.

When all angles in a triangle are acute, it is an **acute triangle**.

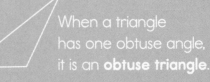

When a triangle has one obtuse angle, it is an **obtuse triangle**.

Aww, What Acute Angle

Circle the **acute triangles**.

Circle the **obtuse triangle**.

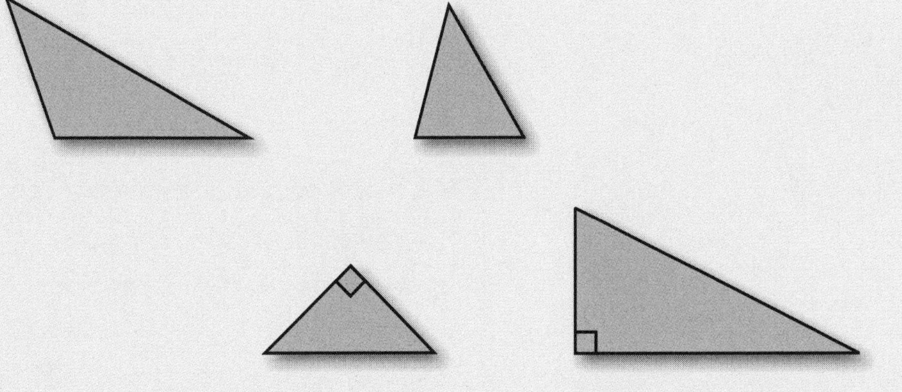

Circle the **right triangles**.

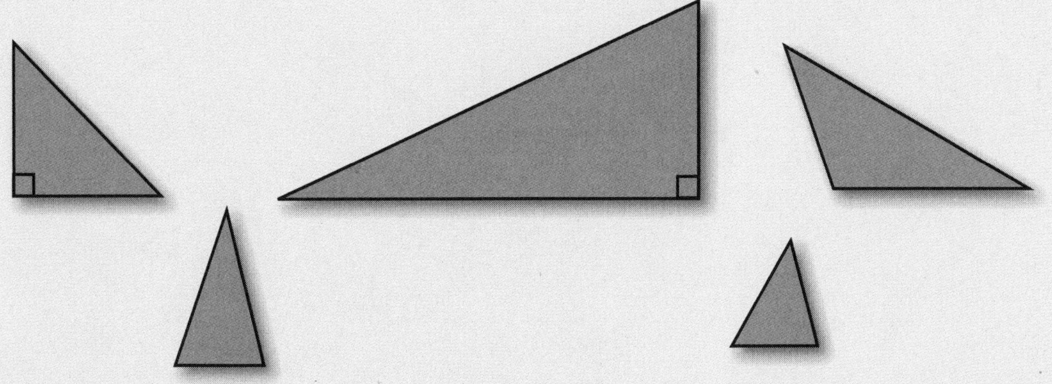

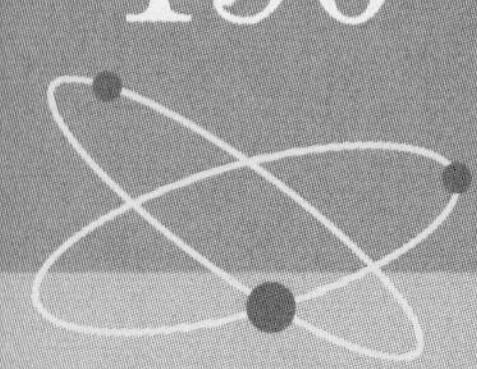

Clean Up!

Put away the **polygons**. Draw a line from the polygon to the box that it should go in based on its properties.

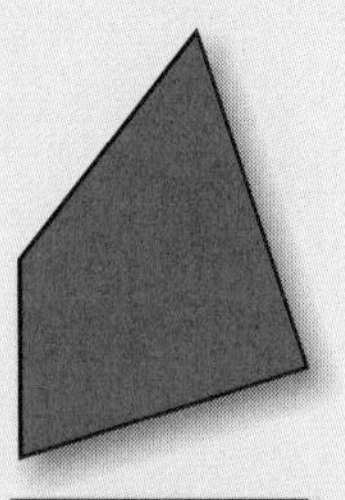

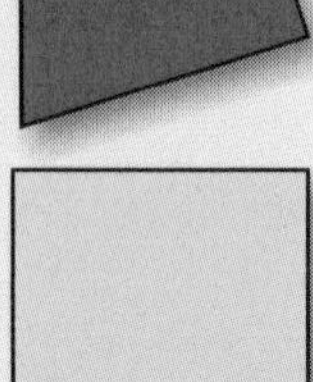

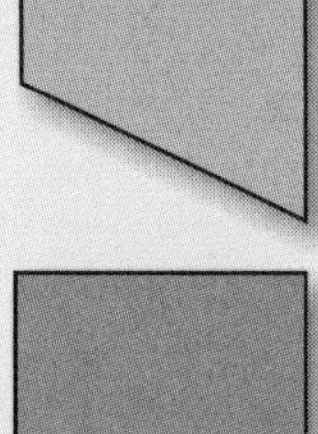

3 congruent sides

3 non-congruent sides

4 congruent sides

2 parallel sides

2 pairs of parallel sides
2 pairs of congruent sides

4 non-parallel, non-congruent sides

Brain Box

A **polygon** is a closed figure with several angles and three or more straight sides. A triangle, a square, and an octagon are just a few examples. Polygons are classified by their characteristics, or properties, like type of angles or sides they have. Polygons can have right, acute, or obtuse angles. Polygons can also be categorized by the number of sides, the number of **parallel** (non-intersecting) sides, or the number of **congruent** (same size) sides.

Four Sure

Read the definitions and study the quadrilateral classification chart. Then circle true (T) or false (F).

A **polygon** has 3 or more sides.

A **quadrilateral** has 4 sides.

A **parallelogram** has 2 pairs of parallel sides.

A **rhombus** has 2 pairs of parallel sides and 4 congruent sides.

A **rectangle** has 4 right angles.

A **square** has 4 right angles and 4 congruent sides.

A **trapezoid** has 1 pair of parallel sides.

Quadrilateral Classification Chart

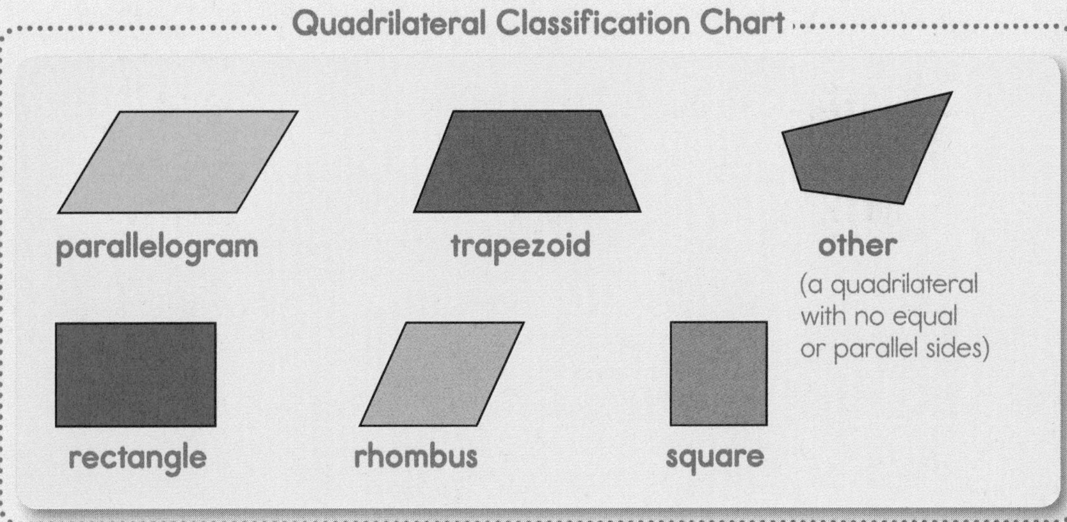

All squares are rectangles. .... T F

All rectangles are squares. .... T F

All rhombuses are parallelograms. .... T F

All parallelograms are rhombuses. .... T F

All quadrilaterals must have at least 1 pair of parallel sides. .... T F

All quadrilaterals are polygons. .... T F

All polygons are quadrilaterals. .... T F

Parallelograms and rectangles have 2 pairs of parallel sides. .... T F

A square and a rhombus both have right angles. .... T F

Brain Box

A **quadrangle** or **quadrilateral** is a polygon with 4 sides. Quadrilaterals can be further classified based on their number of parallel sides, congruent sides, and right angles.

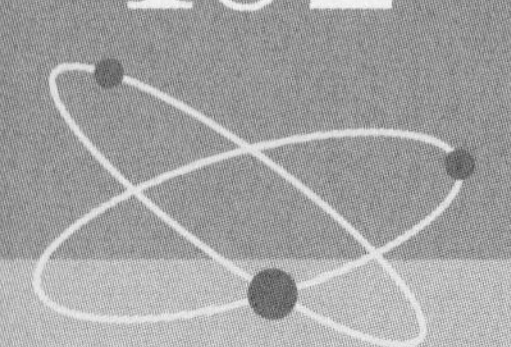

Fence or Tile?

Find the **perimeter** and **area** of each rectangle.

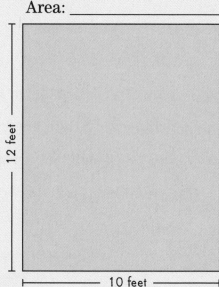

Perimeter: __________

Area: __________

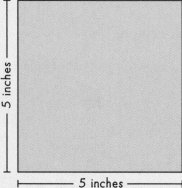

Perimeter: __________

Area: __________

Perimeter: __________

Area: __________

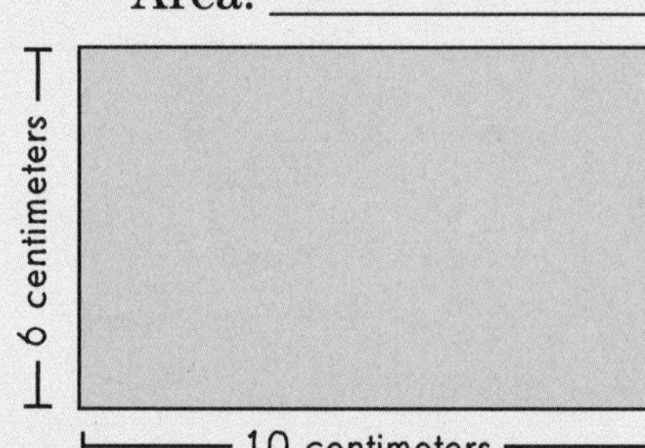

Perimeter: __________

Area: __________

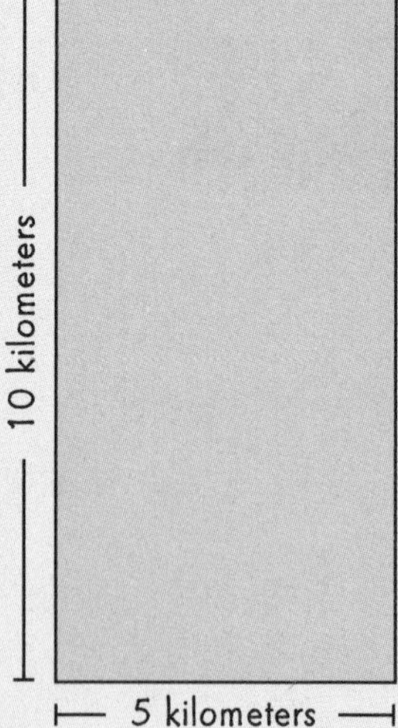

Brain Box

The **perimeter** is the distance along the outside of a figure. If you wanted to build a backyard fence, you need to know the perimeter of the yard. You can find the perimeter by adding the lengths of the sides.

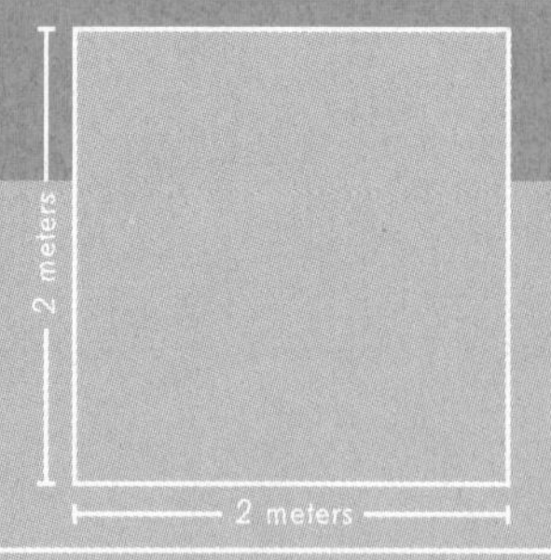

2 + 2 + 2 + 2 = 8 meters
Perimeter = 8 m

The **area** is the number of square units inside a figure. If you wanted to tile a floor, you need to know the area of the floor. You can find the area by multiplying length by width. The unit for measuring area is a square unit.

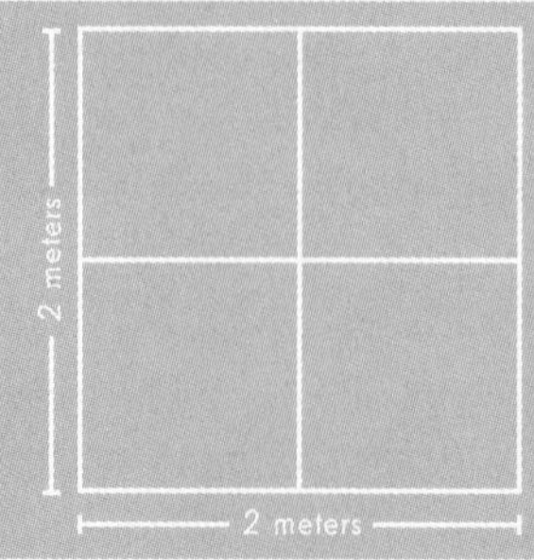

2 × 2 = 4 square meters
Area = $4m^2$

Side by Side

Find the perimeter of each triangle.

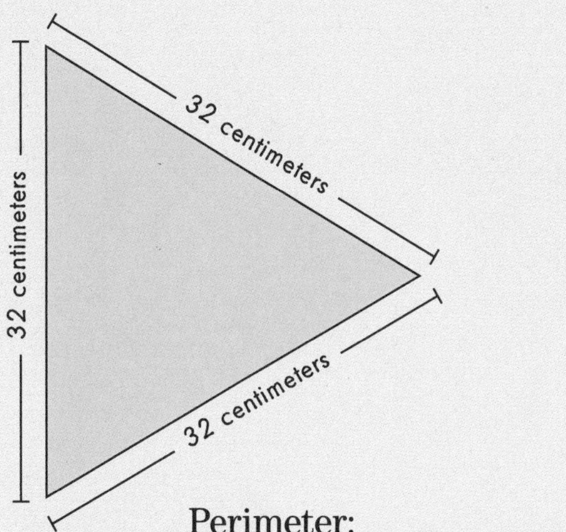

Perimeter: __________

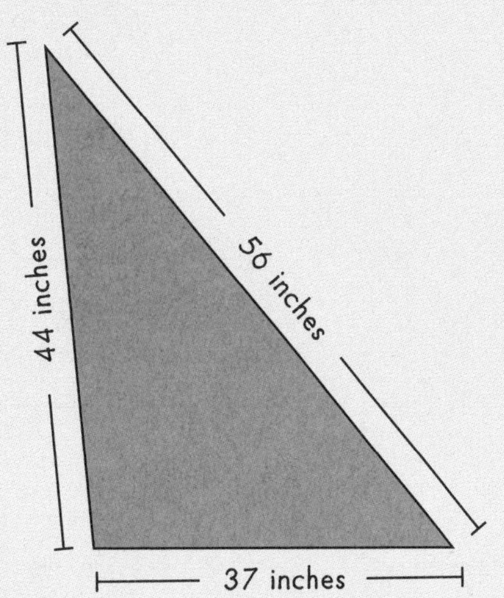

Perimeter: __________

Find the **area** of each triangle.

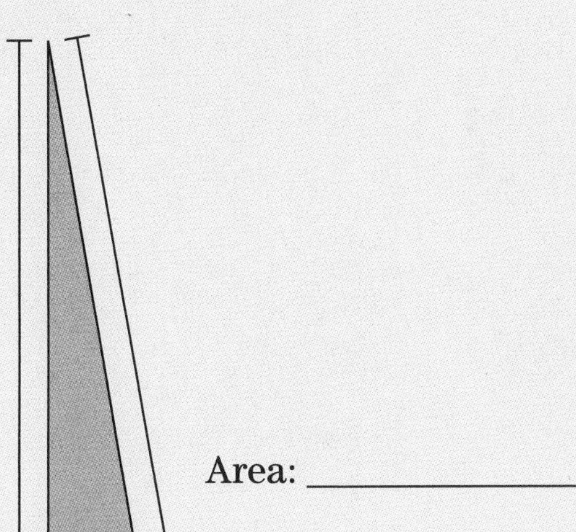

Area: __________

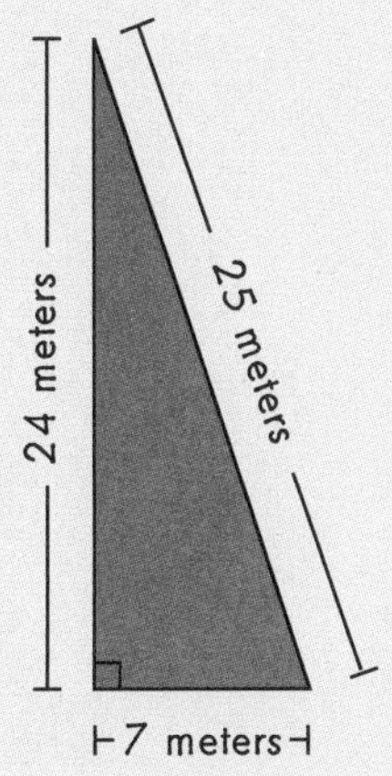

Area: __________

Brain Box

To find the perimeter of a triangle, simply add up the sides.

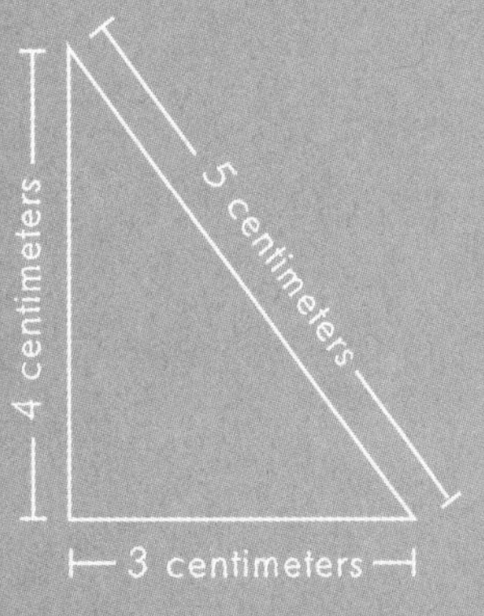

Perimeter = 12 cm

To find the area of a right triangle, use this equation:

$$\text{area} = \frac{\text{base} \times \text{height}}{2}$$

This is like finding the area of a rectangle and dividing it in half.

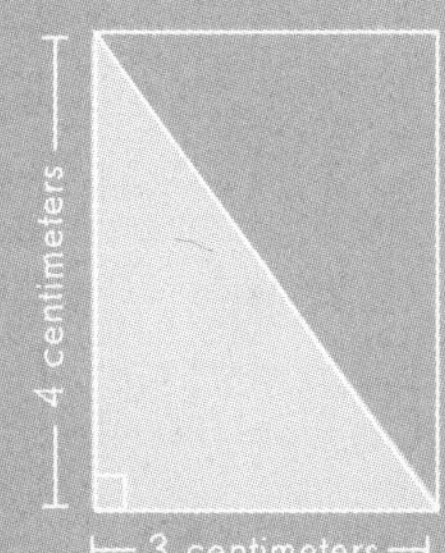

$$\frac{3 \times 4}{2} = \frac{12}{2} = 6$$

Area = 6 cm^2

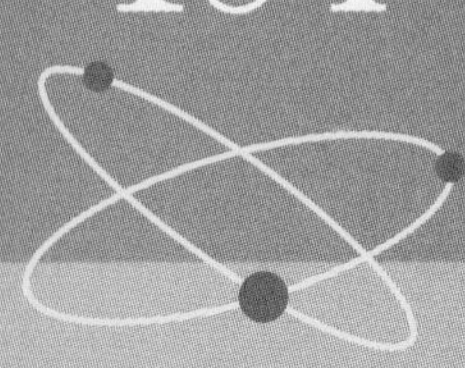

Delivery Truck

Find the **volume** of each.

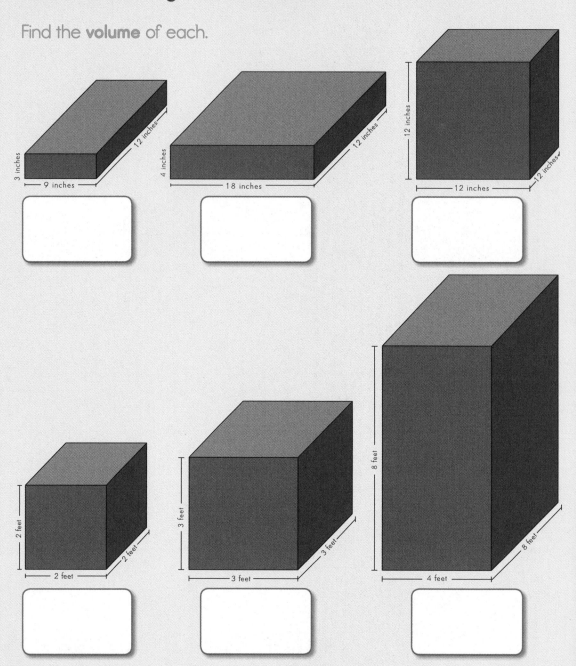

3 inches, 9 inches, 12 inches

4 inches, 18 inches, 12 inches

12 inches, 12 inches, 12 inches

2 feet, 2 feet, 2 feet

3 feet, 3 feet, 3 feet

8 feet, 4 feet, 8 feet

Geometry and Measurement

Volume

Brain Box

Volume is the form of measurement used for solid figures. It is measured in cubic units. Find the volume by multiplying length × width × height.

$2 \text{ cm} \times 2 \text{ cm} \times 4 \text{ cm} = 16 \text{ cm}^3$

4 cm, 2 cm, 2 cm

Ice Cold

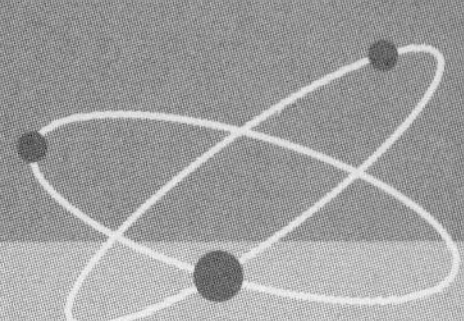

Find the total volume.

2 ice cubes, each $3 \times 3 \times 3$ cm

$3 \times 3 \times 3 = 27$ cubic centimeters per ice cube

$27 + 27 = 54$ cubic centimeters for 2 ice cubes

3 ice cubes, each $3 \times 3 \times 3$ cm

[ ] cubic centimeters

4 ice cubes, each $4 \times 4 \times 4$ cm

[ ] cubic centimeters

5 ice cubes, each $5 \times 5 \times 5$ cm

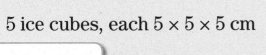

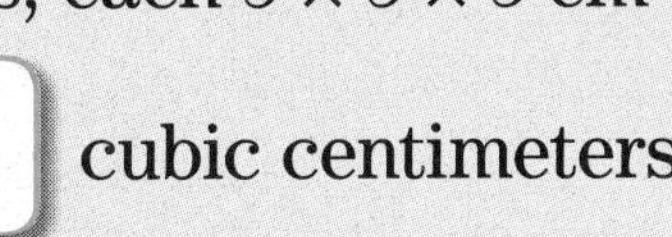

[ ] cubic centimeters

6 ice cubes, each $6 \times 6 \times 6$ cm

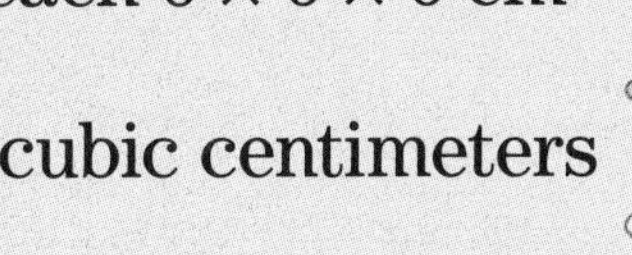

[ ] cubic centimeters

7 ice cubes, each $7 \times 7 \times 7$ cm

[ ] cubic centimeters

8 ice cubes, each $8 \times 8 \times 8$ cm

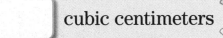

[ ] cubic centimeters

Brain Box

Volume is additive. That means that the volume of two objects combined can be determined by adding them together.

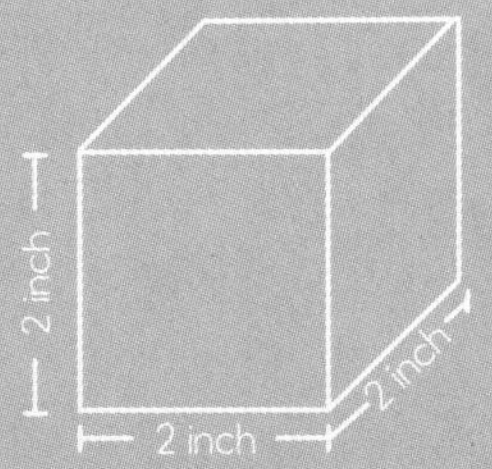

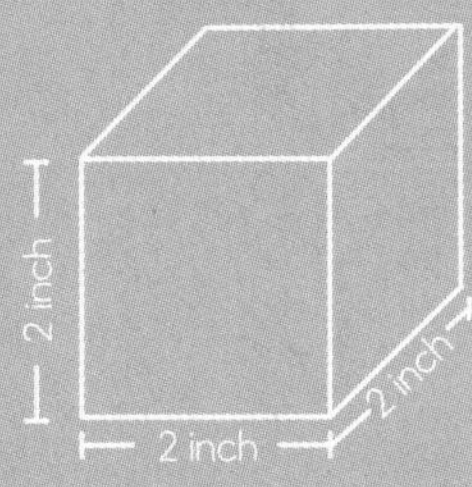

$2 \times 2 \times 2$ inch box
$+ 2 \times 2 \times 2$ inch box
= 8 cubic inches
+ 8 cubic inches
= 16 cubic inches

Geometry and Measurement

Volume

196

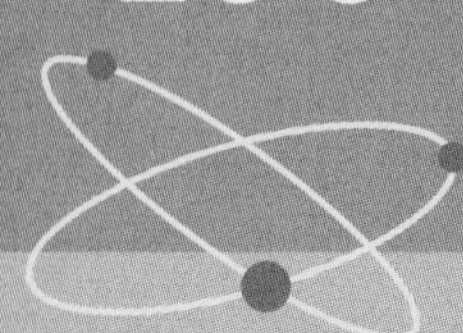

Mmm, Pi

Find the **circumference** of each pie.

6 inches

7 inches

Diameter and circumference

Geometry and Measurement

Brain Box

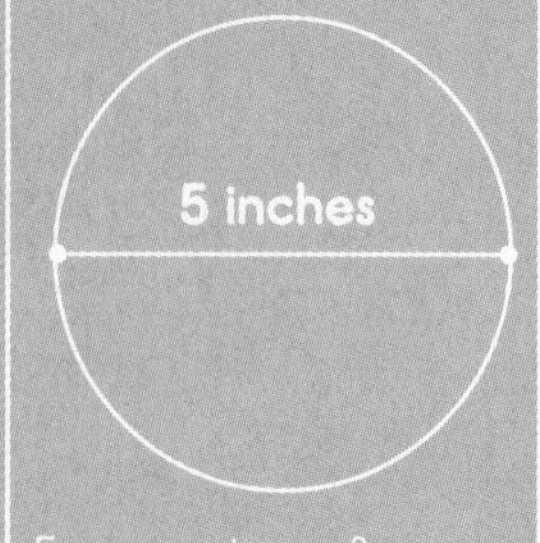

$5 \times \pi$ = circumference

$5 \times 3.14 = 15.7$

The circumference of the circle is 15.7 inches.

The length through the middle of a circle is the **diameter**. The perimeter of a circle is called the **circumference**. To find the circumference of a circle, multiply the diameter by **pi (π)**.

Pi is a special number defined as the ratio of the circumference of a circle to its diameter.

$$\pi = \frac{\text{circumference}}{\text{diameter}}$$

The decimal places of pi go on forever, but pi is approximately 3.14.

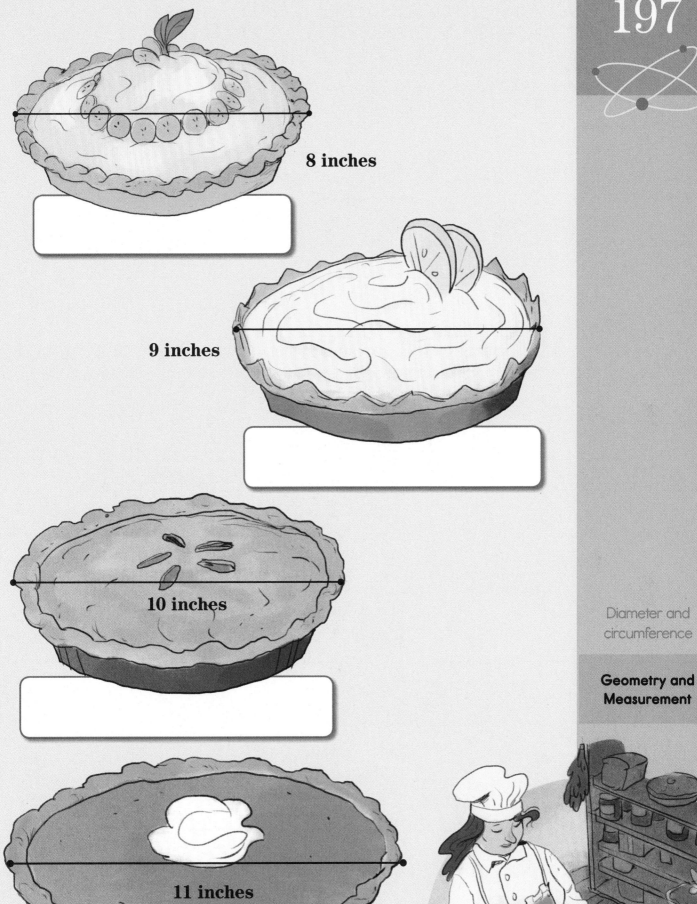

8 inches

9 inches

10 inches

11 inches

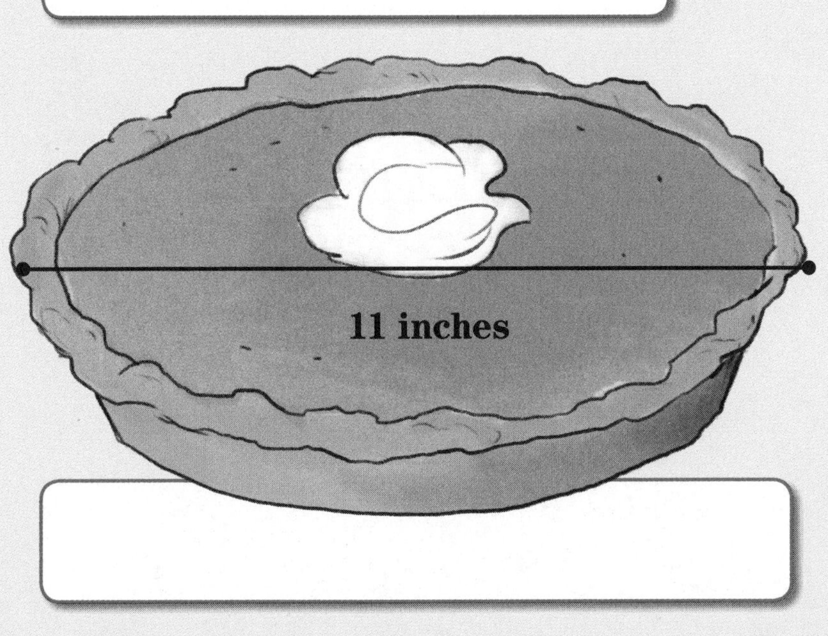

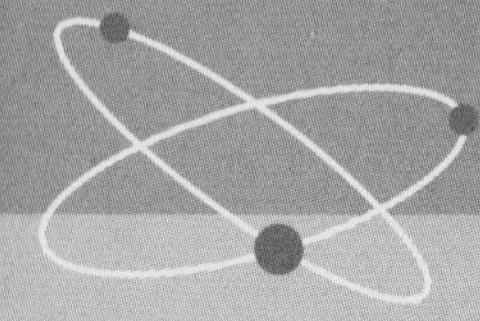

Castle in the Clouds

Find the **area** of the castle turrets.

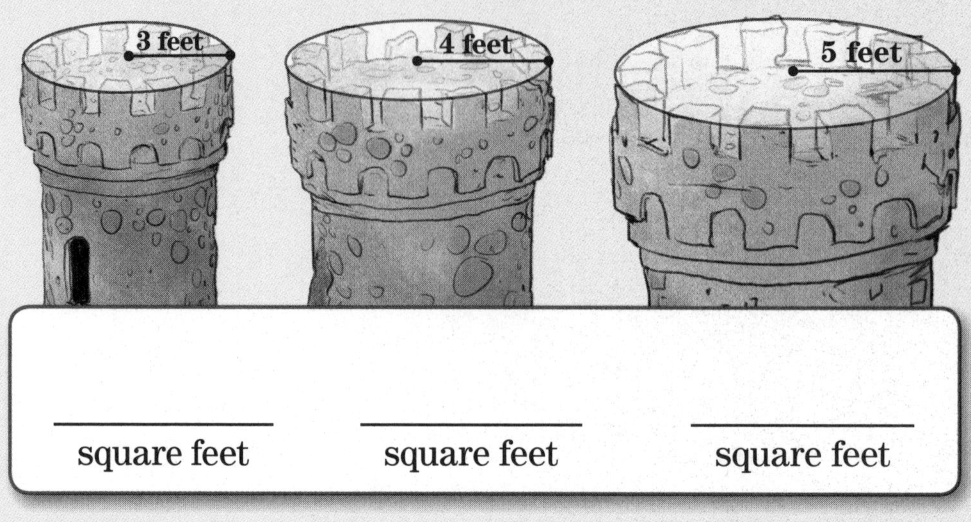

______ square feet ______ square feet ______ square feet

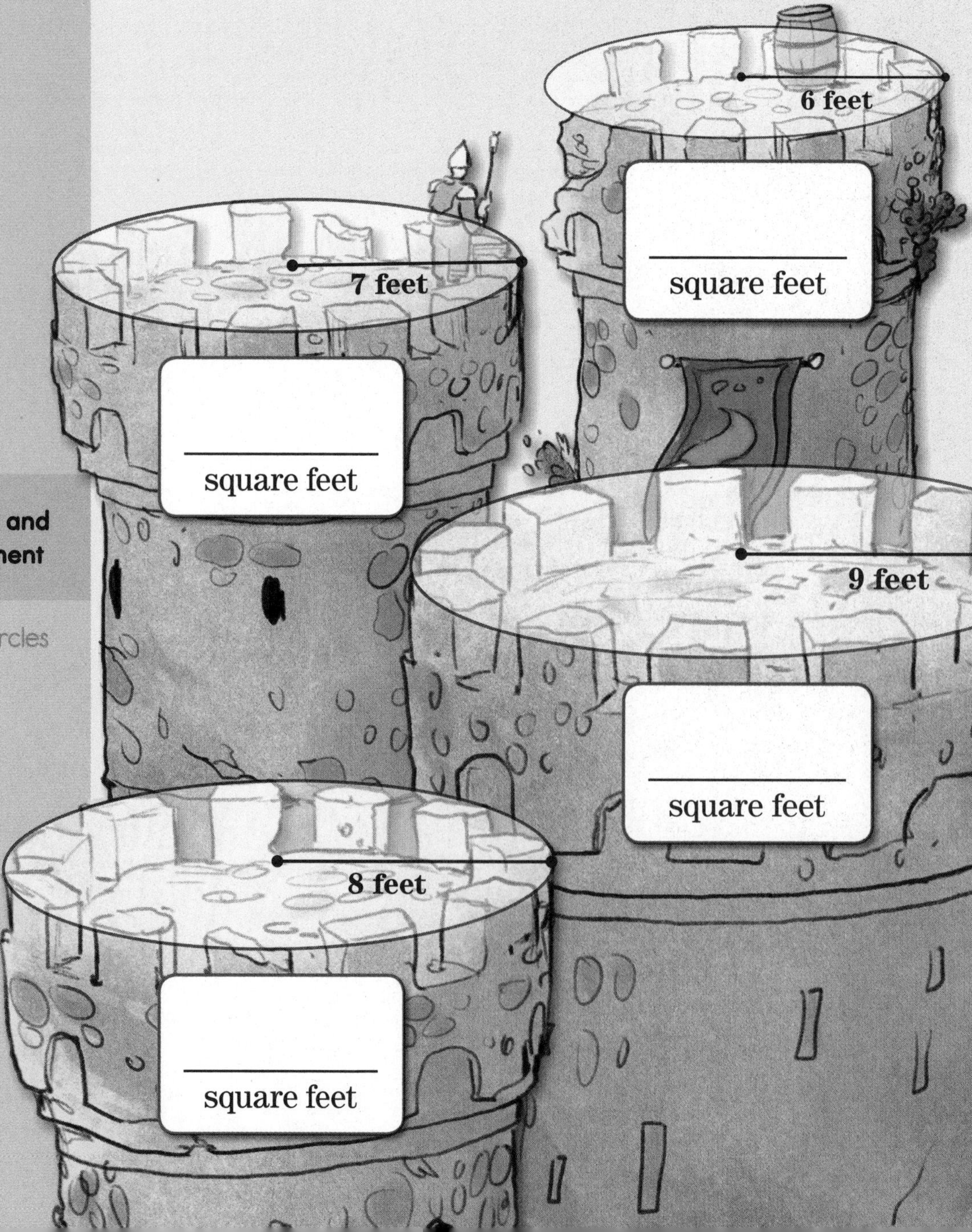

6 feet

______ square feet

7 feet

______ square feet

9 feet

______ square feet

8 feet

______ square feet

Geometry and Measurement

Area of circles

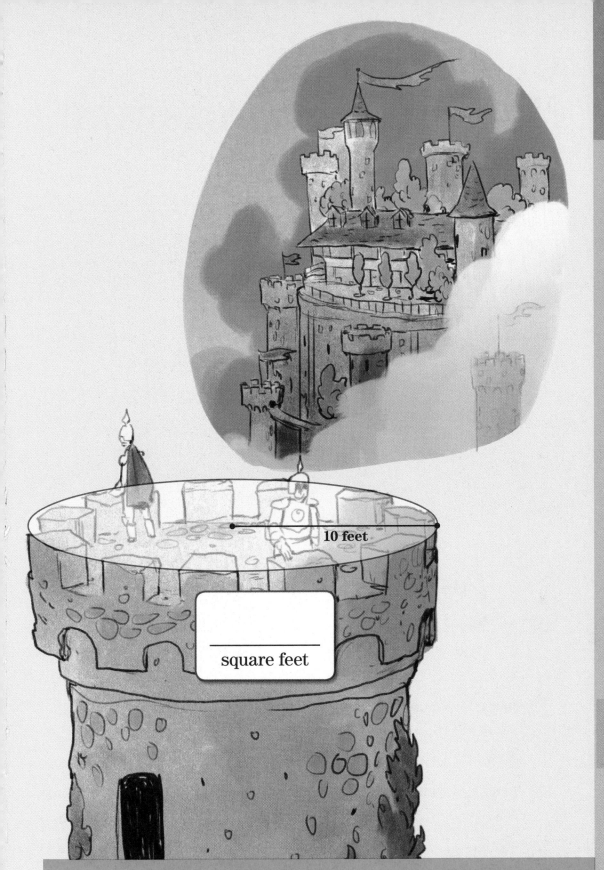

10 feet

_______ square feet

Brain Box

The area of a circle is the product of the radius squared and pi. The **radius** is half of the diameter. A squared number is a number times itself. Area = $\pi \times r^2$

$3.14 \times 5 \times 5 = 3.14 \times 25 = 78.5$
The area of the circle is 78.5 square inches.

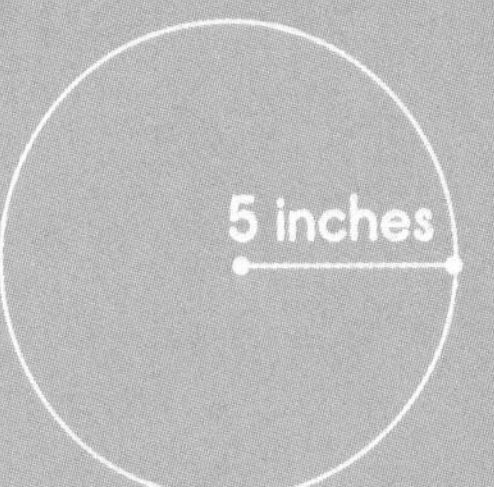

Geometry and Measurement Crossword

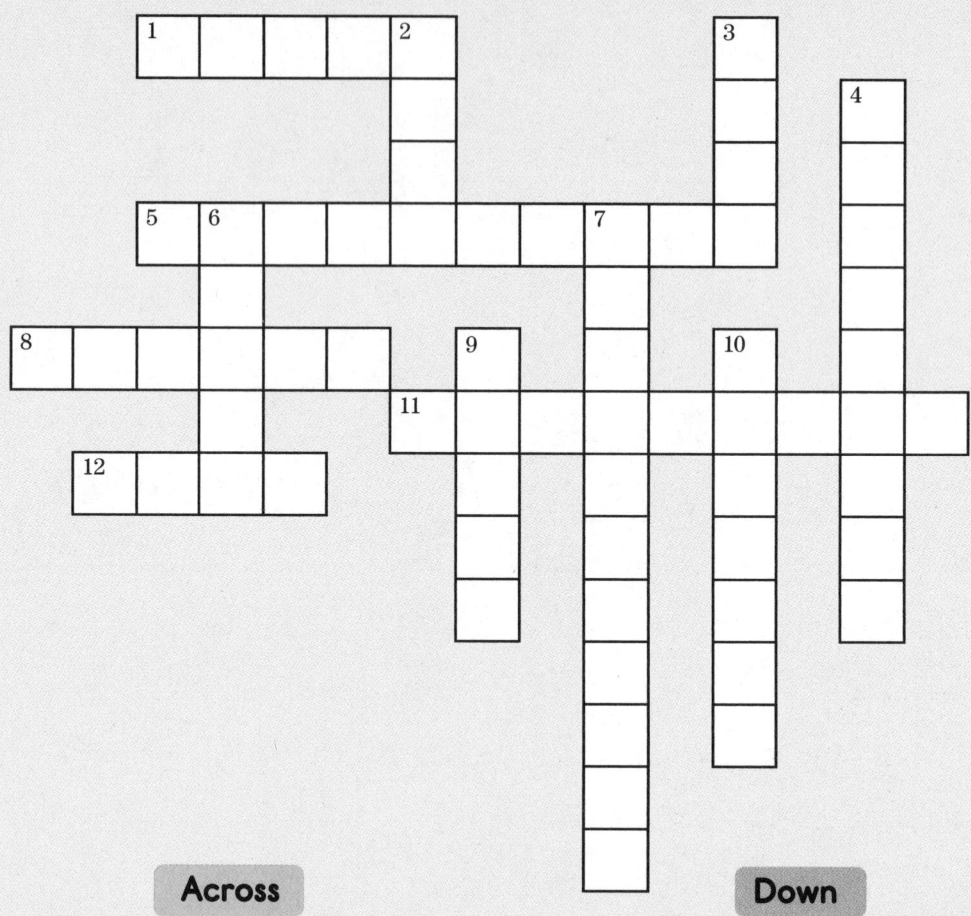

Across

1 A triangle with a 90° angle is a(n) __________ triangle.

5 The U.S. customary unit for temperature is degrees ___________.

8 Length × width × height = ___________.

11 The distance along the outside of a figure is the ________.

12 Length × width=________.

Down

2 There is only one universal way of measuring ____________.

3 A U.S. customary unit for distance is the __________.

4 A triangle with two equal sides is a(n) _______ triangle.

6 An angle less than 90° is ______________.

7 A triangle that has three equal sides is a(n) _______ triangle.

9 A metric unit for distance is the _____________.

10 A metric unit for measuring temperature is degrees _____________.

Data

Fro-yo!

Chart the following **categorical data** by making tally marks on the graph on the following page.

Cameron's favorite frozen yogurt is lemon.

Marita's favorite is chocolate vanilla swirl.

Anika likes vanilla best.

Pete also prefers vanilla.

Elliot likes chocolate.

Carlos also likes chocolate.

Javantre prefers lemon.

Sophia likes vanilla.

John Paul's favorite is peanut butter.

Frank likes chocolate vanilla swirl the best.

Mae prefers vanilla.

Grace likes strawberry.

Favorite Frozen Yogurt	Tally	Number
Chocolate		
Vanilla		
Chocolate vanilla swirl		
Lemon		
Peanut butter		
Strawberry		

Brain Box

Categorical data is data sorted by **characteristics**. For example, frozen yogurt can be sorted by flavor.

When taking a survey about **categorical data**, you can use tally marks to show how many items are in each category.

Shoe Color	Tally	Number
Brown	||||	4
Blue	|||	3
Black	~~||||~~	5
White	||	2

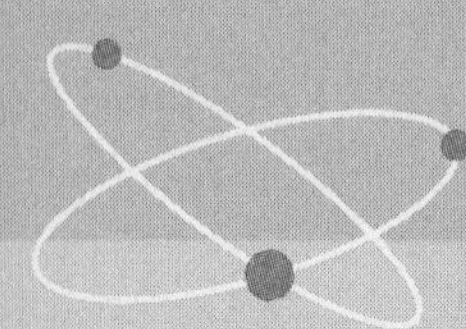

Adventures in Babysitting

Use the **bar graph** to answer the questions on the next page.

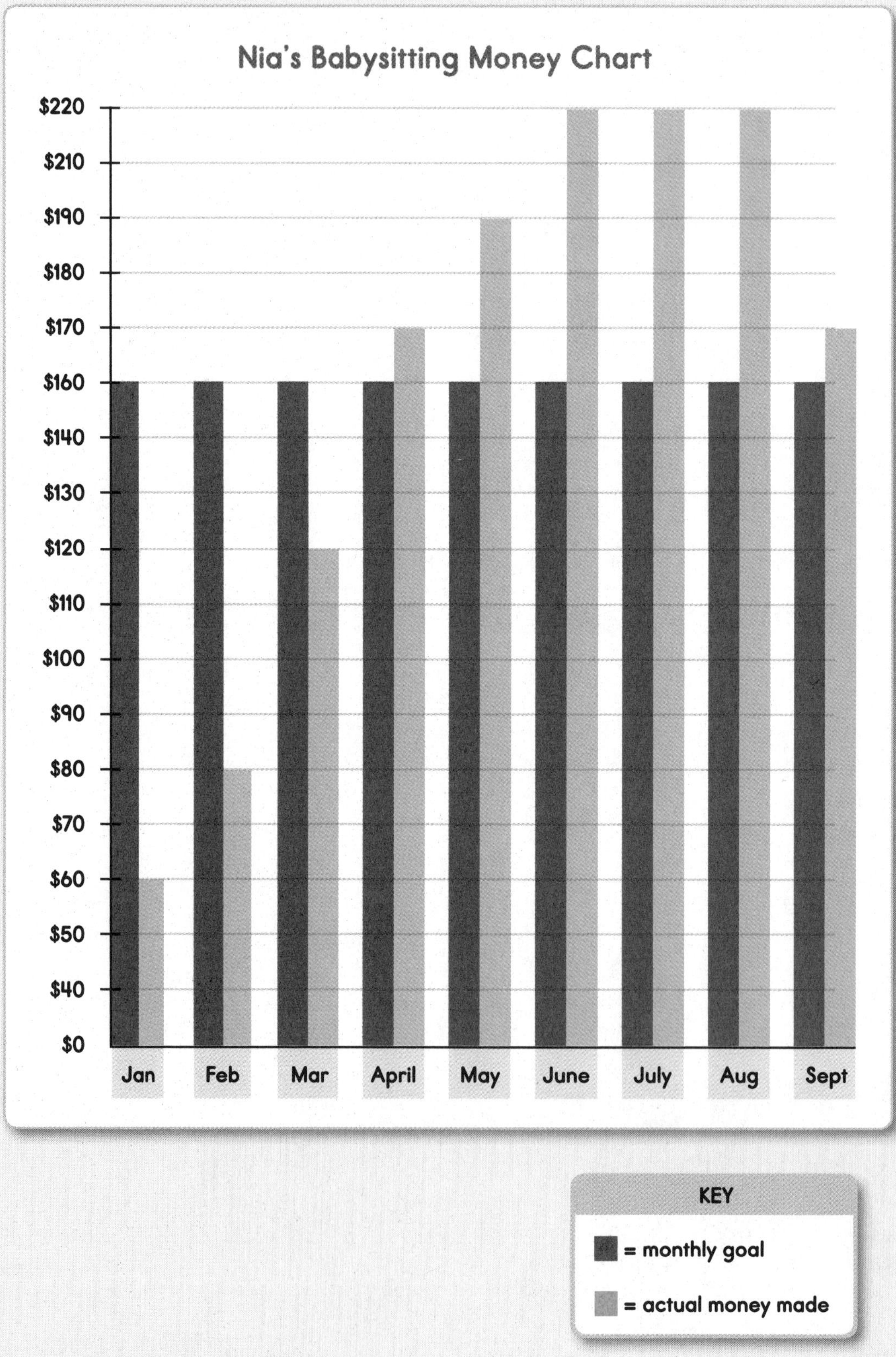

Nia's Babysitting Money Chart
$220
$210
$190
$180
$170
$160
$140
$130
$120
$110
$100
$90
$80
$70
$60
$50
$40
$0
Jan
Feb
Mar
April
May
June
July
Aug
Sept
KEY
= monthly goal
= actual money made

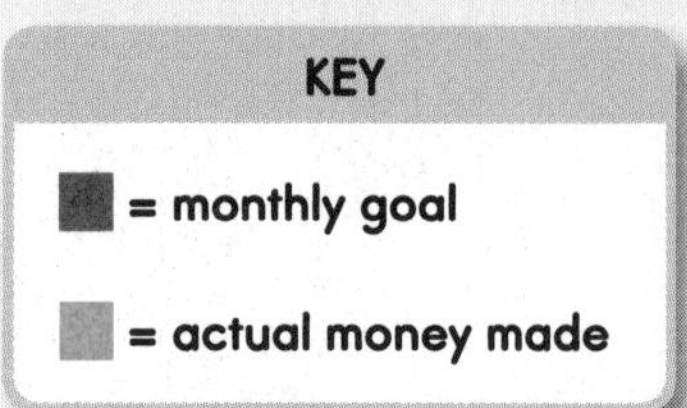

Brain Box

A **bar graph** is a picture, diagram, or drawing that shows how two or more things are related. Some graphs have a key. The **key** gives you information you need to understand the graph.

Data

Bar graphs

This graph shows that Nia hoped to make ________________ every month for ________________ months.

Nia fell short of her goal the months of ________________ , ________________ , and ________________ .

Her goal was to make ________________ total. She actually made ________________ total.

The first month Nia exceeded her goal was ________________ .

Nia made the most money over which three months? ________________

Nia exceeded her goal in the months of ________________ , ________________ , ________________ , ________________ , ________________ , and ________________ .

If Nia's goal had been to make $190 per month, how many months would she have met or exceeded that goal? ________________

Tomato, Tomahto

Fill in the **frequency table** to show how many tomatoes are on each plant.

Number of Tomatoes on the Plant	Tally	Frequency
0–4		
5–9		
10–14		
15–19		

Frequency tables

Data

Brain Box

A **frequency table** shows how often two or more things occur. It can be used for categorical or numerical data.

Example:

Number of Apples on a Tree	Tally	Frequency
100–109	𝍸	5
110–119	𝍸 II	7
120–129	𝍸 III	8
130–139	𝍸 I	6

Showtime

Make a **stem and leaf plot** to show how many people came to each performance of the fifth grade musical.

Number of People Who Attended the Fifth Grade Musical

Stem	Leaf

On Thursday evening, there were 88 people in the audience.

32 people came to the Friday matinee.

Friday evening, 83 people came.

There were 92 people at the Saturday matinee.

Saturday evening, 95 people were in the audience.

At the Sunday matinee, there were 44 people.

Brain Box

A **stem and leaf plot** can be used to show which numbers occur in data. The "stem" on the left-hand side represents the tens digits. The "leaves" on the right-hand side represent the ones digits.

Money Spent on School Supplies by Each Student

Student	Amount
Student 1	$52
Student 2	$64
Student 3	$68
Student 4	$71

Stem	Leaf
5	2
6	4,8
7	1

Note that there are two numbers in the leaf column next to the 6 stem. These numbers represent $64 and $68, respectively.

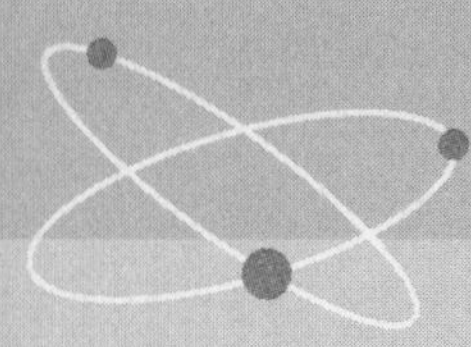

Temperature Rising

On the next page, make a **scatterplot** to show the relationship between the temperature and the number of people at the pool. Then answer the questions.

Saturday, June 1: 80°F, 50 people

Saturday, June 8: 85°F, 75 people

Saturday, June 15: 80°F, 75 people

Saturday, June 22: 90°F, 100 people

Saturday, June 29: 89°F, 100 people

Saturday, July 6: 94°F, 150 people

Saturday, July 13: 95°F, 150 people

Saturday, July 20: 100°F, 200 people

Saturday, July 27: 98°F, 200 people

Brain Box

A **scatterplot** is a way to compare two sets of data. One set is plotted as dots vertically, and the other is plotted as dots horizontally. If the dots cluster around a straight line, the two sets are related.

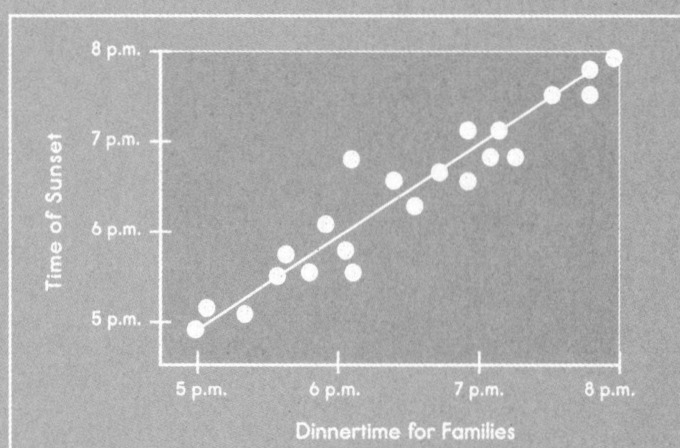

Because the dots are clustered around a line, dinnertime must be related to sunset time.

Scatterplot

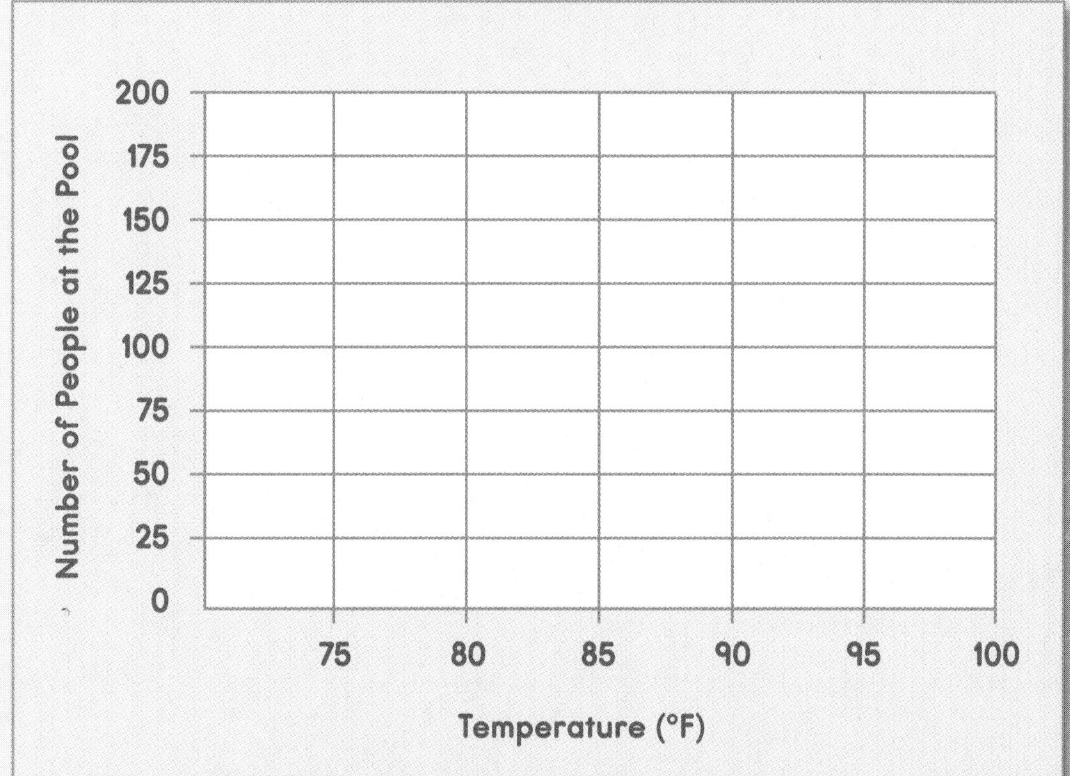

Do most of the dots cluster around a line? ________________

What does that tell you about the two sets of data? __________

____

____

____

Data

Scatterplots

Snack Bar Stats

Show the following data on the **line plot**.

Customer 1 bought a cup of ice for $0.25.
Customer 2 bought a hot dog for $1.50.
Customer 3 bought nachos for $2.00.
Customer 4 bought a hot dog and chips for a total of $2.00.
Customer 5 bought a pack of gum for $0.50.
Customer 6 bought a soda and chips for a total of $1.50.
Customer 7 bought lemonade for $1.00.
Customer 8 bought a snow cone for $0.75.
Customer 9 bought a hot pretzel for $1.00.
Customer 10 bought 2 hot dogs for $3.00.

Brain Box

Line plots (also called **dot plots**), can be used to show numerical data. A number line runs along the bottom of the graph. A dot represents how many times that number occurs.

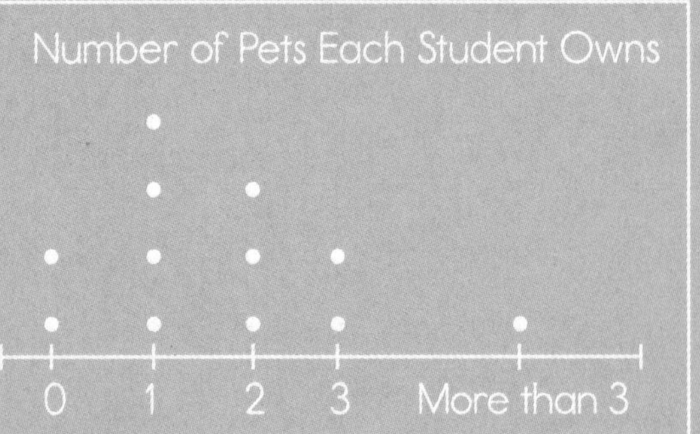

2 students own 0 pets.
4 students own 1 pet.
3 students own 2 pets.
2 students own 3 pets.
1 student owns more than 3 pets.

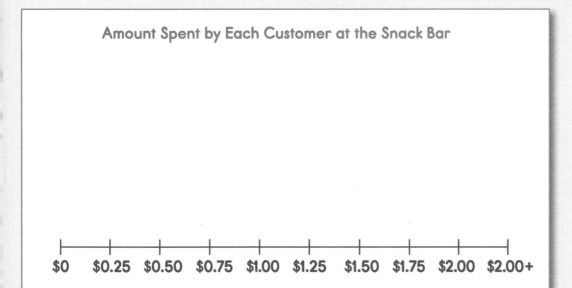

Amount Spent by Each Customer at the Snack Bar

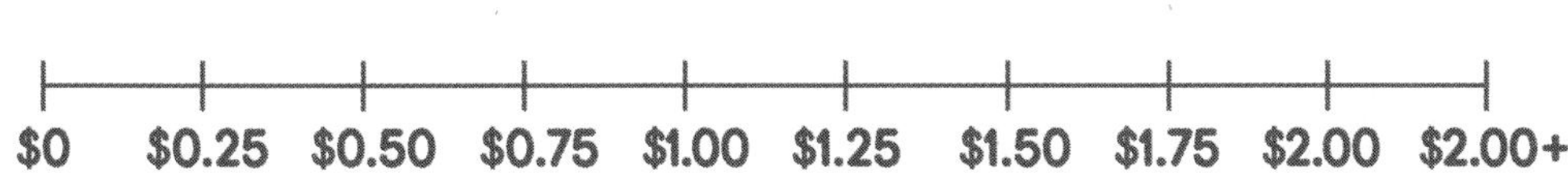

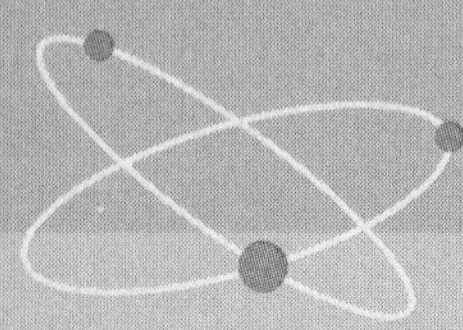

Sour Math

Plot the amount of blueberry juice in each beaker.

Amount of Blueberry Juice in Each Beaker

0 $\frac{1}{8}$ $\frac{1}{4}$ $\frac{3}{8}$ $\frac{1}{2}$ $\frac{5}{8}$ $\frac{3}{4}$ $\frac{7}{8}$ 1L

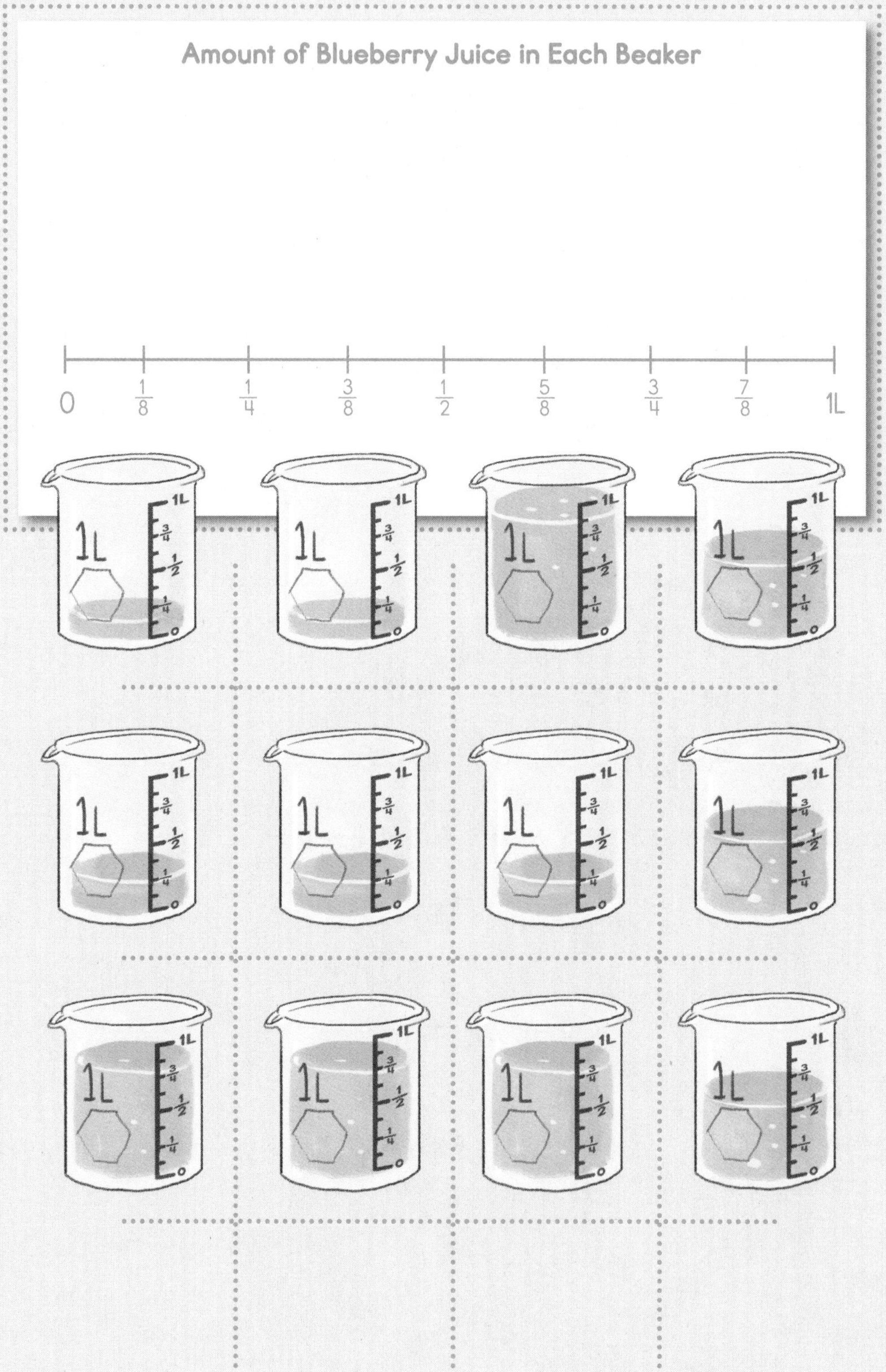

Data

Line plots

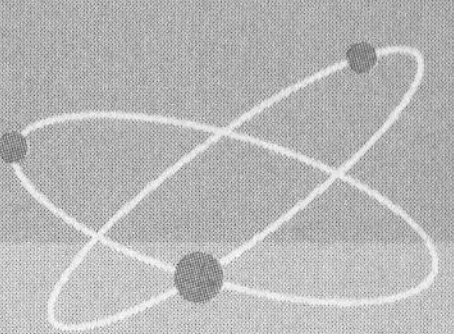

Visualize It

Plot the amount of juice in each beaker. Solve the problems.

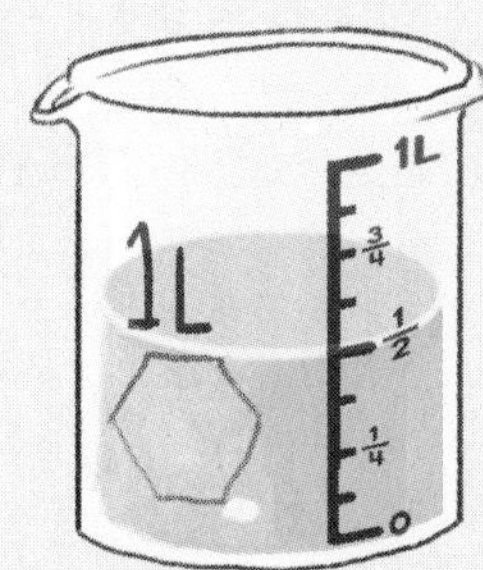

What is the total amount of milliliters that the beakers contain?

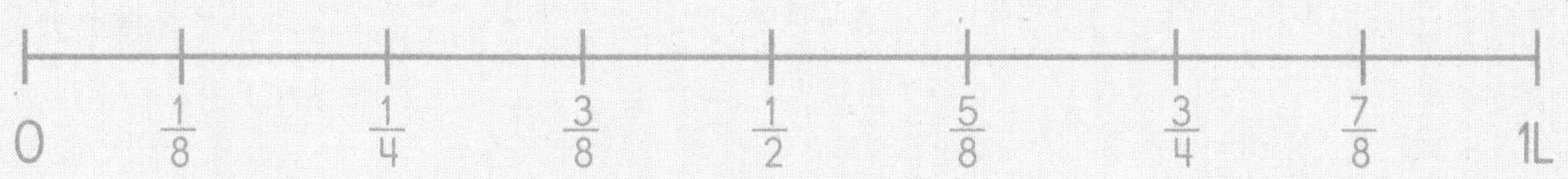

____

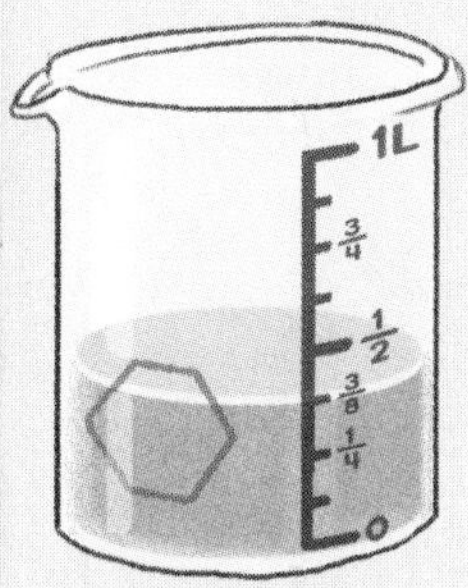

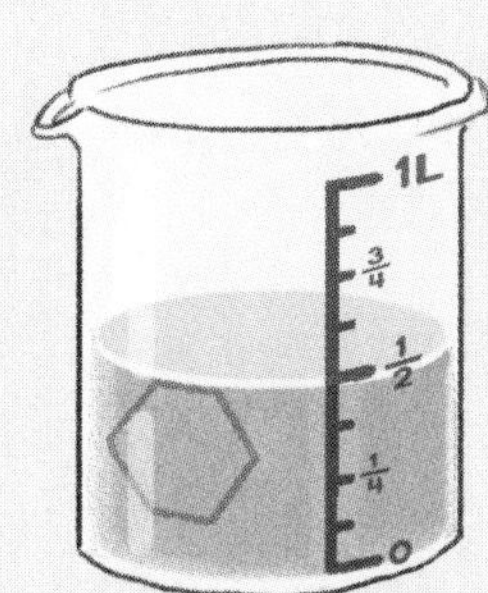

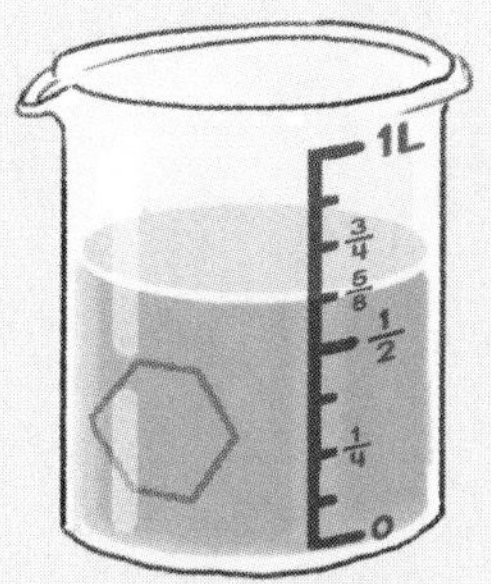

What is the total number of milliliters that the beakers contain?

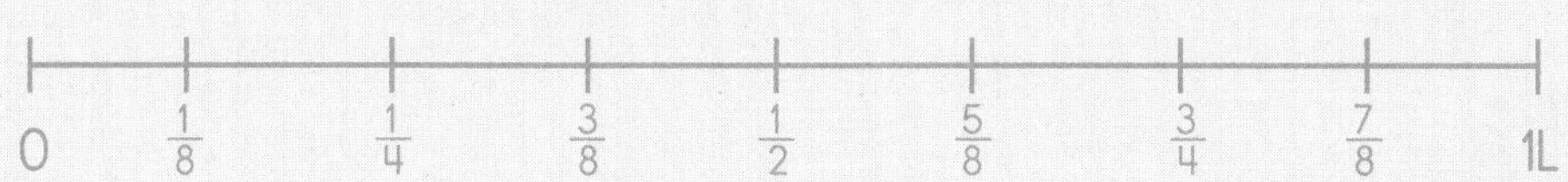

____

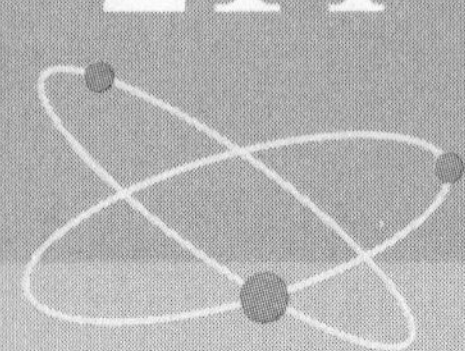

Coin Toss

Conduct the experiments and record your data.

Flip a coin 5 times.

Write a fraction representing how often you get heads.

Write a fraction representing how often you get tails.

Flip a coin 8 times.

Write a fraction representing how often you get heads.

Write a fraction representing how often you get tails.

Flip a coin 10 times.

Write a fraction representing how often you get heads.

Write a fraction representing how often you get tails.

Ask someone else to flip a coin 10 times.

Write a fraction representing how often she or he gets heads.

Data

Data experiments

Algebraic Thinking

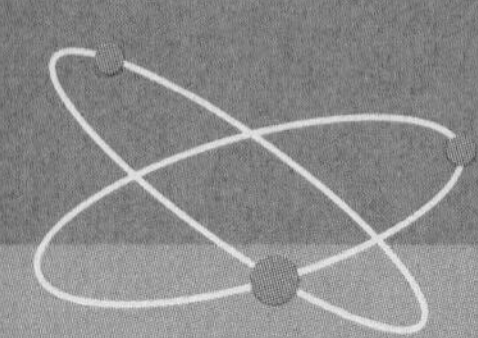

Go PEMDAS!

Write how to solve the problems using the **order of operations, PEMDAS.**

$4 \times (6 + 5)$ Add 6 plus 5 and multiply the sum by 4.

$(2^2 + 4) - 3$

$(4 + 5) \div 3$

Use PEMDAS to solve the problems.

$(5 + 4) \div (1 + 2) =$

$63 \div 3^2 =$

$(7 + 7) \times 3 =$

$111 - (4^2 + 12) =$

$8^2 - 7 \times 2 =$

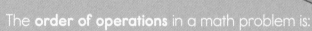

Brain Box

The **order of operations** in a math problem is:

Parentheses/Brackets

Exponents (For example instead of 4 × 4, we use exponents as a shorthand: 4^2)

Multiplication and **D**ivision (in order from left to right)

Addition and **S**ubtraction (in order from left left to right)

The acronym for remembering this is **PEMDAS.** The phrase, "**P**lease **E**xcuse **M**y **D**ear **A**unt **S**ally" is helpful to remember it.

Code Breaker

Explain the **pattern** of each number sequence.
Then compare the two patterns.

0, 3, 6, 9, 12 starting at 0, add 3.
0, 6, 12, 18, 24 starting at 0, add 6.

The numbers in the second sequence are 2 times the corresponding numbers in the first sequence.

0, 2, 4, 6, 8
0, 6, 12, 18, 24

0, 1, 2, 3, 4, 5
0, 5, 10, 15, 20, 25

0, 1, 2, 3, 4, 5
0, 4, 8, 12, 16, 20

Brain Box

Numbers in a sequence can follow a **pattern**. For instance, the numbers may increase by 2. The numbers in a second sequence of numbers can be compared to the numbers in the first sequence. For instance, the numbers in the second sequence may be double the corresponding numbers in the first.

Algebraic Thinking

Patterns

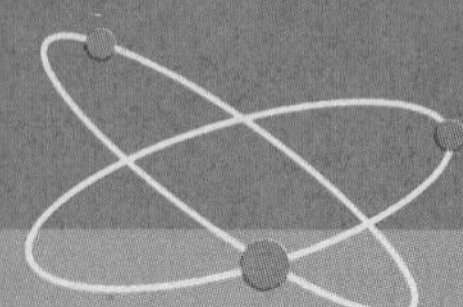

218 On the Grid

Write the number sequences as **coordinates**. Then **graph** the coordinates.

Brain Box

The corresponding numbers of two sequences of numbers can be written as pairs, or **coordinates**.

0, 1, 2, 3, 4
0, 2, 4, 6, 8
can be paired and written as (0,0) (1,2) (2,4) (3,6) (4,8).

Then they can be **graphed** as points on a grid. The ***x*-axis** goes across. The ***y*-axis** goes up and down. The first number in the pair represents the ***x* coordinate**, and the second number represents the ***y* coordinate (*x*,*y*)**. To graph *x*, go across *x* number of squares. To graph *y*, go up *y* number of squares.

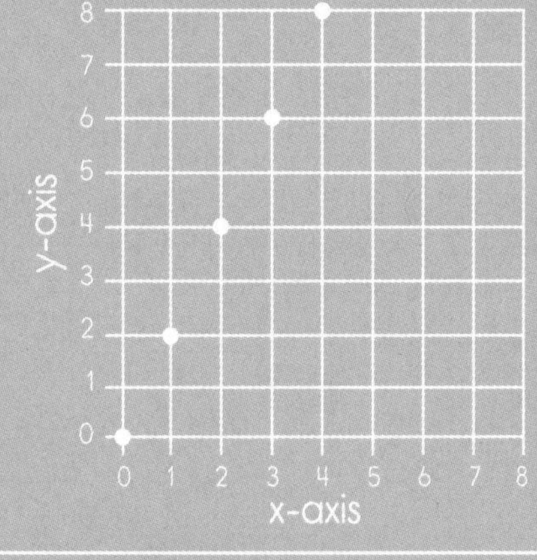

Notice that the points on the graph move up two squares for every one square they move over.

0, 1, 2, 3, 4, 5
0, 3, 6, 9, 12, 15

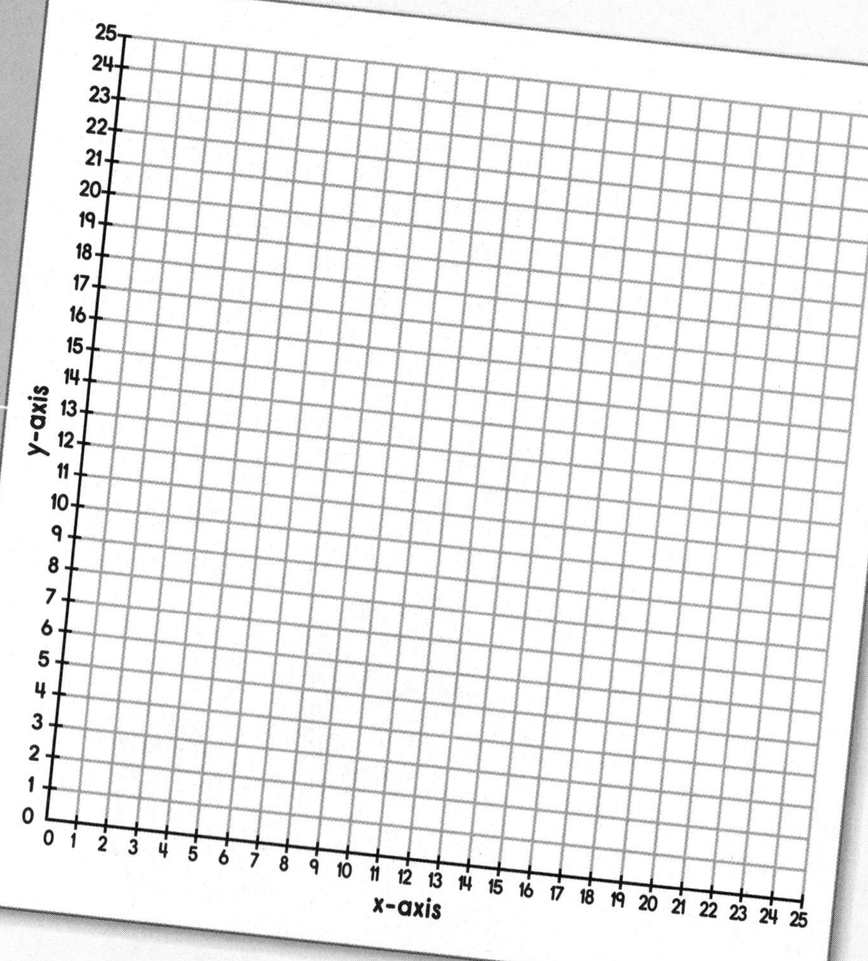

Algebraic Thinking

Graphing

On the Grid II

Write the number sequences as coordinates.
Graph the coordinates.

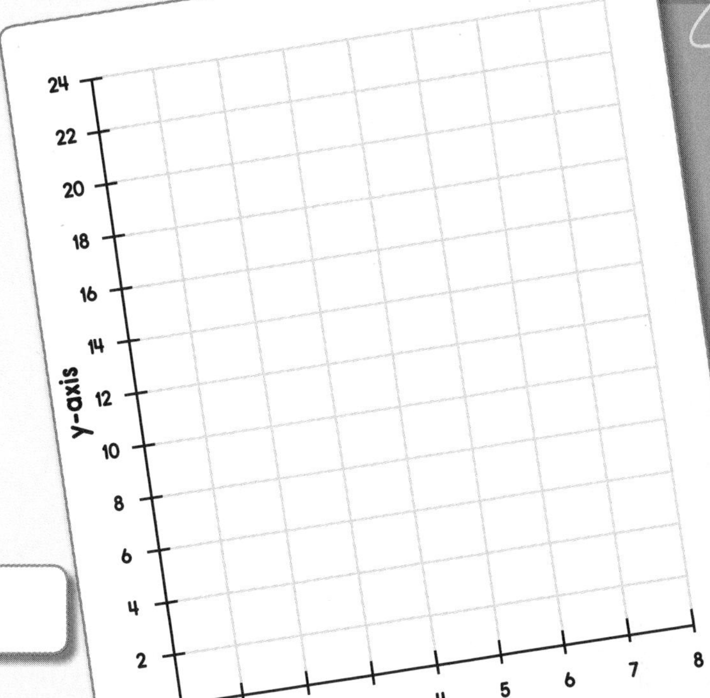

0, 2, 4, 6, 8

0, 6, 12, 18, 24

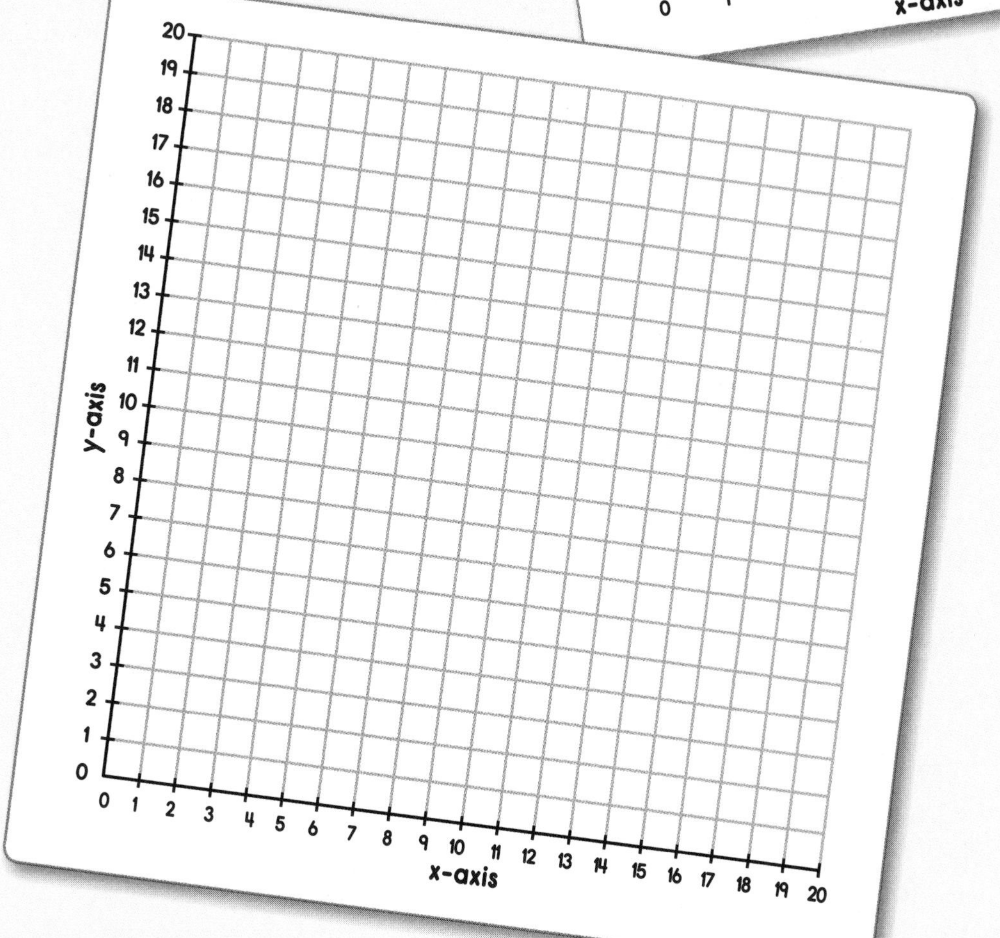

0, 1, 2, 3, 4, 5

0, 4, 8, 12, 16, 20

Algebraic Thinking

Graphing coordinates

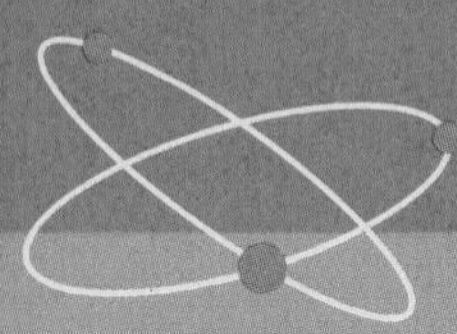

Snow Much Money

Graph the coordinates for the problems.

Leo makes $0.50 per lemonade he sells. Graph the relationship between the lemonades sold and money earned.

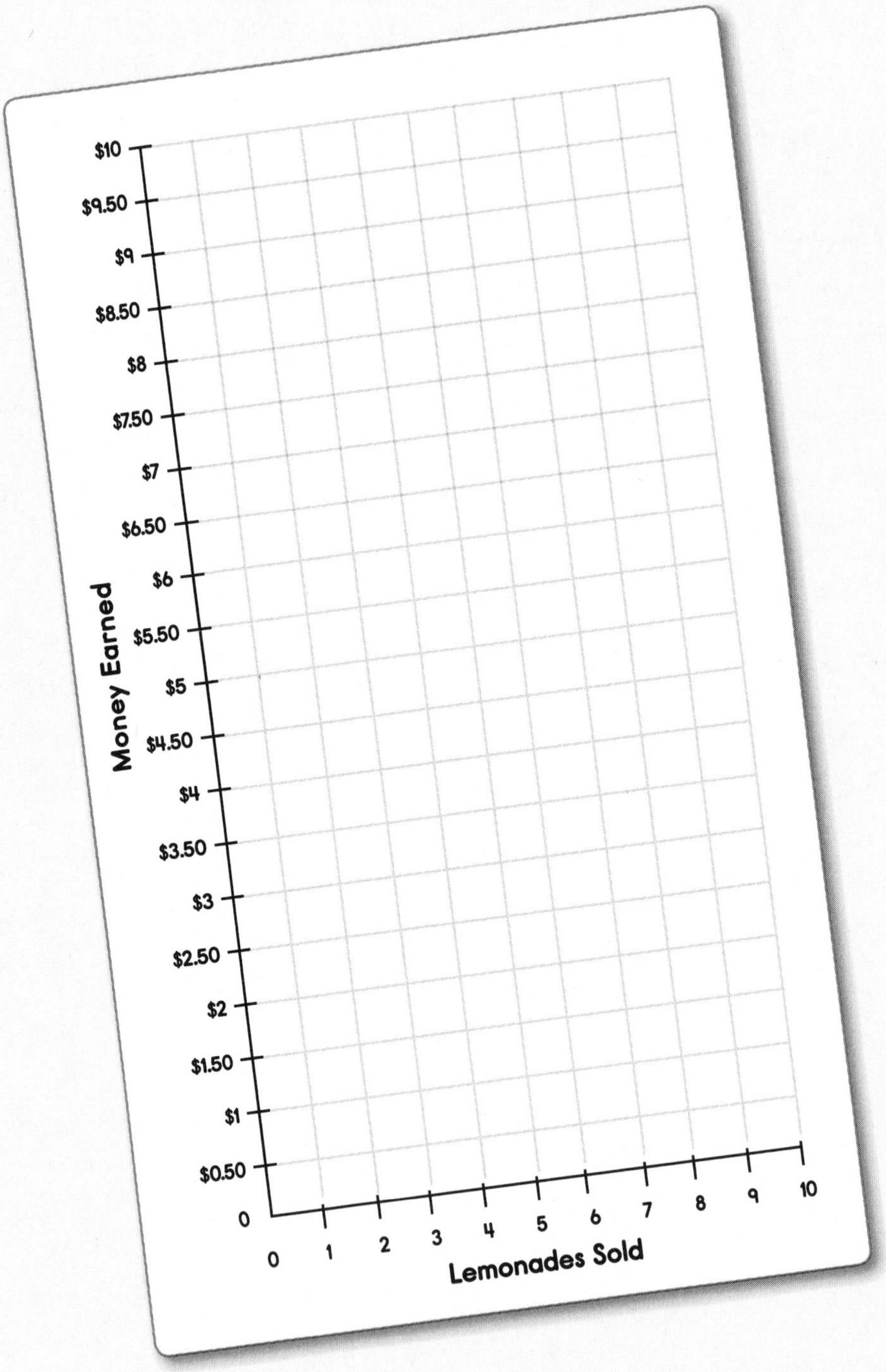

Money Earned: 0, $0.50, $1, $1.50, $2, $2.50, $3, $3.50, $4, $4.50, $5, $5.50, $6, $6.50, $7, $7.50, $8, $8.50, $9, $9.50, $10

Lemonades Sold: 0, 1, 2, 3, 4, 5, 6, 7, 8, 9, 10

Maya earns $5 for every sidewalk she shovels. Graph the relationship between the sidewalks shoveled and the money earned.

Money Earned

$25
$24
$23
$22
$21
$20
$19
$18
$17
$16
$15
$14
$13
$12
$11
$10
$9
$8
$7
$6
$5
$4
$3
$2
$1
$0

0 1 2 3 4 5 6 7 8 9 10

Sidewalks Shoveled

Speed Round

Answer the following questions based on the graphs.

How many seconds does it take Tommy to complete a math problem? ______

How many problems has Tommy completed after 7 seconds? _______

How many problems has Tommy completed after 14 seconds? _______

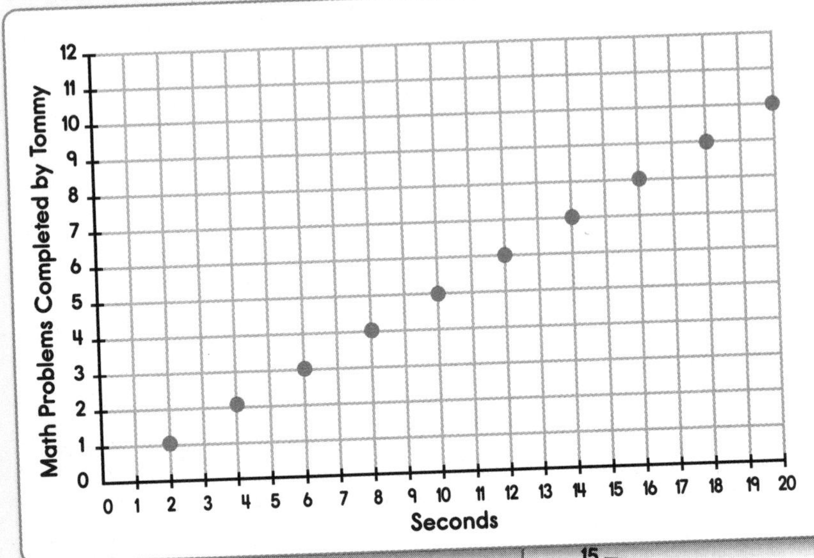

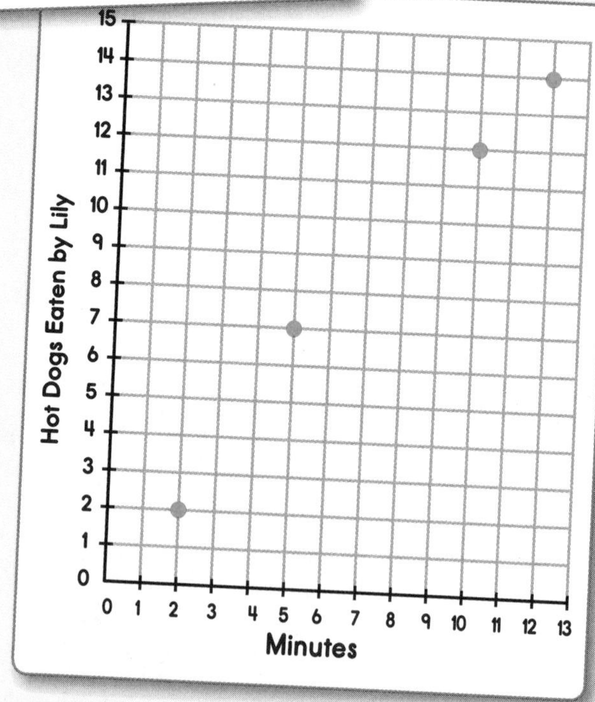

How many hot dogs can Lily eat per minute? ________

How many hot dogs has she eaten after 5 minutes? ______

How many hot dogs has she eaten after 10 minutes? ______

How many hot dogs will she have eaten after 12 minutes? ________

Word Problems

The Big Apple

Solve the word problems.

Use numerals to write "fifty-three billion one hundred twenty-seven million four hundred seventeen thousand five hundred and six."

Rosie just moved to New York City and makes $2,700 per month at her new job. Each month, she pays $2,000 for rent, $100 for the subway, and $200 for groceries. She saves $100 a month for a rainy day. How much can she spend on other things, like going out to eat or seeing a play?

Write the number 4,681 in expanded notation.

Write 2,000 + 400 + 60 + 8 in standard notation.

Aggie has 17 cupcakes and 7 friends at her party. Can the cupcakes be evenly divided among her friends?

Jack is selling 138 potatoes. Can he evenly divide them among 3 customers?

Mary is selling 135 apple fritters. Can she evenly divide them among 5 customers?

Word Problems

Math skills

The Legend of Zero

Solve the word problems.

R. J. bought a dozen doughnuts for his Spanish club. There are 10 members in the club. If the doughnuts are divided evenly, how many should each member get? How many doughnuts are left over?

Joe starts out with 7 tickets. After playing games at the carnival, he has 10 times as many. How many tickets does he have now?

Frank makes $0.40 for each lemonade he sells. By the end of the day, he has sold 100 lemonades. How much money did he make?

How many zeroes does 70 billion have?

How many zeroes does 300 million have?

Write all the prime numbers between 1 and 10.

Wedding Feast

Solve the word problems.

At the wedding, there were 6 platters, each with 58 slices of prime rib. How many slices of prime rib were there in all?

There were 5 casseroles, each with 398 vegetables. How many vegetables were there in all?

There were 8 fruit bowls, each with 204 pieces of fruit. How many pieces of fruit were there in all?

There were 3 cakes, which were each sliced into 156 pieces. How many pieces were there in all?

There were 363 guests. As party favors, each guest took home 3 Italian wedding cookies. How many cookies were there in all?

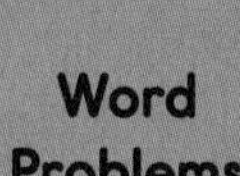

Tree-mendous

Solve the word problems.

443 leaves fell from the maple tree every day for 38 days. How many leaves fell in all?

557 gumballs fell from the gumball tree every day for 17 days. How many gumballs fell in all?

389 helicopter seeds dropped from the box elder tree every day for 26 days. How many helicopter seeds fell in all?

792 petals dropped from the magnolia trees every day for 41 days. How many petals fell in all?

114 hedge apples fell from the hedge apple trees every day for 16 days. How many hedge apples fell in all?

Party Treats

Solve the word problems.

Brendan baked 48 cupcakes for 10 guests. How many cupcakes were left over after they were divided evenly among the guests?

Maya baked 56 cookies for 15 guests. How many cookies were left over after they were divided evenly among the guests?

Ian made 38 fruit skewers for 8 guests. How many fruit skewers were left over after they were divided evenly among the guests?

Francie made 74 cake pops for 44 guests. How many cake pops were left over after they were divided evenly among the guests?

Ryan made 118 bags of trail mix for 52 guests. How many bags of trail mix were left over after they were divided evenly among the guests?

Animal Snackers

Solve the word problems.

7 bats eat an equal number of mosquitoes. They eat 3,192 mosquitoes total. How many do they each eat?

11 frogs eat an equal number of flies.
They eat 1,397 total. How many do they each eat?

8 anteaters eat an equal number of ants.
They eat 7,168 total. How many do they each eat?

9 puffins eat an equal number of herring.
They eat 1,044 total. How many do they each eat?

6 squirrels eat an equal number of acorns.
They eat 2,064 total. How many do they each eat?

3 koalas eat an equal number of eucalyptus leaves.
They eat 2,046 total. How many do they each eat?

Hot Dog!

Solve the word problems.

Brady bought a used car for $8,460, which he paid for over 36 months. He paid the same amount each month. How much did he pay each month?

Sam owed $9,384 in student loans. She paid them off over 24 months. She paid the same amount each month. How much did she pay each month?

Grace's braces cost $5,786. Her parents paid for them over 22 months, and they paid the same amount each month. How much did they pay each month?

Calvin bought an oven for his restaurant for $4,788. He paid for it over 18 months, and he paid the same amount each month. How much did he pay each month?

Kara bought a hot dog stand for $5,064. She paid for it over 12 months, and she paid the same amount each month. How much did she pay each month?

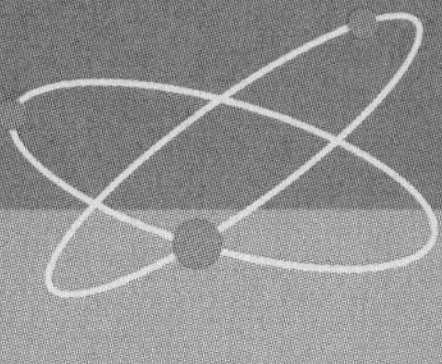

Lunch Room Leftovers

Solve the word problems.

There were 386 fish sticks for 88 students. How many fish sticks were left over after each student got an equal number?

The school cook prepared 548 chicken nuggets for 96 students. How many chicken nuggets were left over after they were divided evenly among the students?

There were 853 apple slices for 79 students. How many apple slices were left over after each student got an equal number of slices?

There were 275 ounces of applesauce for 68 students. How many ounces were left over after each student got an equal amount?

There were 523 ounces of sloppy joe filling for 76 students. How many ounces were left over after each student got an equal amount?

Not Exactly

Solve the word problems.

The grocery store has 28 32-ounce bags of flour. Estimate (by rounding to the nearest 10) how many total ounces of flour the store has.

The store has 64 32-ounce cans of tomato sauce. Estimate (by rounding to the nearest 10) how many total ounces of tomato sauce the store has.

At the tournament, there are 28 teams, and each team has 14 players. Estimate (by rounding to the nearest 10) how many total players are at the tournament.

A ship contains 49 boxes filled with 68 tennis balls each. Estimate (by rounding to the nearest 10) how many total tennis balls the ship is carrying.

A box contains 34 candy bars with 82 peanuts each. Estimate (by rounding to the nearest 10) how many total peanuts are in all the candy bars.

Be Our Guest

Solve the word problems. Reduce if possible.

Mae had 8 pieces of rhubarb pie. She served 5 pieces to her guests. What fraction describes the amount of pie that remains?

Liam had 24 chocolate drop cookies. His guests ate 18. What fraction describes the amount of cookies his guests ate?

Kynthia ordered 2 large turkey club subs for her 6 guests. What fraction of a sub should each guest get?

Brooks ordered 3 chocolate chip cookie cakes for his 12 guests. What fraction of a cookie cake should each guest get?

Lucibell bought 2 gallons of rainbow sherbet for her 24 guests. What fraction of a gallon should each guest get?

Sarah fixed 3 large bowls of pimento cheese dip for her 72 guests. What fraction of a bowl should each guest get?

School Supplies

Solve the word problems.

Dalen combined a box of pencils that was $\frac{3}{8}$ full with a box of pencils that was $\frac{1}{4}$ full. The boxes were equal in size. How full was the combined box?

Mary Ellen added a $\frac{3}{5}$ full box of markers to a $\frac{1}{4}$ full box of markers. The boxes were equal in size. How full was the combined box?

Justin's box of crayons was $\frac{3}{4}$ full. He gave half the crayons in the box to Daniel. How much remained in Justin's box?

Mrs. Layton found the box of glue sticks $\frac{2}{3}$ full. She took $\frac{1}{4}$ of the remaining glue sticks out of the box. How much of the box remained?

Mrs. Randolph borrowed a box of books from the library. She loaned $\frac{3}{5}$ to the students. How much of the box remained?

Maggie combined a $\frac{1}{6}$ full box of erasers with a $\frac{4}{5}$ full box. The boxes are equal in size. How full was the box now?

The After Picnic

Solve the word problems.

$\frac{1}{2}$ a fluffernutter sandwich was left in the grass. 4 mice shared it. How much of the sandwich did each mouse get?

$\frac{1}{3}$ of a grape freeze pop lay on the sidewalk. 3 flies shared it. How much of the freeze pop did each fly get?

$\frac{1}{4}$ of a bag of cheese puffs spilled. 4 birds shared it. How much of the bag did each bird get?

$\frac{2}{5}$ of a can of strawberry soda pop spilled. 10 ants shared the spilled soda. How much of the can did each ant get?

2 raccoons shared $\frac{2}{3}$ of a deviled egg that fell in the mud. How much of the egg did each raccoon get?

5 squirrels shared $\frac{3}{4}$ of a canister of mixed nuts that was left on the table. How much of the canister did each squirrel get?

Dot Dot Dot

Solve the word problems.

The science student added 10.2 milliliters of lemon juice to 20.45 milliliters of milk. How much total liquid was there?

The scientist combined 3.4 milliliters of water and 2.1 milliliters of hydrogen peroxide. How much total liquid was there?

Which is greater: $\frac{4}{5}$ or 0.85?

What is the decimal equivalent of $\frac{3}{4}$?

How much money is 2 quarters, 2 dimes, 2 nickels, and 2 pennies?

What is the product of 43.5 and 0.87?

Extreme Tree House Makeover

Solve the word problems.

Kids are adding glass to the windows of a tree house. The windows are 18 inches wide and 24 inches high. How many square inches of glass do they need for each window?

The kids are carpeting the tree house. The floor is 8 feet wide by 10 long feet. How many square feet of carpeting do they need?

The kids are painting one interior wall with chalkboard paint. The wall is 8 feet wide and 7 feet tall. How many square feet do they need to paint?

The kids are adding a glow-in-the-dark wallpaper border. This will go along the top of the walls. Two of the walls are 8 feet across, and two are 10 feet across. How many feet of border do they need?

The kids are painting the outside of the tree house purple. Two walls are 8 feet × 7 feet, and two walls are 10 feet × 7 feet. How many square feet need to be painted altogether?

This and That

Solve the word problems.

What is the volume of a 12 × 12 × 12 centimeter cardboard box?

Maddie swam 30 laps. Each lap was 50 meters. How many kilometers did she swim?

The temperature on Monday was 89°F but dropped to 51°F overnight. What was the difference in temperature?

The diameter of the story-time circle is 10 feet. What is the circumference (using 3.14 as π)?

Mr. Tapko painted a circle with a 5-foot radius for a tetherball court. What is the area of the court (using 3.14 as π)?

Diona needed 32 cups of milk.
How many gallons did she need?

Social Studies

Know Your States

Label the states on the map that are missing their names.

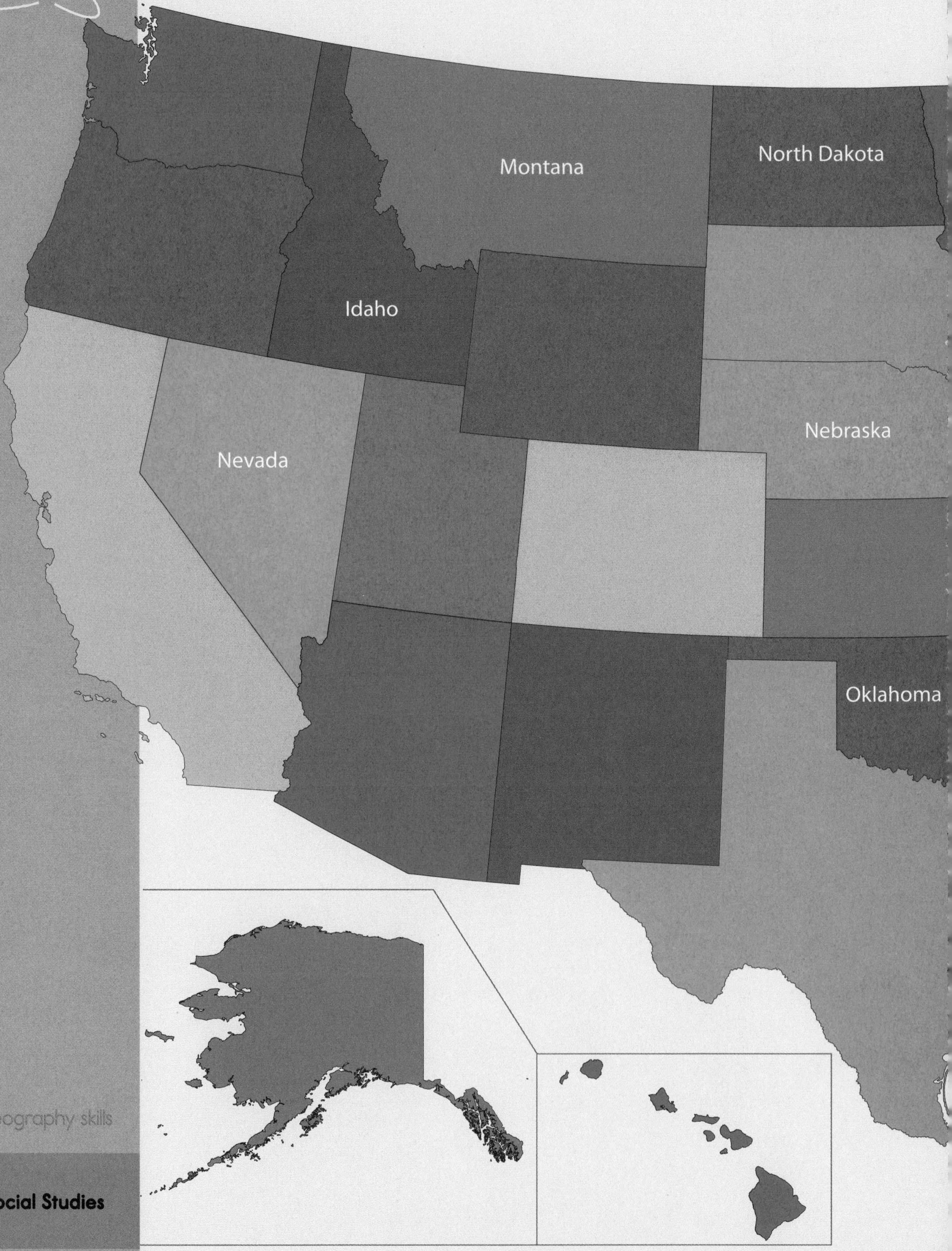
Montana
North Dakota
Idaho
Nevada
Nebraska
Oklahoma

Geography skills

Social Studies

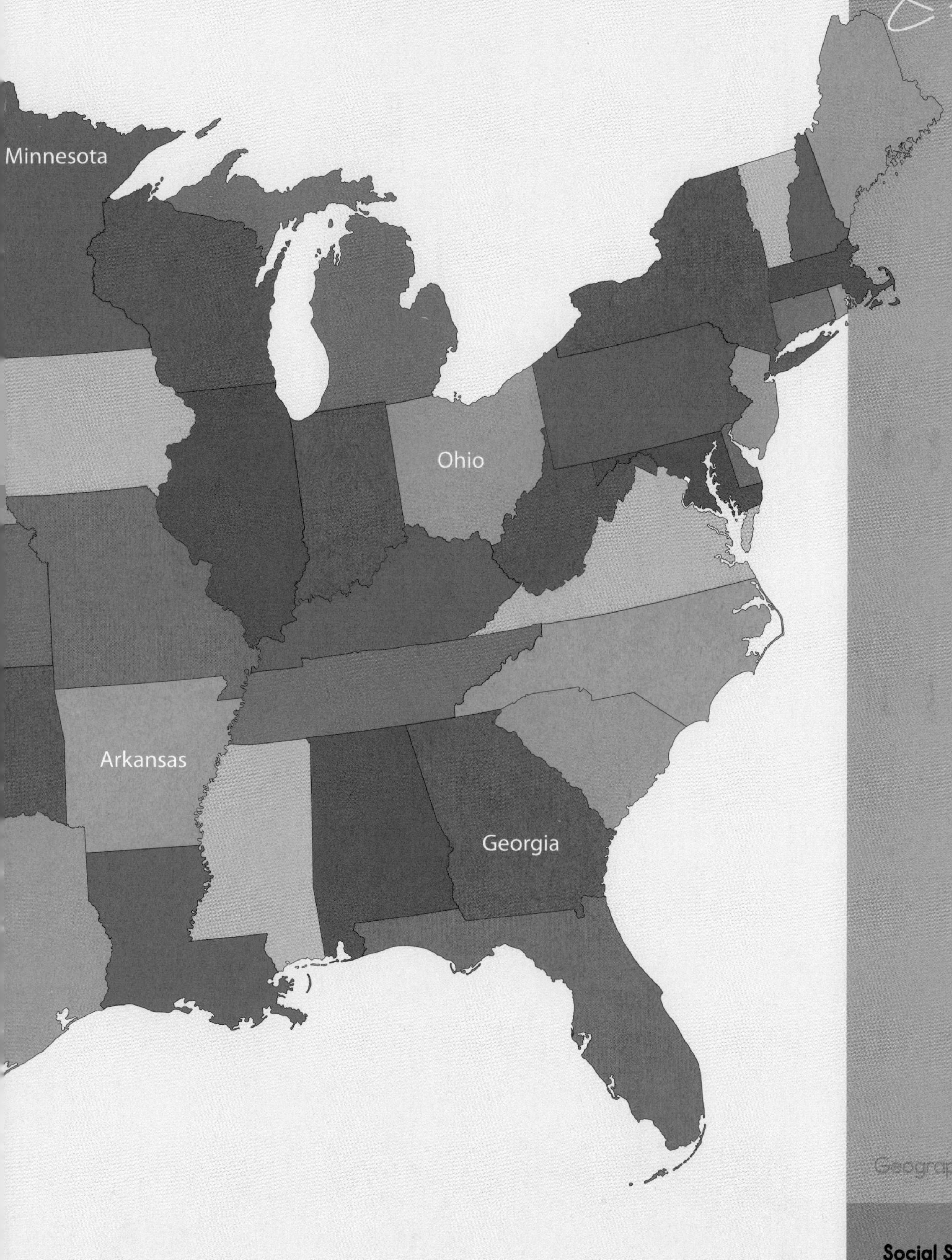

Minnesota
Ohio
Arkansas
Georgia

The Abbreviated States of America

Read the list of states and their abbreviations.
Then follow the directions below.

State	Abbreviation
ALABAMA	AL
ALASKA	AK
ARIZONA	AZ
ARKANSAS	AR
CALIFORNIA	CA
COLORADO	CO
CONNECTICUT	CT
DELAWARE	DE
FLORIDA	FL
GEORGIA	GA
HAWAII	HI
IDAHO	ID
ILLINOIS	IL
INDIANA	IN
IOWA	IA
KANSAS	KS
KENTUCKY	KY
LOUISIANA	LA
MAINE	ME
MARYLAND	MD

HELLO my NAME IS AL

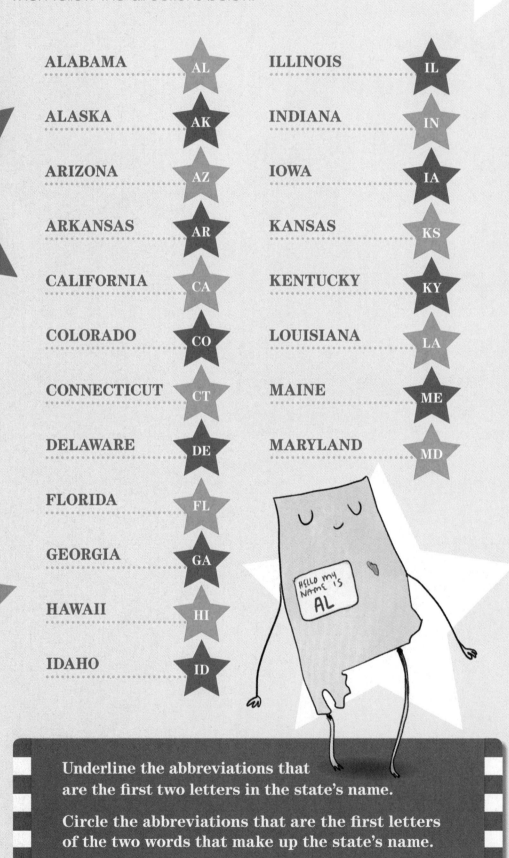

Underline the abbreviations that are the first two letters in the state's name.

Circle the abbreviations that are the first letters of the two words that make up the state's name.

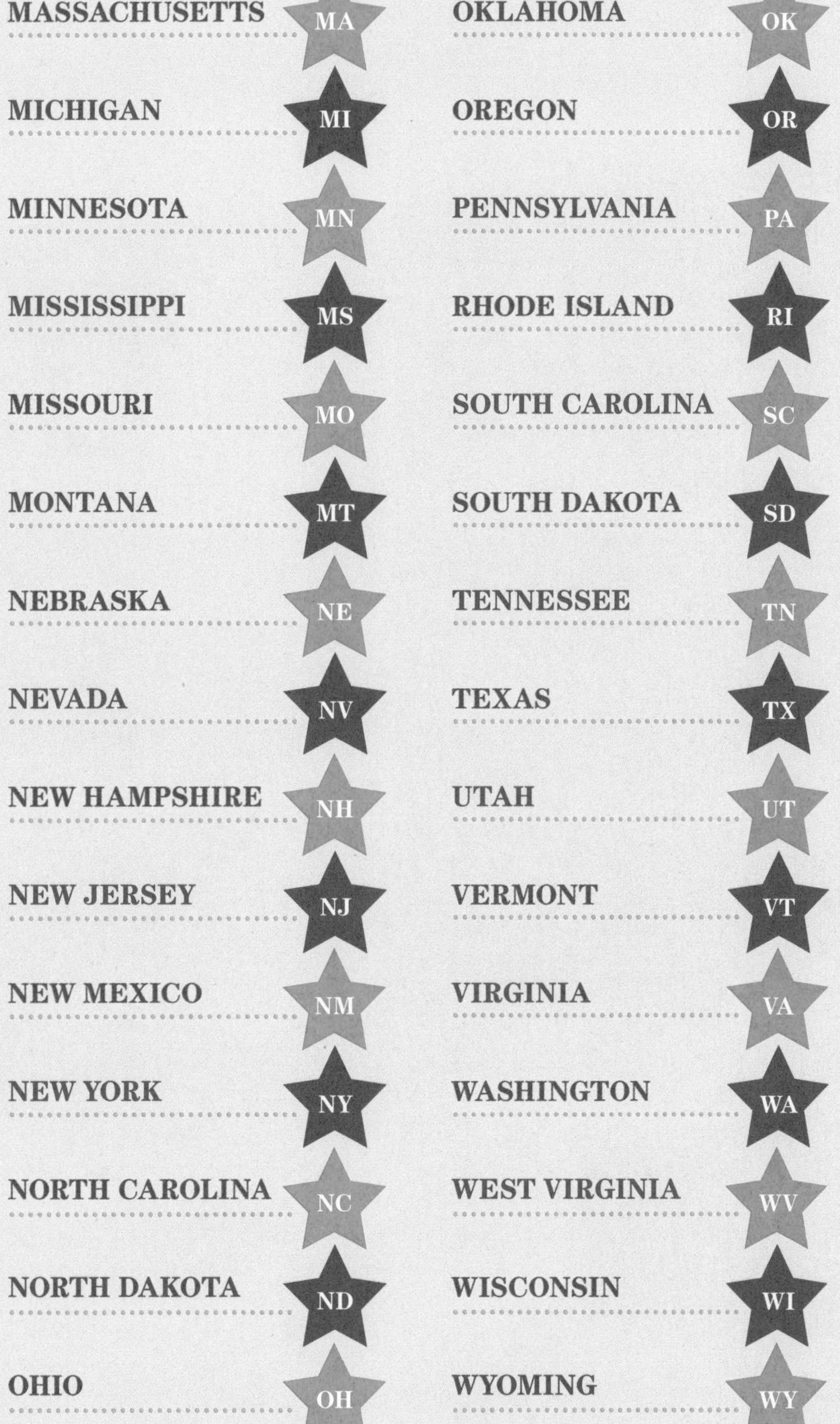

MASSACHUSETTS MA
MICHIGAN MI
MINNESOTA MN
MISSISSIPPI MS
MISSOURI MO
MONTANA MT
NEBRASKA NE
NEVADA NV
NEW HAMPSHIRE NH
NEW JERSEY NJ
NEW MEXICO NM
NEW YORK NY
NORTH CAROLINA NC
NORTH DAKOTA ND
OHIO OH
OKLAHOMA OK
OREGON OR
PENNSYLVANIA PA
RHODE ISLAND RI
SOUTH CAROLINA SC
SOUTH DAKOTA SD
TENNESSEE TN
TEXAS TX
UTAH UT
VERMONT VT
VIRGINIA VA
WASHINGTON WA
WEST VIRGINIA WV
WISCONSIN WI
WYOMING WY

Put a star next to the abbreviations that are the first and last letters in the state's name.

Put a plus sign next to abbreviations that follow none of these patterns.

State abbreviations

Social Studies

Bright Lights, Big Cities

Study the map and answer the questions.

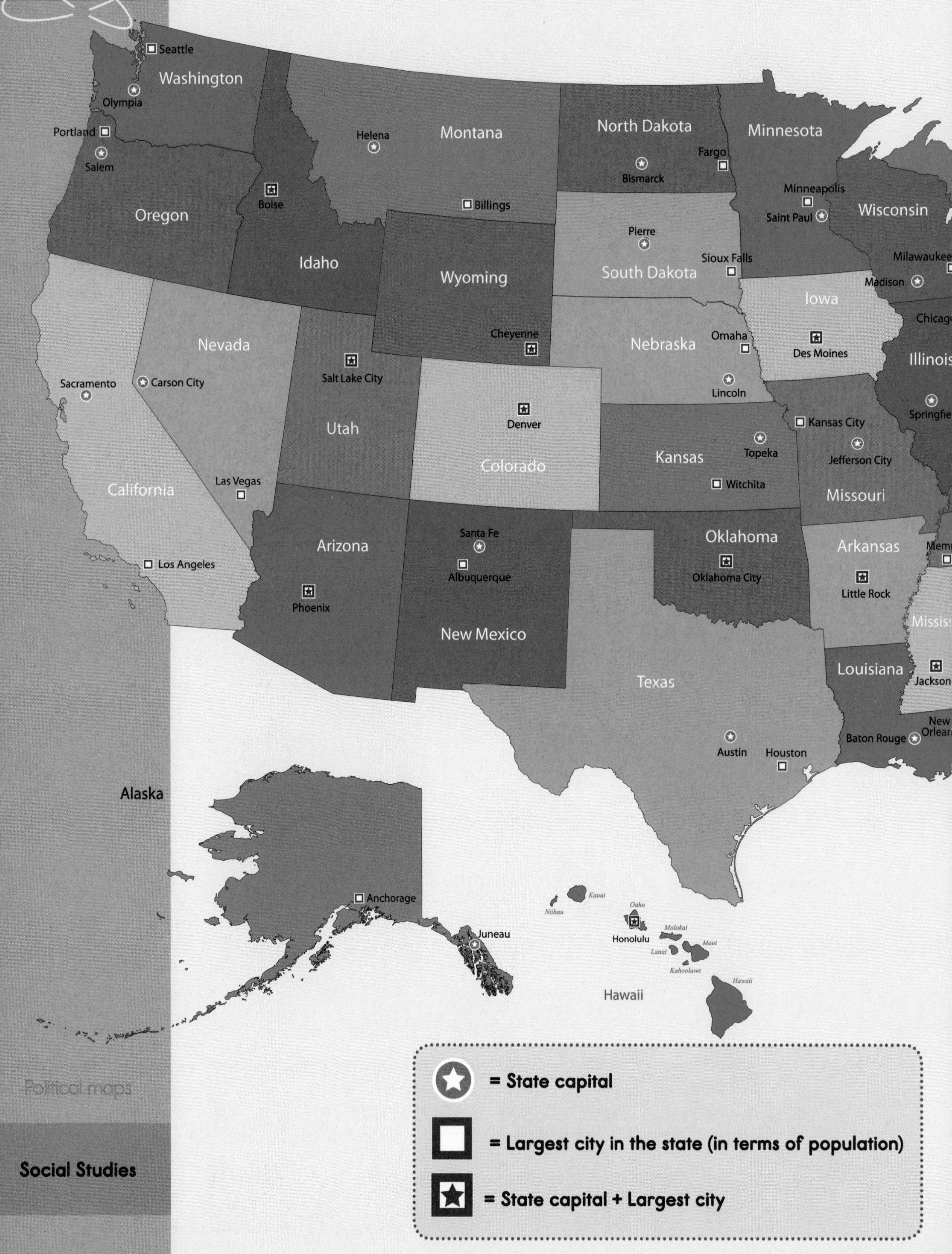

Political maps

Social Studies

What is the largest city in Wisconsin?

Which city is both the capital and largest city in Utah?

What city is both the capital and the largest city in Arkansas?

What is the largest city in Kansas?

What is the capital of Louisiana?

What is the capital of Tennessee?

What is the largest city in South Dakota?

What is the capital of Alaska?

In which 17 states is the capital also the largest city?

________	________	________
________	________	________
________	________	________
________	________	________
________	________	________
________	________	________

Brain Box

Political maps show government boundaries, such as state and country borders. They also show the location of cities. Note that some cities are also state capitals, and some cities have the largest population in the state.

Mountains Majesty

Study the physical map and answer the questions.

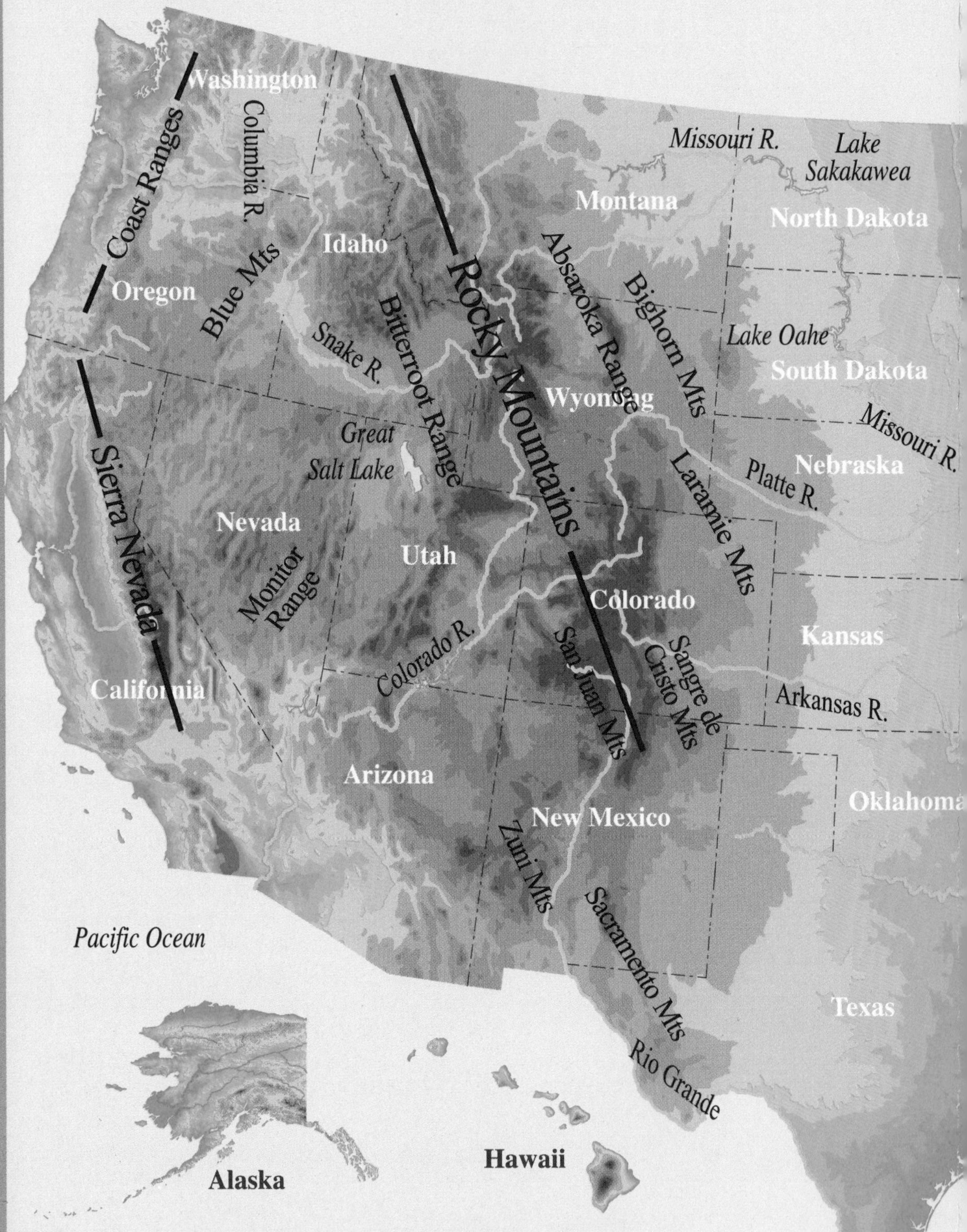

What mountain range spans Georgia to Maine?

From which state does the Mississippi River empty into the Gulf of Mexico?

Which states border Lake Michigan?

Physical maps

Social Studies

In which state is the Great Salt Lake located?

What body of water is between Texas and Florida?

If you drive west through Kansas, does your elevation increase or decrease?

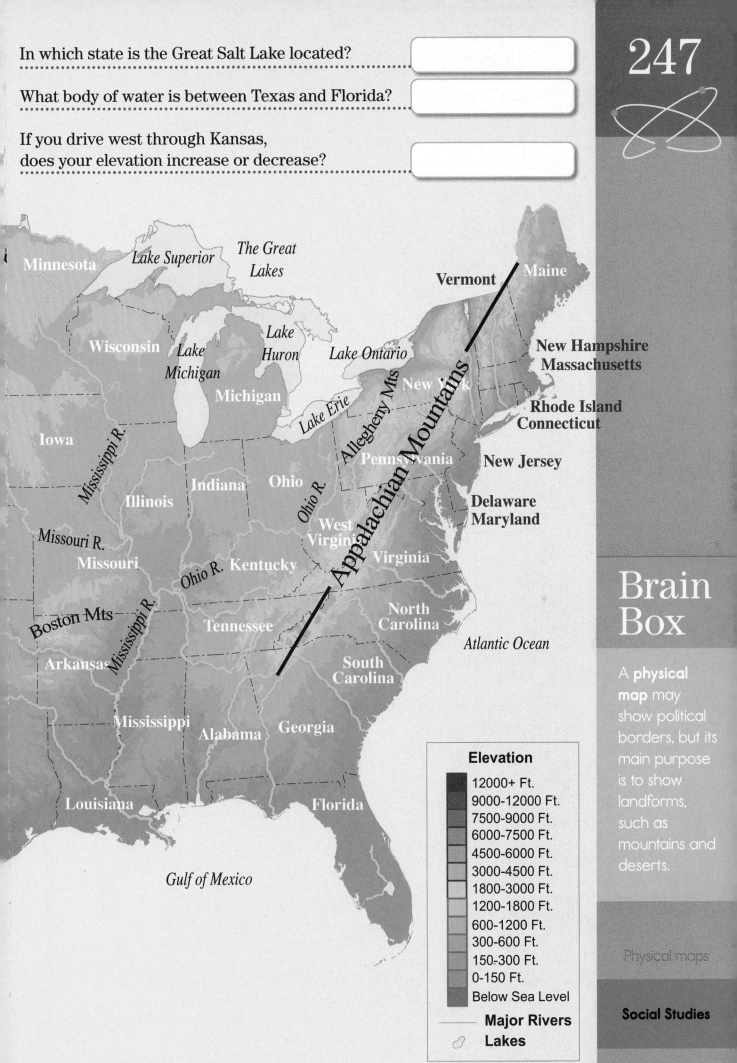

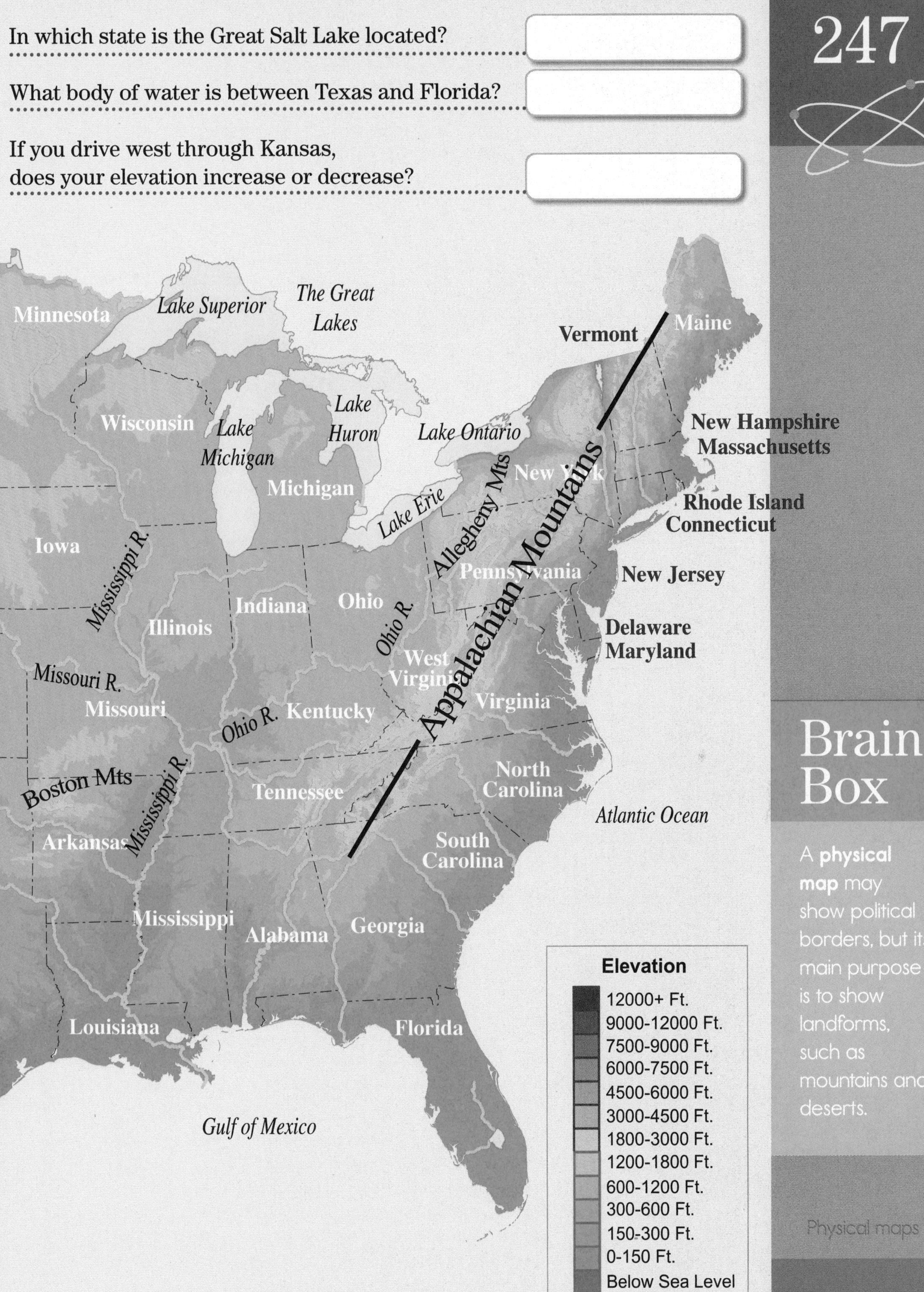

Brain Box

A **physical map** may show political borders, but its main purpose is to show landforms, such as mountains and deserts.

Physical maps

Social Studies

Many Cultures

Read about how people lived in some of the **regions** of early America.

The original inhabitants of America were here thousands of years before the Europeans. Their natural resources varied by region, as did their cultures and ways of making a living. There were many groups of people living in each region. The descriptions below describe some of the things the groups had in common within each region.

Pacific Northwest

Peoples of the Pacific Northwest enjoyed a mild climate and ample rain. For this reason, food was plentiful. They fished for salmon and hunted for whales, otters, bear, deer, and elk. Food was so abundant that some people could specialize in making art rather than gathering food all day. For this reason, art flourished in the Pacific Northwest. Elaborate totem poles are one example. The bounty of food also allowed people to acquire personal wealth and status. Even within families, there were ranks, just as royal families are ranked today.

Southwest

The Southwest was desert land. Southwest peoples grew beans, corn, and squash, and because water was scarce, they used irrigation on their farms. With little rainfall, few trees grew with which to build homes. Instead, the people built adobe homes. Adobe is a mixture of mud and straw that is dried in the sun. Some southwest peoples built homes in the sides of cliffs. In this case, they used ladders to access their homes. The ladders could be pulled up so that enemies couldn't gain access.

Great Plains

Prior to the arrival of Europeans, most peoples of the Great Plains settled in river valleys, where water was abundant and rainfall fairly reliable. They were primarily farmers. On the western Great Plains, however, water was scarce and the weather could be very hot or cold. This land was not conducive to farming, but the prairie grasses that thrived there fed huge herds of bison. The people of the western Great Plains followed the migration of the bison as nomadic hunters. When the Europeans arrived with horses, hunters could follow their prey on horseback, which led to more successful hunts. In the 17th and 18th centuries, many native peoples moved to the Great Plains to become bison hunters, and a rich hunting culture emerged. The 17th- and 18th-century Great Plains hunters are commonly depicted in art and movies. But this was only one Native American culture in the region, and one that existed only briefly. In fact, there were many Native American peoples, and their ways of life varied greatly.

Answer the questions.

What are three of the major regions in which Native Americans lived?

____

____

How did an abundance of food allow art to flourish in the Pacific Northwest? What is an example of such art?

____

____

What is one way that the people of the Southwest adapted to a lack of water?

____

____

What were two differences between life in the Pacific Northwest and life in the Southwest?

____

____

Prior to the arrival of Europeans, what did most Great Plains people do for a living?

____

____

Why were there so many bison on the western Great Plains?

____

____

What led to there being more bison hunters on the western Great Plains?

____

____

Brain Box

The **regions** of the Americas are not political entities, as countries or states are. Instead, each has its own history, climate, and cultural features.

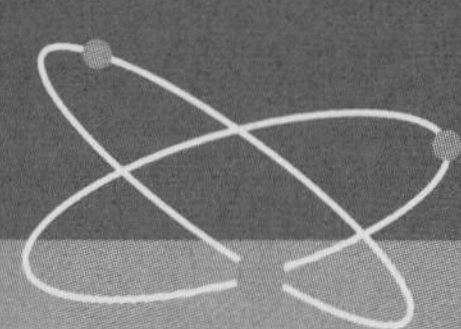

Ship Ahoy!

Fill in the blanks using the innovations and inventions from the cards below.

Innovations and Inventions

Seaworthy ships were essential for crossing the Atlantic and Pacific Oceans en route to new lands. One such ship was the **caravel**. As early as the 1200s, the caravel was a type of shipping boat. Through the years, however, the ship became faster and more maneuverable. By the 1400s, it was a favorite ship of explorers.

The **magnetic compass** had been invented by the Chinese in the 1000s, but it came into use in Europe in the 1300s. The compass allowed explorers to know in which direction they were headed on the open sea.

Chinese scientists discovered **gunpowder** in the year 850. They used it to propel their arrows in wars against the Mongols. The technology spread to Europe and the Islamic world in the 1200s. The gunpowder was used first in cannons, and then in handguns. Guns, along with swords, allowed explorers to conquer powerful civilizations, such as the Inca, who lacked similar weapon technology.

Christopher Columbus spoke of the great speed and maneuverability of his prized ________________, the *Niña*.

Columbus didn't tell his crew that in the Atlantic, the ____________ behaved unpredictably, so that it was difficult to determine whether it was really pointing north.

In 1532, 168 Spanish explorers known as conquistadors managed to defeat 80,000 Inca troops because of their horses, knowledge of past battles, and weapon technology, including ________________.

Brain Box

The **Age of Exploration** refers to the time period from 1400 to 1600 when Europeans traveled the world to acquire raw materials, land, and other assets. Inventions and innovations made it possible to take sea journeys to new lands and to conquer the peoples in these lands.

Age of Exploration

Social Studies

Life at Sea

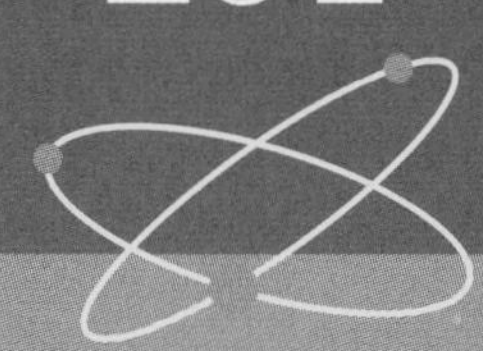

Read the firsthand account of life at sea during the **Age of Exploration.** Then answer the questions.

"We were three months and twenty days without refreshment from any kind of fresh food. We ate biscuit which was no longer biscuit but its powder, swarming with worms, the rats having eaten all the good. It stank strongly of their urine. We drank yellow water already many days putrid. We also ate certain ox hides that covered the top of the yards to prevent the yards from chafing the shrouds, and which had become exceedingly hard because of the sun, rain and wind. We soaked them in the sea for four or five days, then placed them for a short time over the hot embers and ate them thus, and often we ate sawdust. Rats were sold for half a ducat apiece, and even so we could not always get them."

—The explorer Antonio Pigafetta describing the conditions on Ferdinand Magellan's ship in 1521

How long had the men gone without fresh food?

____

Name three things the men on the ship ate in lieu of fresh food.

____

____

____

What had happened to the supply of biscuits?

____

____

Brain Box

During the **Age of Exploration**, seafarers would go on journeys across unknown territory. Sometimes, this led them to lands they didn't know existed, as was the case with Columbus landing in America. But it would sometimes cause them to run out of food before they reached their destination. This happened to Ferdinand Magellan, who believed his crew could sail across the Pacific in 3 weeks, a journey that in fact took more than 3 months.

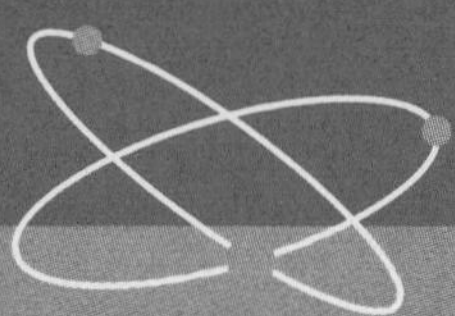

Brain Box

Many colonial settlements existed in America. They were ruled by the French, Dutch, Spanish, Russians, and English. The **thirteen English colonies** along the eastern coast of North America went on to become the United States. The colonies were formed in the early 1600s, and they persisted until the end of the Revolutionary War in 1783.

Thirteen colonies

Social Studies

The Originals

Fill in the names of the original **thirteen colonies** with the help of the clues.

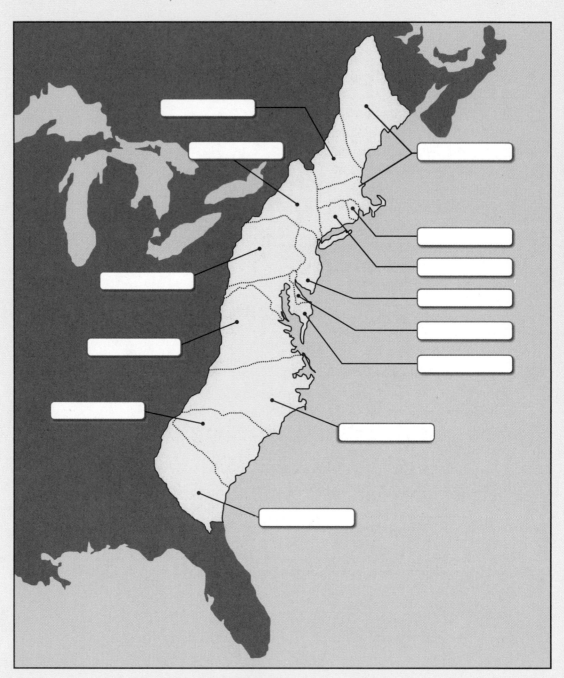

The southernmost colony is Georgia.

Maryland and Delaware share a peninsula.

Pennsylvania is the only colony that does not touch the Atlantic Ocean.

Rhode Island is nestled between Massachusetts and Connecticut.

A large island is part of New York.

New Jersey is below New York and above a peninsula.

Massachusetts has two land areas separated by New Hampshire.

Virginia is above North Carolina and South Carolina.

We the People

Read the preamble of the **U.S. Constitution** and the definitions of some of the words. Then rewrite the preamble in your own words.

We the People of the United States, in Order to form a more perfect Union, establish Justice, insure domestic Tranquility, provide for the common defence, promote the general Welfare, and secure the Blessings of Liberty to ourselves and our Posterity, do ordain and establish this Constitution for the United States of America.

union: a country made up of states

justice: fairness and moral rightness

domestic: relating to a people's home country

tranquility: peace

welfare: health and happiness

liberty: freedom from unfair government rules

posterity: future generations

ordain: decree

establish: set up

We the people, ____

____

____

____

____

____

____

____

____

Brain Box

The **U.S. Constitution** is the law of the land. Established in 1789, it describes the U.S. system of government, including the three branches (executive, legislative, and judicial) and states' rights and responsibilities. It has been amended 27 times. The first 10 amendments make up the **Bill of Rights**.

Jamestown, 1607

Read the story about the first permanent British colony in America.

Jamestown:
The First Permanent British Colony

In 1607, 104 British colonists arrived in what would become Jamestown, Virginia. The colonists were employed by a group of investors called the Virginia Company to find gold and silver, which had already been found by the Spanish in Mexico and Peru.

An earlier group of English settlers had disappeared from the region. It was believed that the Native American inhabitants had attacked the earlier settlers for trespassing on their land. This time, however, the new settlers were careful to settle on unclaimed territory.

Such land was difficult to come by. The region was home to a Native American chiefdom called Tsenacomoco. Approximately 14,000 people lived in villages and grew corn in the surrounding fields. These people were ruled by Chief Powhatan, who had united several chiefdoms to form Tsenacomoco.

The Jamestown settlers resorted to marshy land that was infested with mosquitoes and riddled with bad drinking water. Powhatan's people didn't dispute this land claim, as the land was bad anyway. Many colonists died from water-borne illnesses. Others died of starvation because a drought made food hard to grow, and with so many sick, there were few to tend the crops. But more colonists arrived, along with a new leader, John Rolfe. Rolfe married Powhatan's daughter, Pocahontas, which helped to keep the peace between the natives and the colonists.

The Jamestown settlers continued to die at alarming rates (it's believed that only 1 in 4 survived), but new colonists from England kept arriving. The English farms, along with their domesticated animals crowded out the Tsenacomoco people, who needed room to hunt and rotate their crops. At the same time, many English settlers arrived in America infected with malaria, a sickness spread by mosquitoes. The disease was quickly passed on to Powhatan's people. If they had wanted to fight the colonists for land, they may have been too sick to do so. Eventually, the English colonists took the land that had once been Tsenacomoco.

Answer the questions.

When did the Jamestown colonists first arrive in America?

____

What were the Jamestown colonists hoping to find in America?

____

Write three facts about Tsenacomoco.

____

____

____

Describe the land on which the Jamestown settlers lived.
Include at least 2 details.

____

____

____

What fraction of Jamestown colonists are believed to have died due to illnesses and starvation?

____

Give two reasons that explain how the English colonists came to control the land that had once been Tsenacomoco.

____

____

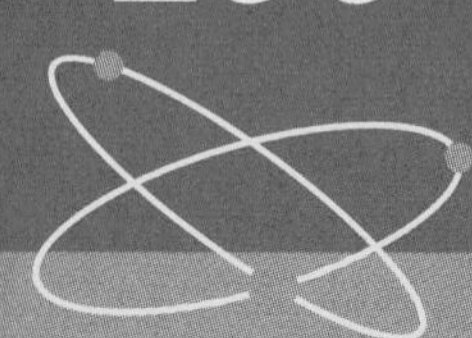

Revolutionary Players

Read the cards about the **Revolutionary War**.

King George III

Claim to Fame: King of England for 59 years

Born: 1738

Died: 1820

Personal Fact: He and his wife, Charlotte, had 15 children.

Role in the Revolution: Along with Parliament, he led the British in the war against the American colonists.

George Washington

Claim to Fame: 1st U.S. President

Born: 1732

Died: 1799

Personal Fact: After the war, Washington wanted to return to farming, but was talked into running for president.

Role in the Revolution: He was the commander in chief of the Continental Army.

John Adams

Claim to Fame: 2nd U.S. President

Born: 1735

Died: July 4, 1826

Personal Fact: His son, John Quincy Adams, became the 6th U.S. president.

Role in the Revolution: He was a delegate to the Continental Congress and a leader in the American quest for independence.

Thomas Jefferson

Claim to Fame: 3rd U.S. President

Born: 1743

Died: July 4, 1826

Personal Fact: He died within hours of his friend John Adams.

Role in the Revolution: He was a delegate to the Continental Congress and writer of the Declaration of Independence.

Brain Box

The **Revolutionary War** (or the **American Revolution** or the **U.S. War of Independence**) lasted from 1775 to 1783, and ended with the 13 North American colonies winning their independence from the British crown.

Mary Ludwig (aka Molly Pitcher)

Claim to Fame: Revolutionary War soldier

Born: 1754

Died: 1832

Personal Fact: She was nicknamed Molly Pitcher because she carried pitchers of water to the soldiers during the war.

Role in the Revolution: When her husband collapsed during the Battle of Monmouth, she fired his cannon in his place.

Abigail Adams

Claim to Fame: 2nd U.S. First Lady

Born: 1744

Died: 1818

Personal Fact: She encouraged her husband to give women rights equal to those of men in the U.S. Constitution.

Role in the Revolution: She advised her husband and interrogated Massachusetts women who remained loyal to the British crown.

Draw a line from each person to the statement that is true about him or her.

King George III	was the second U.S. president.
George Washington	was nicknamed for her work during the war.
John Adams	worked alongside Parliament.
Thomas Jefferson	was talked into running for president.
Mary Ludwig	questioned Massachusetts residents who remained loyal to the British crown.
Abigail Adams	wrote the Declaration of Independence.

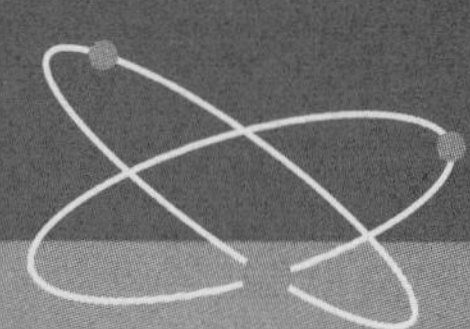

You Be the Judge

Read the summary of the **Bill of Rights**.

The Bill of Rights

Amendment I

The right to freedom of religion, freedom of speech, freedom of the press, and freedom to peaceably assemble

Amendment II

The right to bear arms as part of a well-regulated militia

Amendment III

The right not to be required to house soldiers

Amendment IV

The right not to be searched or to have your home or belongings searched without a warrant

Amendment V

The right to due process, which includes a grand jury for a capital crime, the right not to testify against oneself, and the right not to be tried twice for the same crime

Amendment VI

The right to a speedy and fair trial, including an attorney and an impartial jury

Amendment VII

The right to a trial by jury

Amendment VIII

The right not to be charged excessive bail or fines, or to suffer from cruel and unusual punishment

Amendment IX

The right to not be denied rights not listed in the Bill of Rights

Amendment X

The right of states to make and uphold laws not in the power of the federal government

Brain Box

The first ten amendments to the U.S. Constitution are collectively called the **Bill of Rights**, which grants basic rights to Americans. When these rights are violated, a person may have a case against the person or people who violated those rights.

Bill of Rights

Social Studies

Write which amendment may have been violated.

A man is fined $200 for mistakenly catching a fish out of season. He cannot afford to pay the fine, so he is fined another $1,000 for failure to pay. Unable to pay the new amount, he is jailed for one month. Then he is required to pay $500 for his room and board in jail, which he also can't afford. So he is fined another $200 for not paying that. He now owes $1,900.

____

A student wears a political T-shirt to school. Even though he has not violated the dress code, the student is told not to wear the shirt again.

____

A man has been in prison for five years awaiting his trial.

____

A homeless person lives in a box. When she is suspected of committing murder, the police search the box without a search warrant.

____

After a natural disaster, the governor of Florida declares martial law and requires residents to provide room and board to soldiers.

____

Go West!

Read about the **Westward Expansion.**

While the British colonies on the East Coast were fighting the Revolutionary War and forming the United States, other countries still laid claim to parts of America. In 1803, the French government made a surprise offer to sell its land, the Louisiana Territory, to the United States. President Thomas Jefferson jumped at the offer: 828,000,000 square miles of land for $15 million—about 4 cents an acre.

The land, extending from the Mississippi River to the Rocky Mountains, and from the Canadian border to the Gulf of Mexico, doubled the area of the United States. Fifteen U.S. states would eventually form from the new land.

The Westward Expansion was the movement of Americans west in search of farmland and other opportunities in the newly acquired territory. Settlers believed that owning land was part of the freedom that America offered (as opposed to the low-wage jobs, which they may have had in their home countries). President Jefferson and others shared this idea. The journalist John O'Sullivan coined the phrase "manifest destiny," which expressed the idea that America was a gift from God and that Americans were meant to populate the rest of the continent.

The land to the west first became territories, and then states. This process pushed Native Americans off their land (a process that had already happened in the East). In addition, as the states formed, there arose the question of whether new states would allow slavery. The Missouri Compromise was a law that allowed Missouri to have slaves but that prohibited slavery in states that formed north of Missouri within the Louisiana Purchase. States that formed outside of the Louisiana Purchase did not necessarily have to follow this rule. The government later decided that states that formed from the Louisiana Purchase could choose whether or not they would allow slavery. In the 1850s, this issue caused a war in Kansas known as Bleeding Kansas. The next decade, the issue erupted into the Civil War.

Consult the order in which the states were admitted into the Union. Then label each state with the correct number.

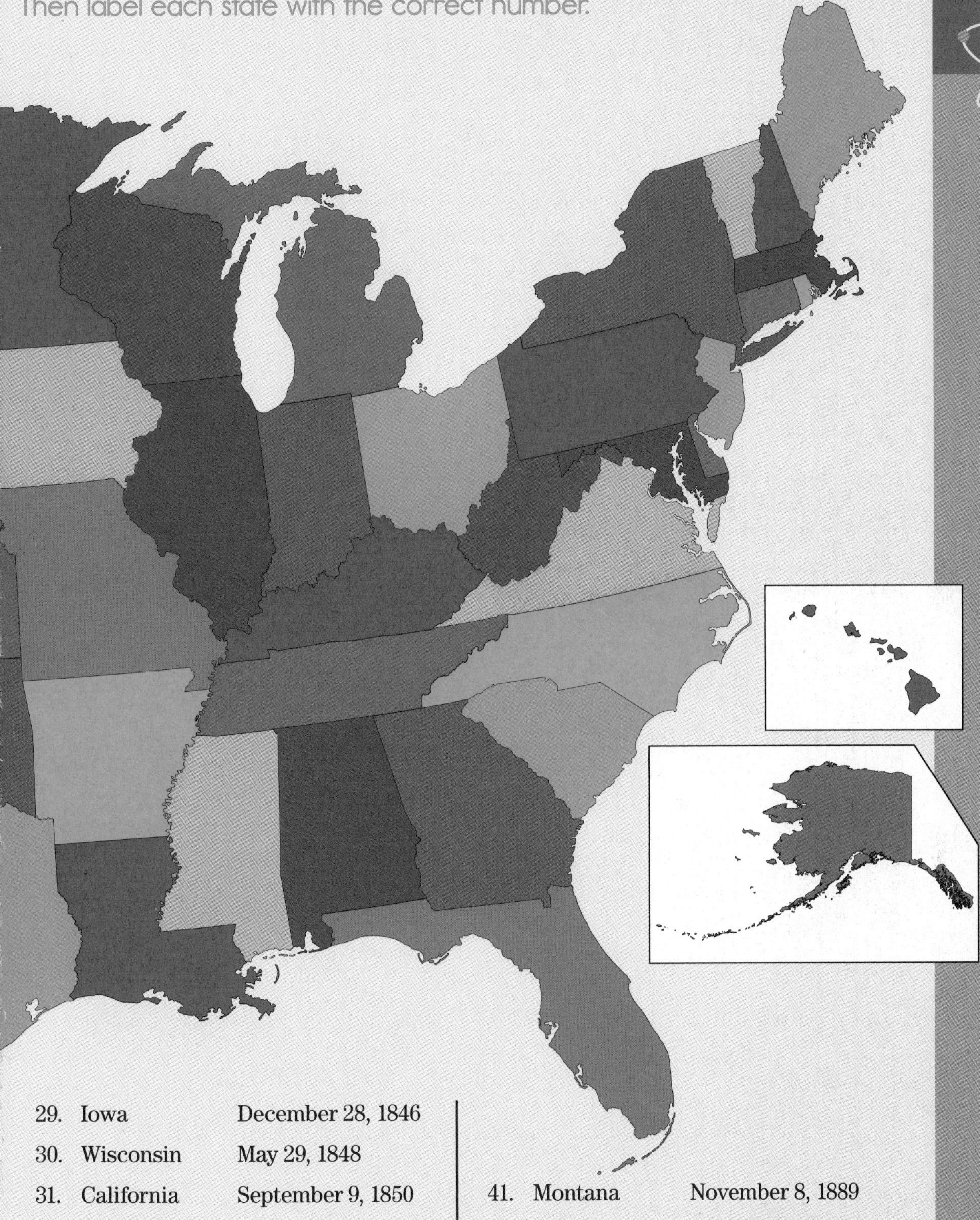

29.	Iowa	December 28, 1846
30.	Wisconsin	May 29, 1848
31.	California	September 9, 1850
32.	Minnesota	May 11, 1858
33.	Oregon	February 14, 1859
34.	Kansas	January 29, 1861
35.	West Virginia	June 20, 1863
36.	Nevada	October 31, 1864
37.	Nebraska	March 1, 1867
38.	Colorado	August 1, 1876
39.	North Dakota	November 2, 1889
40.	South Dakota	November 2, 1889
41.	Montana	November 8, 1889
42.	Washington	November 11, 1889
43.	Idaho	July 3, 1890
44.	Wyoming	July 10, 1890
45.	Utah	January 4, 1896
46.	Oklahoma	November 16, 1907
47.	New Mexico	January 6, 1912
48.	Arizona	February 14, 1912
49.	Alaska	January 3, 1959
50.	Hawaii	August 21, 1959

Little Houses on the Prairie

Read the story about prairie life on the Great Plains.

In 1862, the U.S. Homestead Act allowed citizens to claim 160 acres of land in the Great Plains region, the grassland stretching from the Missouri River to the Rocky Mountains. For new immigrants and others living in crowded eastern cities, it was a chance for a better life. But to keep the land on which they settled, the newcomers had to build a home within six months of arriving.

For those who settled on wooded lands, a log cabin was the obvious choice. But on the prairie, a settler could walk for miles without seeing a single tree. Instead, these settlers built earthen homes known as soddies.

Prairie grass had strong roots that held the soil beneath together. This mixture of grass and soil is known as sod. To make sod bricks, settlers would wait for a rainstorm or snowmelt. Afterward, they would cut long strips of wet sod using a horse-drawn plow. With an ax, they would chop the strips into bricks. Then they would stack the sod bricks on top of each other like blocks. The roof was constructed with twigs and branches that they also covered with sod. Only the home's door and window frames were made of wood.

Soddies had good points and bad. The sod kept the home warm in the winter and cool in the summer. However, when it rained, the water seeped through the roof, creating a muddy mess inside. Dry spells presented their own problems. The sod would dry out, and dirt would rain down on the inhabitants. And because sod is a natural habitat for mice and rattlesnakes, the homes were constantly infested with vermin.

Nevertheless, people managed to make the soddies homey. They built wood floors or plastered the walls, which helped ward off critters. Throwing flower seeds on the roof created a beautiful display in spring and summer. And in spite of the cramped space, people would take in a cat, dog, or bird to liven up the place.

Eventually, the inhabitants would save money to build a frame house on their land. Then the sod house would be used as a shed. One such structure, the McCully House, still stands today as part of a museum in Oklahoma—a testament to the sturdiness of the soddies.

Dear Diary

Pretend that you and your family have just arrived on the prairie. In your diary, describe either what it was like to build a soddy or what it was like to live in a soddy.

This Means War

Read the **Civil War** timeline. Then answer the questions.

The Beginning of the Civil War

November 6, 1860
Abraham Lincoln becomes the 16th president of the United States. The new president opposes the expansion of slavery into new U.S. territories, angering people in many states where slavery is legal.

December 20, 1860
In response to Lincoln's electoral victory, South Carolina legislators vote to secede from the Union.

January 9–February 1, 1861
Mississippi, Florida, Alabama, Georgia, Louisiana, and Texas also secede from the Union.

January 29, 1861
Kansas becomes the 34th state. It does not allow slavery.

February, 1861
The seceded states, now called the Confederate States of America, elect Jefferson Davis as their president.

April 12, 1861
The first shot of the Civil War is fired at Fort Sumter in Charleston Harbor, South Carolina.

April 15, 1861
Lincoln calls for 75,000 volunteers to enlist in the Union Army and fight the Confederate states.

April 17–May 20, 1861
Virginia, Arkansas, Tennessee, and North Carolina join the Confederate States of America.

April 19, 1861
Lincoln directs the Union Army to cut off supplies from reaching Confederate ports.

April 21, 1861
Union troops from New York and Massachusetts defend Washington, D.C., against the rebels.

May 24,1861
Union troops capture Alexandria, Virginia.

What does it mean to secede from the Union?

___

Which state was the first to secede from the Union?

___

Name all the states that seceded from the Union.

___

Why did these states secede from the Union?

___

Why did Lincoln call for volunteers to enlist in the Union Army?

___

What was the name of the government of the seceded states?

___

Who was the president of the seceded states?

___

Name three actions that the Union Army took during the war.

___

Brain Box

The **Union** is another word for the United States. When a state seceded from the Union, it was withdrawing from the United States. The southern states, which relied on slavery for free labor, seceded because they feared that, with President Lincoln's election and the growing power of the northern states, slavery would soon come to an end in the U.S. During the Civil War, the **Union Army** referred to the army of the United States (the states that did not secede from the Union). The **Confederate Army** fought for the Confederate States of America (the states that seceded).

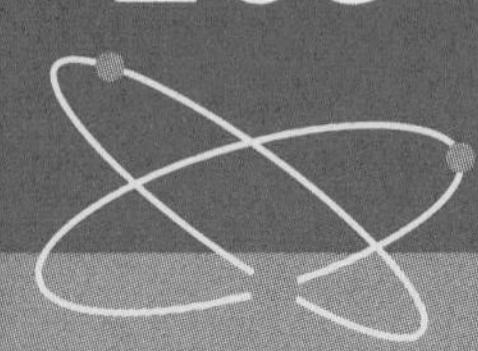

No Money, No Friends

Read the excerpt from an article in the May 8, 1887, *Sun* newspaper about immigrants landing in **Castle Garden**.

Several hundred immigrants had just arrived by a German steamer, and were undergoing registration. The castle officials are not inclined to use unseemly haste in their work, and yet the formalities take very little time. Each immigrant, as he passed the clerk's desk, had to show his passport and tell whether he had any family, friends in this country, or money in his pocket. The vast majority of all immigrants answer these questions satisfactorily. That is, they have families and a little money, and they are able-bodied. In such case they are passed without further query. Able-bodied young men are passed if they have friends here who will agree to look out for them, even if they have no money. The reporter stood by the clerk during the registration. A young German presented his passport, and the name was transcribed upon the clerk's book. Then the questions:

"Have you any money?"

"No, sir." [Through an interpreter.]

"Friends in this city?"

"No, sir."

"Anywhere in the country?"

"No sir."

"What do you expect to do?"

"I am a baker, and I purpose to look for work here."

"How are you going to live until you find it?"

The young man hesitated, and the interpreter explained that he would have to satisfy the officials that he would not be compelled to resort to charity. He thereupon pulled from his trousers' pocket a large and heavy gold watch and laid it upon the clerk's desk.

"I was intending," he said, "to call on the German Consul and ask him to take it as surety for my board at some house he should recommend until such time as I should receive my first wages. It's mine by rights," he continued quickly: "you will find my father's name inscribed inside the case. It was his only legacy, and I would not sell it for anything."

He was held for further examination by the Commissioners, but was "allowed to land," as the saying is, when an officer of a Germany society agreed to assure the community that the young man would not become a charge upon it for a year.

Brain Box

Before Ellis Island opened in 1892, **Castle Garden** was where immigrants arriving in New York City landed and were questioned before being allowed into the United States. Some would stay in New York; others moved on to other states.

Immigration

Social Studies

Pretend you are an immigrant who has just arrived in New York City. Write a letter home to a friend.

Include the following:

- Your home country
- Your reason for immigrating to America
- What it was like at Castle Garden
- What you are doing for work
- How your family is doing
- What you like about America
- What you miss about home

Big Ideas

Read the timeline. Match the inventions to their correct categories.

1784
Benjamin Franklin invents bifocal eyeglasses, one of his many inventions.

1794
Eli Whitney gets a patent for the cotton gin, which removes seeds from cotton used to make clothing and other goods.

1837
John Deere invents the steel plow, that is specialized for the tough Midwest prairie farm soil.

1876
Alexander Graham Bell and Thomas Watson invent the telephone.

1879
Thomas Edison invents the first practical incandescent lightbulb.

1903
The Wright Brothers fly the first successful airplane.

Invention	Category
Bifocals	Energy
Steel plow	Clothing
Telephone	Communication
Lightbulb	Health/Well-being
Cotton gin	Food

The Three Branches

Read the paragraph and study the diagram. Then fill in the blanks with the correct branch of government.

The writers of the Constitution wanted a system of government that didn't give any one person or group too much power. So they separated the power into three branches of government. The legislative branch (Congress) is in charge of making the laws. The executive branch (the President) leads the country and makes sure laws are obeyed. The judicial branch (the Supreme Court) interprets laws and decides whether certain laws are unconstitutional.

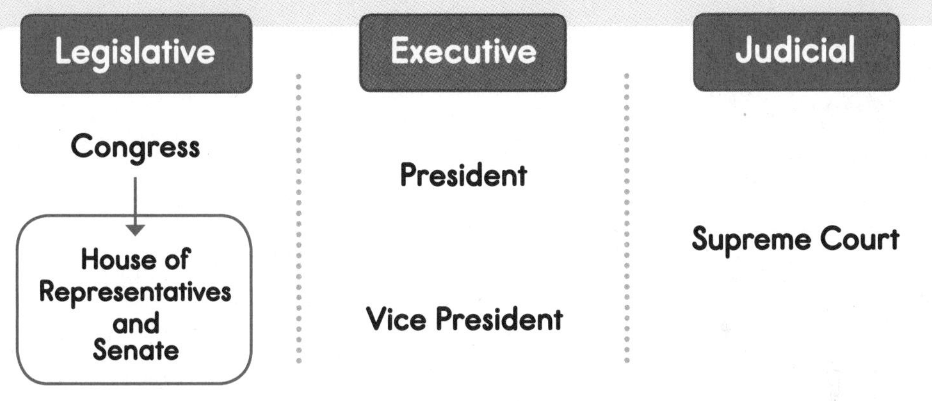

A law is passed by Congress, the __________________ branch, requiring power plants to reduce their carbon dioxide emissions.

The President, as the __________________ branch, directs the Environmental Protection Agency (EPA) to enforce the new carbon dioxide reduction law.

The Supreme Court, acting as the the__________________ branch, rules that this law can be enforced by the EPA because carbon dioxide emissions are a threat to human health.

Government

Social Studies

Stars and Stripes

Read about the American flag.

The first American flag, created in 1777, had 13 stars and 13 stripes, one of each for each of the states. When Vermont and Kentucky became states in 1795, two more stars and two more stripes were added.

However, as more states joined the union, it became clear that if a stripe were added for each one, the flag would soon become crowded with too many stripes. Instead, Congress decided the flag should go back to having 13 stripes, but that a new star would be added for each state. In 1912, Arizona and New Mexico became the 47th and 48th states. The flag was almost complete. Finally, in 1959, Alaska and Hawaii also joined the Union, bringing the number of stars up to 50. Will more stars ever be added? It is possible that Puerto Rico, whose residents are already U.S. citizens, will one day become a state and the flag's 51st star.

Based on what you learned in the paragraph, match the flags to the right year.

Draw a picture of today's American flag, including the correct number of stars and stripes.

American symbols

Social Studies

I Pledge Allegiance

Read the facts below.

Facts about the Pledge of Allegiance

The Pledge of Allegiance was written by Francis J. Bellamy in 1892.

The owner of the magazine *Youth's Companion* asked Bellamy to write the pledge to increase patriotism among kids.

The magazine also published directions for saluting the flag during the pledge. At the time, people held their right arm out straight toward the flag.

During World War II, Americans decided the straight-arm salute was too similar to Germany's Nazi salute. In 1942, Congress changed the salute to the hand-over-heart gesture we use today.

In 1954, with President Dwight D. Eisenhower's support, the words "under God" were added after "one nation."

Complete the timeline.

1892	1942	1954
____________	____________	____________

Write the Pledge of Allegiance from memory.

____

____

____

____

____

____

____

____

____

____

____

____

____

Brain Box

If you don't know the Pledge of Allegiance, go to the website publications .USA.gov.

American symbols

Social Studies

A Monumental Vacation

Read about the national monuments.

The White House

Construction began on the official residence of the president in 1792. That house burned during the War of 1812 but was rebuilt in 1817. President Theodore Roosevelt renovated the house in 1902, adding the West Wing, where the president's Oval Office is located. Roosevelt also named the residence the White House. Today, the White House has 132 rooms, including 35 bathrooms and 3 kitchens.

The Statue of Liberty

The Statue of Liberty was a gift from the people of France as a tribute to the United States' freedom. Sculpted by Auguste Bartholdi, it was unveiled in 1886. For immigrants arriving on nearby Ellis Island, the statue was a symbol of welcome after weeks at sea. In 1903, a poem by Emma Lazarus was added to the base of the statue. It ends with these words: "Give me your tired, your poor, / Your huddled masses yearning to breathe free, / The wretched refuse of your teeming shore. / Send these, the homeless, tempest-tost to me, / I lift my lamp beside the golden door!"

The Lincoln Memorial

Completed in 1922, the Lincoln Memorial symbolizes President Lincoln's belief in the freedom of all people. The 36 columns represent the 36 states that made up the United States when Lincoln died. Located in a chamber of the memorial, and visible from the outside, is a statue of Lincoln sitting. It is 19 feet tall and weighs 175 tons (including the pedestal.) The Gettysburg Address is engraved on the south wall of the monument.

Choose one national monument that you would like to visit. It can be one from the facing page or any other monument. Research it online.

Write four facts or details about the monument.

1. ____

____

2. ____

____

3. ____

____

4. ____

____

Write a postcard to a friend, describing your visit to the memorial.

PLACE STAMP HERE

MADE IN U. S. A

POST CARD

Social Studies Crossword

Across

2 ________________ was the first permanent British settlement.

3 Theodore Roosevelt named the ________________.

6 Another name for the United States and the name of one army in the Civil War is the ________________.

9 The Jamestown company settled in the chiefdom of ________________.

11 The U.S. ________________ is the law of the land.

12 A ________________ map shows government boundaries.

13 The American flag has 13 ________________.

Down

1 ________________ was reluctant to run for office.

4 The abbreviation for Hawaii is ________________.

5 The abbreviation for Utah is ________________.

7 The ________________ Memorial celebrates a president's belief in the freedom of all people.

8 The 13 English ________________ became the United States.

10 The first 10 amendments to the U.S. Constitution are known as the ________________ of Rights.

Science

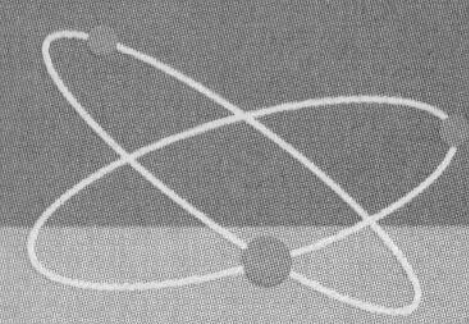

Classified Information

Read the **animal classification** chart and bullet points.

Animal Classification

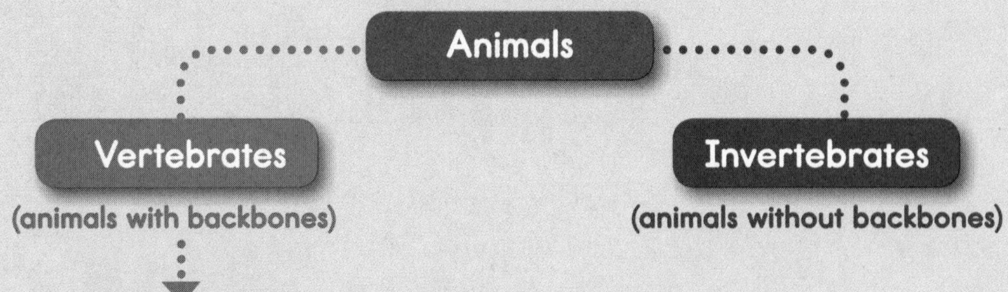

Fish

- live in water
- breathe using gills
- most are cold-blooded

Amphibians

- spend time both on land and in water
- use gills to breathe for part or all of their lives
- do not have scales
- most go through metamorphosis
- are cold-blooded

Reptiles

- have scales
- breathe with lungs
- most lay eggs
- most are cold-blooded

Birds

- have feathers
- have wings (but not all fly)
- lay eggs
- are warm-blooded

Mammals

- produce milk to feed their babies
- have hair or fur
- most give birth (as opposed to laying eggs)
- are warm-blooded

Brain Box

Animals are **classified** by their relationships to each other. They are first divided into vertebrates and invertebrates. Vertebrates are more closely related to each other than to invertebrates. Vertebrates are further divided into fish, amphibians, reptiles, birds, and mammals. In each category, animals share certain characteristics. For exampe, all birds have feathers and lay eggs.

Living science

Answer the questions.

In a puddle, you find an animal with gills swimming along. Explain why this could be either a fish or an amphibian.

___

___

You see a creature that spends most of its time in the water. It has a bill shaped like the bill of a duck, has flippers, and lays eggs. It also has fur. Explain why this animal could be a mammal.

___

___

An animal spends most of its time in the water. It has a layer of fat under its skin. The animal is covered with feathers but doesn't fly. Explain why this animal is a bird.

___

___

An animal looks like a big fish, but you see that it comes to the surface of the water frequently to take breaths. It has only a few hairs on its head. Underwater, it can be seen feeding milk to its young. Explain why this animal is a mammal.

___

___

___

___

___

___

Brain Box

When classifying animals, pay attention to characteristics that all animals in that category have, and characteristics that only most of them have. For instance, all mammals have hair and feed milk to their young, but not all mammals give birth. Some lay eggs.

Life Cycles

Read about the **life cycles** of a frog and a moth, then answer the questions.

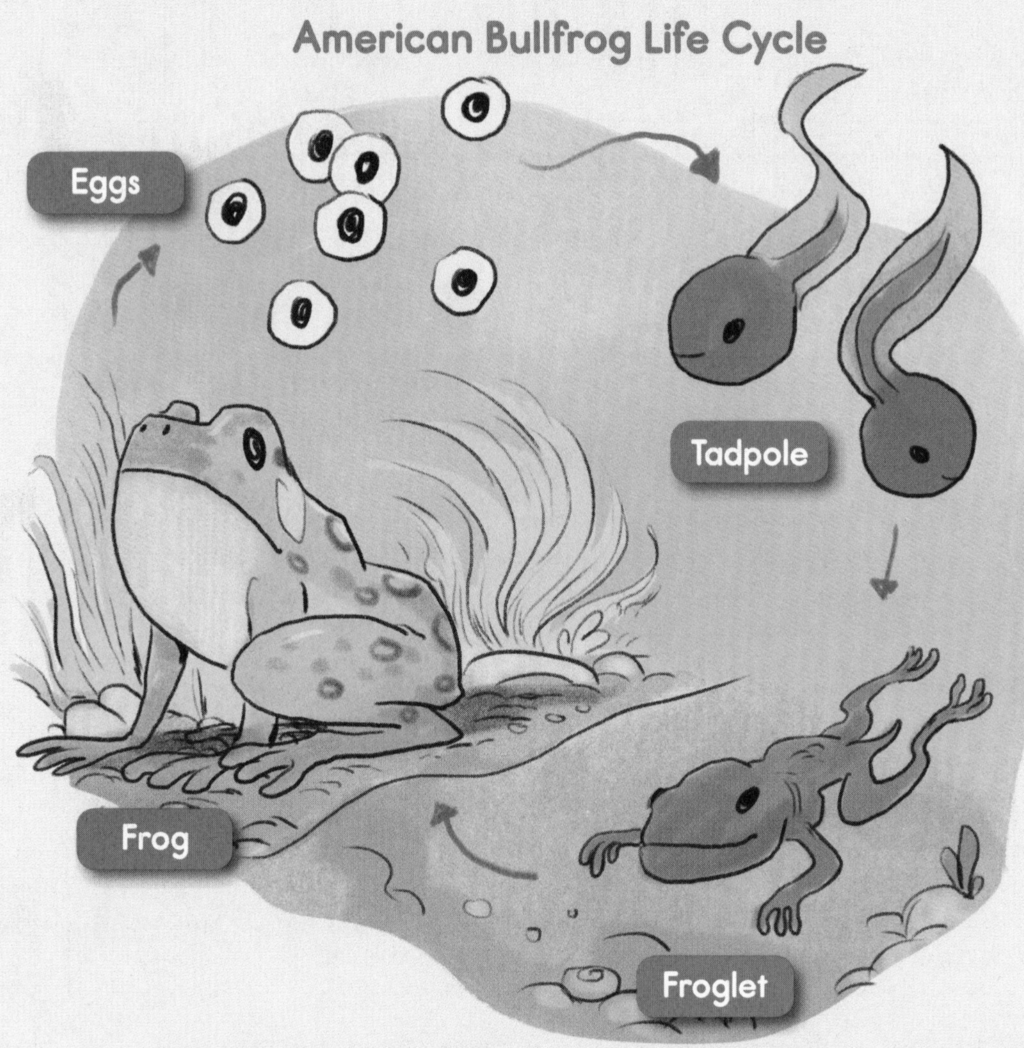

First, female frogs lay several unfertilized eggs in water, and males come along to fertilize them.

After about 4 days, tadpoles hatch out of the eggs. The legless tadpoles live exclusively in the water and breathe through gills.

After about 3 weeks, the tadpoles sprout legs and arms, but still have a tail. They are froglets.

Gradually, the froglets outgrow their tails and become frogs.

Five years after hatching, the frogs are ready to have tadpoles.

Silkworm Moth Life Cycle

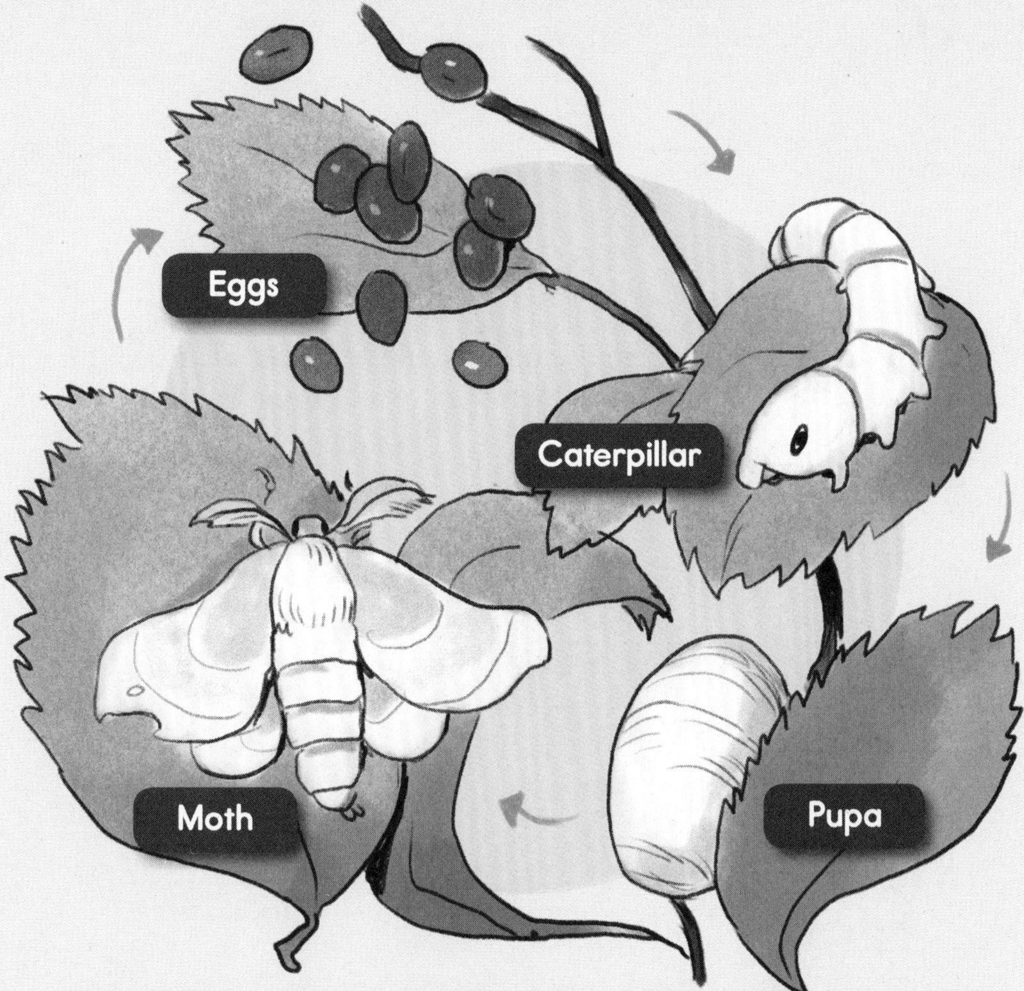

The male and female silkworm mate, and the female lays several fertilized eggs on milkweed leaves.

Caterpillars hatch from the eggs and eat the milkweed. They grow bigger and bigger.

Next, they spin cocoons out of silk. Inside the cocoons, the caterpillars become pupas. This is the stage in which they transform from caterpillars into moths.

The new adult moths eat their way out of their cocoons. The whole process occurs in a matter of weeks, and now the moths are ready to lay eggs that will become caterpillars.

List three things that are similar about a frog's and a moth's life cycle.

____

____

List three things that are different about a frog's and a moth's life cycle.

____

____

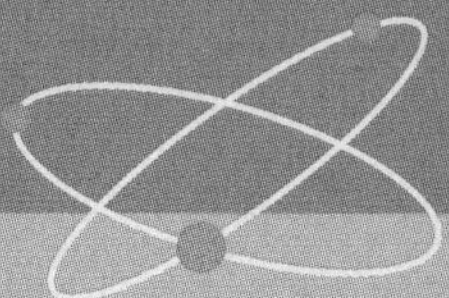

Brain Box

A **life cycle** describes an animal's stages of development from the egg stage to maturity, when it can have babies. Some insects and amphibians go through **metamorphosis.** That means that the young animals transform so that, as adults, they look and act completely different. For instance, a tadpole looks like and lives like a fish until it becomes a full-grown frog. A caterpillar is flightless until it transforms into a moth.

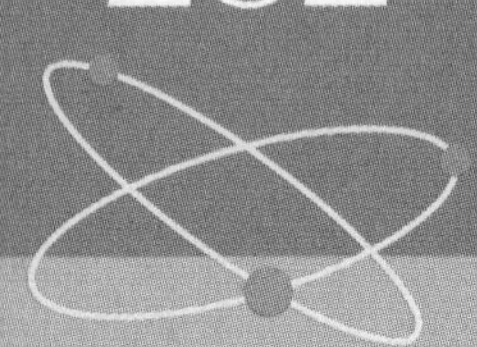

Neat Feet

Read about the different kinds of feet that animals have. Then answer the questions.

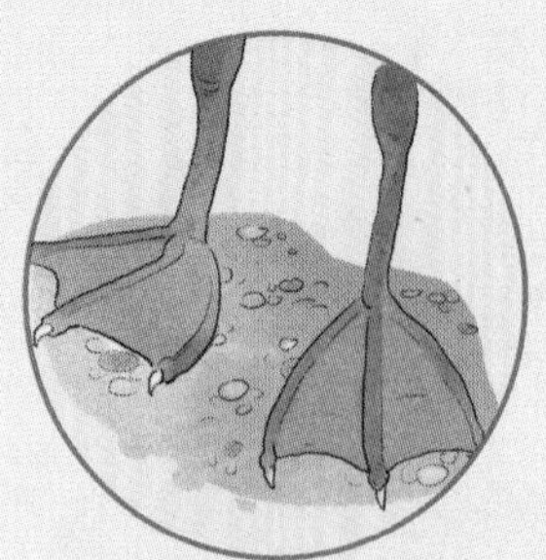

webbed feet

Animals that live in the water have webbed feet, which help them swim faster or farther to catch prey.

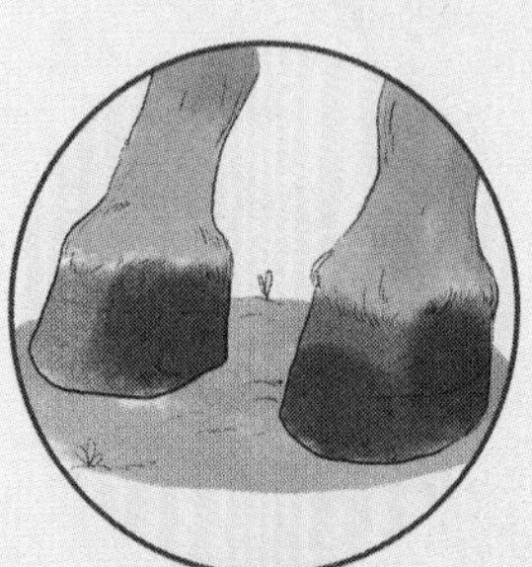

solid hooves

Prey animals that live in grasslands have solid hooves, which are built for speed. This allows hooved animals to escape predators.

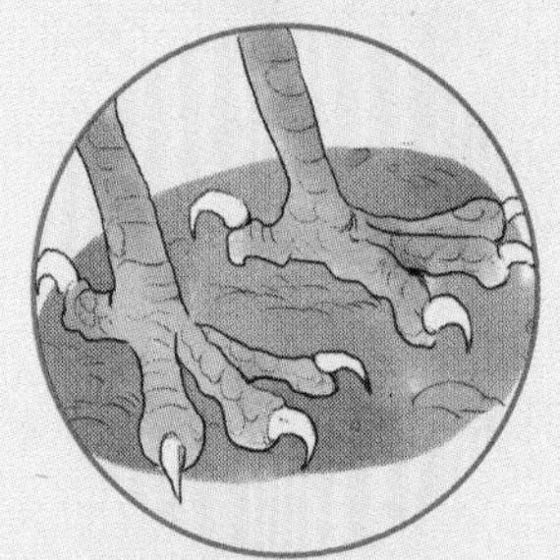

talons

Birds of prey have talons in order to grab their prey and hold on to it as they fly to a safe place to eat it.

paws

Paws can be used for climbing trees to find food. The claws on paws can be used to dig for food or to grasp prey.

Explain why ducks have webbed feet.

____

Why are solid hooves helpful to horses?

____

Why do eagles have talons?

____

Why does a bear have paws?

____

Brain Box

Adaptations are traits, such as having feet instead of flippers, that help animals survive in their environment. Specific traits, called **chararteristics**, are better suited to certain environments than to others.

Circle of Life

Use the words below to fill in the blanks and explain how plants and animals interact within the **food chain** and **carbon cycle.**

photosynthesis	carnivores	bacteria
herbivores	decomposers	

The Food Chain and Carbon Cycle

In a process called _____________, plants use chlorophyll to convert sunlight, water, and carbon dioxide into glucose and oxygen. The plants release the oxygen into the air. Animals breathe in this oxygen, which is necessary to live.

The plant uses the glucose to build its stem and leaves. The glucose is made up mainly of carbon. If the plant dies, the carbon is released back into the air as the plant rots. The carbon combines with oxygen to form carbon dioxide. New plants absorb the carbon dioxide once again.

Animals called _____________ eat plants. The glucose gives the animals energy to live and to find more food. In turn, these animals might be eaten by _____________. When the animals die, they release carbon back into the air.

Dead plants and animals are both eaten by _____________. These include animals such as insects and worms, but also smaller organisms such as fungi and _____________. By digesting the dead plants and animals, the organisms turn them into soil. New plants grow in the soil, and the cycle continues.

Brain Box

A **food chain** illustrates how each organism uses another as a source of food. The **carbon cycle** is the series of processes in which carbon dioxide is used by organisms to create nutrients that are eventually restored into the atmosphere.

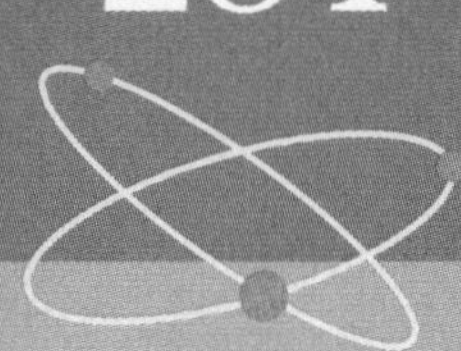

Biomes

Read the story and answer the questions.

Grasslands!

Plants and animals in a biome help each other survive. They are also aided by the climate in the biome, to which they have adapted. Grassland biomes exist throughout the world. In America, they are called prairies. In Africa, they are called savannas.

As the name suggests, grasses are the primary plants in grasslands. Grazing animals eat the grass. The grass, which has a vast system of roots underground, grows back (just as mowed grass grows back). Because grasslands have few trees, and, therefore, few places to hide from predators, large grazing animals must be able to run away from danger. The hooved feet and long legs of grazers, such as horses, antelopes, and camels, make them fast. Even American bison, which weigh 2 tons, can run 35 miles per hour.

Prairie grasses and flowers also feed smaller animals, including a wide array of insects. Insects, in turn, pollinate prairie plants. They also decompose dead plants and animals, returning nutrients to the soil, which feeds the grass.

The climate in grasslands is extreme. Weeks can pass with no rain, followed by a large thunderstorm. For this reason, grassland grasses have deep roots that can store water. In temperate grasslands like the American prairie, the temperature can be very hot in the summer and very cold in the winter. The grassland animals are adapted to these extremes. For instance, bison have a thick coat during the winter, which they shed in the spring.

How have large grassland animals adapted to there being few hiding places from predators?

____

What are two ways that insects help grassland plants grow?

____

How are grassland grasses adapted to dry spells?

____

How are bison adapted to the hot and cold extremes of the prairie?

____

Brain Box

Biomes are types of land or water environments that have similar climates, plants, and animals no matter where they are in the world. Major biomes include prairies, forests, deserts, wetlands, and coral reefs.

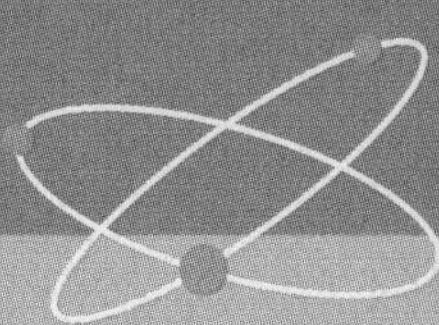

Cells

Using the clues, label the parts of the animal **cell**.

The **cell membrane** is the outer layer of the cell. It holds the cell together, but allows material to pass in and out.

In the middle of the cell, the **nucleus** controls the cell so that the cell carries out its function.

The nucleus contains **DNA**, which looks like a twisted ladder.

The **cytoplasm** lies between the cell membrane and the cell's nucleus.

The cytoplasm contains **mitochondria**, which produce chemical energy for the cell, and **vacuoles**, which store water and remove waste from the cell.

Brain Box

Cells are the building blocks of all living things. They have various functions. For instance, cells can make up muscles or an organ. Multiple cells that have the same function form **tissue**.

Journey to the Center of the Earth

Using the clues, label the Earth's layers with words from below.

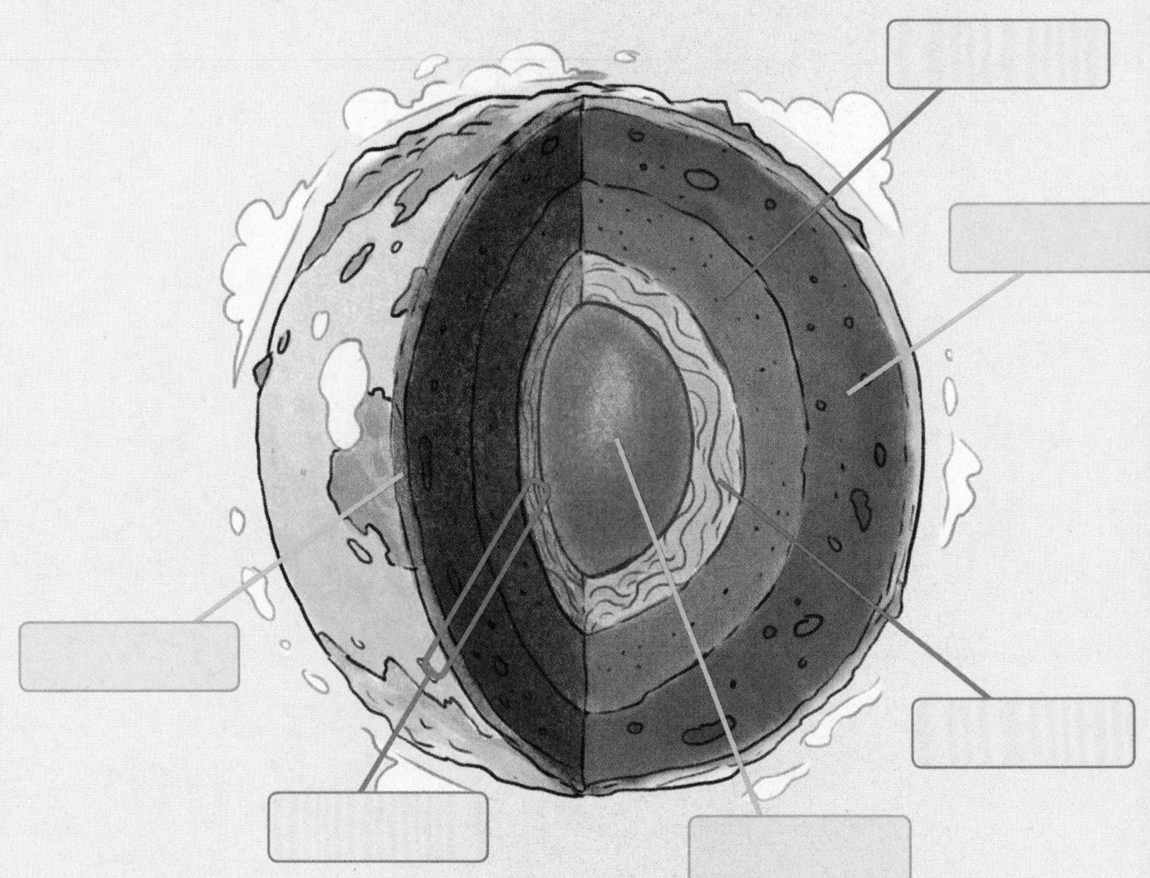

Brain Box

The Earth has different layers: the **core**, **mesosphere**, **asthenosphere**, **lithosphere**, and **crust**. Some layers are solid and others liquid. Each layer also has a different chemical makeup.

Earth science

The center of the Earth is called the **core**.

Above the core is the **mantle**. The mantle includes the mesosphere, asthenosphere, lithosphere, and crust.

The **mesosphere** is closest to the core.

The **crust** is the topmost layer of the earth—it includes the land and oceans.

The **lithosphere** includes the crust but also extends deeper into the mantle.

The **asthenosphere** is between the mesosphere and lithosphere.

Rock It!

Read about the 3 kinds of rocks. Then choose the highlighted category for each type of rock.

Igneous rocks form when molten (hot, liquid) rock cools and hardens. This occurs after a volcano erupts.

Sedimentary rocks form when sediment piles up and then hardens. The sediment can include rock, sand, shells, and bones.

Metamorphic rocks form when existing rocks are heated and put under pressure. Rocks buried deep in the Earth's crust are under pressure because of the weight of the Earth above them. They are also exposed to heat from the magma in the asthenosphere.

Limestone forms as plants, shells, and animal bones settle on the ocean floor. Over time, they harden to become rock. Limestone is:

AN IGNEOUS ROCK **A SEDIMENTARY ROCK** **A METAMORPHIC ROCK**

Marble is limestone that was heated and put under pressure. It is:

AN IGNEOUS ROCK **A SEDIMENTARY ROCK** **A METAMORPHIC ROCK**

Pumice is a lightweight rock ejected from volcanoes. It is:

AN IGNEOUS ROCK **A SEDIMENTARY ROCK** **A METAMORPHIC ROCK**

Sandstone forms when layers of sand harden over time to form rock. Sandstone is:

AN IGNEOUS ROCK **A SEDIMENTARY ROCK** **A METAMORPHIC ROCK**

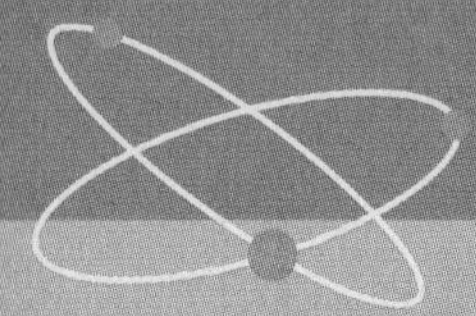

Consider the Alternative

Match the descriptions of **alternative energy sources** to the correct illustrations.

Brain Box

Fossil fuels are fuels created by ancient plants and animals. They include oil, gasoline, coal, and natural gas. When burned, they produce **energy**. However, these fuels release the pollutant carbon dioxide into the air. Alternative fuels like wind and solar energy do not release carbon dioxide into the air.

Hydroelectric power comes from river water flowing through large dams. It supplies 19 percent of the world's energy.

Nuclear energy comes from splitting an atom at a nuclear power plant. Nuclear power supplies 19 percent of electricity in America.

Wind currently produces 6 percent of America's electricity. Wind power is produced by turbines, which look like giant fans.

Solar energy is captured by solar panels. In Hawaii, 10 percent of homes have solar panels on their roofs.

Biofuels are an alternative to gasoline. They are made from recently living things such as switch grass or algae.

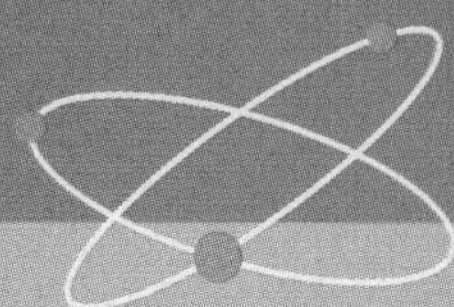

Landforms

Read about the forces that create **landforms**.

Erosion is the wearing away of land by wind, water, or ice. Deposition is the flip side of erosion. Sediment that is scraped off the land by wind, water, or ice is then deposited somewhere else, building up the land in that location.

Plate tectonics refer to the movements of the Earth's lithosphere. The lithosphere is made up of large plates of rock, which fit together like puzzle pieces. These plates float on the semi-magma asthenosphere beneath the lithosphere. The plates can crash into each other, forming mountains, or pull away from each other, causing the land to spread out. These effects occur over very long periods of time.

A rise in sea level can swallow areas of land, leaving islands or peninsulas. A drop in sea level can expose land, causing an island to become part of another land mass.

Circle which highlighted force created the landform.

During the last ice age, glaciers extended into what is now the northern United States. They cut deep valleys through the land. When the glaciers melted, the water filled these valleys and formed the Great Lakes.

Erosion **Deposition** **Plate Tectonics** **Rising Sea Level**

Because ice age glaciers eroded the land, they contained a great deal of sediment, pebbles, and even large boulders. When the glaciers melted, they released the sediment and rocks. In many places, boulders now stand alone in otherwise empty fields. These are called glacial erratics.

Erosion **Deposition** **Plate Tectonics** **Rising Sea Level**

During the last ice age, England and Ireland were part of mainland Europe. As the glaciers melted, sea levels rose worldwide, inundating some of the land so that Ireland and England became islands.

Erosion **Deposition** **Plate Tectonics** **Rising Sea Level**

250 million years ago, the continents were in a different place. Africa collided with North America. This squeezed the land, causing it to rise up and form the Appalachian Mountains.

Erosion **Deposition** **Plate Tectonics** **Rising Sea Level**

Each year, the Mississippi River deposits 500 million tons of sediment into the Gulf of Mexico. At the mouth of the river, this sediment has built up over time to create the Mississippi River Delta.

Erosion **Deposition** **Plate Tectonics** **Rising Sea Level**

Brain Box

A **landform** is any naturally occurring feature on land. Mountains, valleys, canyons, peninsulas, and sand dunes are all landforms. Landforms can be caused by many factors, including **erosion**—the wearing away of land—and **deposition**—the building up of sediment.

Earth science

Chemistry Lab

Read the definitions on the cards and fill in the blanks.

atom the smallest particle of an element that can exist while still being that element. Everything that is a solid, a liquid, or a gas is made up of atoms.

atomic number the number of protons in an atom's nucleus. An element always has the same atomic number.

element a chemical substance made up of one type of atom.

molecule two or more atoms bonded together.

compound a chemical substance made from two or more elements that are chemically bonded in a set ratio. For instance, water (H_20) has two hydrogen atoms for every one oxygen atom. Compounds can only be separated by chemical methods.

bond the attraction between atoms that results in two or more elements forming a compound.

mixture two or more elements or compounds mixed but not chemically bonded together. They can be separated by physical methods, such as occurs when large particles are filtered out.

Calcium has 20 protons in its nucleus. Its ________________ is 20.

Josie wanted to perform an experiment on a bucketful of muddy lake water. She fastened a coffee filter to a jar. Then she poured the lake water over the filter. The filter caught some of the mud so that the water in the jar was clearer than the water in the bucket. This means that the muddy water was a ________________, not a compound.

Sodium and chlorine form a ________________ and thereby become the compound sodium chloride, or salt.

Gold exists as an ________________ in nature. It is made up of one type of atom and not bonded to another substance.

Carbon dioxide is a ________________ that has a ratio of one carbon ________________ for every two oxygen atoms.

Brain Box

Chemistry is the study of the **elements** and **compounds** that make up all things. Chemists explore how elements and compounds react to one another and to chemical changes, such as heating.

Light

Read about **light**. Then circle true or false.

What Is Light?

Light is a form of energy. It moves in waves that have different wavelengths. The different wavelengths are what give things their color. Substances absorb some wavelengths of light and reflect others. We see the wavelengths that are reflected. For instance, plants are green because their chlorophyll absorbs blue and red wavelengths and reflects green wavelengths.

Light is composed of a stream of particles called photons. Light travels in a straight line until it strikes an object. At that point, the object reflects the light. Light can be seen at its source and also where it is reflected from something. For instance, the sun can be seen (though it shouldn't be viewed directly) because it is a source of light. The moon can be seen because it reflects sunlight. Everything on Earth can be seen by day, because everything reflects sunlight. In pitch darkness, on the other hand, nothing can be seen because light is not being reflected.

Besides reflecting light, objects can allow light to pass through. These objects, which include glass, are transparent. Light can also be bent. This is called refraction. It happens when light passes from one substance to another, such as from air to water. This is why if you stand over water and see a fish, it appears to be a few inches away from where it really is. The light that you see reflecting off the fish is bent.

The colors that we see are the wavelengths that have been absorbed by objects.

TRUE **FALSE**

The moon can be seen because it is a source of light.

TRUE **FALSE**

In pitch darkness, objects cannot be seen because they are not reflecting light.

TRUE **FALSE**

If something is transparent, it allows no light to pass through.

TRUE **FALSE**

If you view a fish through water, it appears to be a few inches away because of refraction.

TRUE **FALSE**

Be a Scientist

Read about the **scientific method**.

The scientific method is a way of testing a scientific theory to see if it is true. To use the scientific method, follow these steps:

1. **Observe.**

   Example: How does temperature affect the number of lightning bugs in my yard?

2. **Make a hypothesis.**

   A hypothesis is an educated guess. The answer should be measurable.

   Example: As the temperature increases, there be more fireflies in my yard.

3. **Experiment.**

   The conditions should be as consistent as possible during the experiment.

   Example: Each night at the same time, record the outdoor temperature. Then count the number of firefly flashes that occur within 5 minutes in your yard. Do this for one month. The time of day and the number of minutes should be the same each day.

   In the course of your experiment, take notes. For instance, you might notice that there are fewer firefly flashes on a rainy night.

4. **Analyze.**

   Using your observations, decide whether your hypothesis was correct or incorrect. It is okay if your hypothesis proves incorrect. The point is not to be right, but to find the truth.

5. **Accept or reject hypothesis.**

   If your hypothesis was correct, repeat the experiment to accept or reject the hypothesis. If it was incorrect, come up with a new hypothesis and start the process all over again.

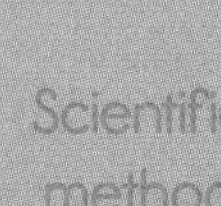

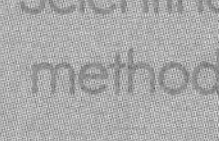

Conduct an experiment using the **scientific method**. If you live in a region that has fireflies, it can be the firefly experiment. You can also find experiments in books about science projects. Or you can come up with your own experiment!

Ask a question. Write it here.

Research. Write the name of the book you read or website you visit.

Write your hypothesis. Remember, the answer should be measurable.

Write how you will conduct your experiment.

Record the results of your experiment.

Record any other observations.

Write whether your hypothesis was correct or incorrect.

Circle one:

I need to repeat my experiment.

I need to come up with a new hypothesis.

Scientific method

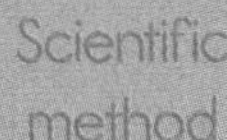

Science Crossword

Across

3 The ______________ is the building block of all living things.

5 The ______________ is the smallest unit of an element.

6 A(n) ______________ is a substance that always has the same atomic number.

8 The central part of a cell or an atom is called a(n) ______________. It holds the cell's genetic material.

10 A(n) ______________ is a naturally occurring feature of land.

11 Different ______________ are what give things their color. Substances absorb or reflect them.

Down

1 A(n) ______________ is two or more atoms bonded together.

2 The innermost layer of Earth is the ______________.

3 ______________ is located between the nucleus and the cell membrane.

4 We see light when it is ______________ off objects.

7 ______________ is a substance that is shaped like a twisted ladder and is located in a nucleus.

9 Feet that help an animal run fast are ______________.

Answer Key

(For pages not included in this section, answers will vary.)

page 6
com, combine
ob, oblong
sub, submerge
sub, subheading
com, companion
ob, obnoxious
com, comrade
ob, obstruct
sub, subway
sub, subplot

page 7
inadequate: unacceptable
disadvantage: a situation that puts one behind others
iaccurate: incorrect or inexact
untimely: happening at an inconvenient time

page 8
adaptable
breakable
comfortable
desirable
distinguishable
inflatable
lovable
notable
believable

Four words ending in able:
adorable
bearable
memorable
preferable
(Answers may vary)

page 9
Hey, Charlie,
I just heard the horrable news that your cupcakes were stolen. That's terrable! I hope there is tangable evidence pointing to whoever is responsable! I always felt comfortible leaving my food unattended, but not after this unbearible event. I guess none of us is invincable. We are all susceptable to thievery. The sad thing is: the cupcakes probably had incredable frosting.

Sincerely,
Your Lovible Dog, Junior

P.S. Please excuse the crumbs.

horrible, terrible, tangible, responsible, comfortable, unbearable, invincible, susceptible, incredible, lovable

page 10
collision
nation
duration
division
persuasion
editions
addition
revision
decision
ambition

page 11
transferred, transferring
controlled, controlling
equipped, equipping
permitted, permitting

referred, referring
expelled, expelling
regretted, regretting
tapped, tapping
committed, committing

page 12
interesting, no
forgetting, yes
appearing, no
treating, no
stopping, yes
acting, no
explaining, no
exiting, no
beginning, yes
editing, no

page 13
signaled
criticized
criminal
electricity
financial
authenticity
residential
publicity
circumstantial
influential

page 14
āt
it
it
āt
it

Both
Meaning
Meaning
Both
Both

page 15
batter; bank; novel; bluff; cobbler; loom; hail; crane; patient; peer

page 16
I love you're hat! Its so cute!
I didn't know you went to Silver Beach this summer! Its my favorite place!
Your so photogenic!
Did you ever get ice cream at Mimi's? Its across the street from the beach.
Where did you're family buy they're great sunglasses?
My cousins live in that town. We stayed at they're house last year.
Kaitlyn, I played beach volleyball with you're cousins. Their cool.
Let's all meet up next summer if your around when I am.

your, It's, It's, You're, It's, your, their, their, your, They're, you're

page 17
Although
In addition
For instance
Similarly
However
Moreover
Therefore

page 19
tele
meter
photo
ambi
amphi
aero
anti
audi
logy, astro
phobia

Geology, Claustrophobia, ambivalent

page 21
something unusual
to repay money spent
to buy
dirty and unhealthy
to guess what will happen in the future

to separate
to have taken away
family
doing things on one's own
having the power to affect others' decisions

page 23

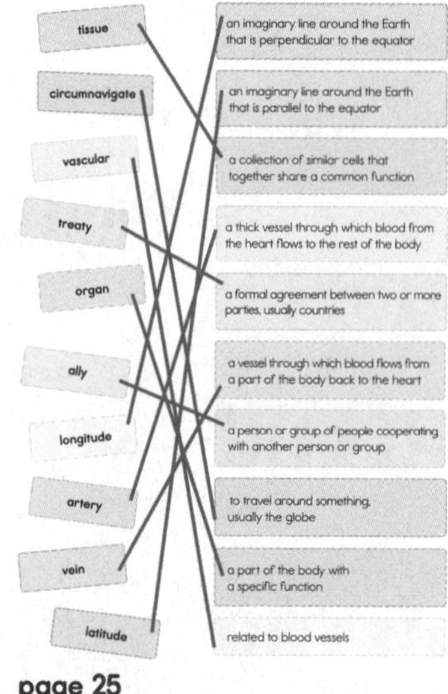

page 25
long a
a noun
Answers will vary: The two sides parleyed in an attempt to make peace.
loot
interjection
stop
Answers will vary: friend, comrade
noun
avast and matey

page 26
the whole nine yards
cool as a cucumber
apple of my eye
bee's knees
piece of cake
have a cow
pie in the sky
dressed to the nines
bell the cat
in a pickle

page 27
h
h
h
s
s
s
m, h
m, s
h
s

page 29
Practice makes perfect.
A stitch in time saves nine.
Actions speak louder than words.
The early bird gets the worm.
No man is an island.
Rome wasn't built in a day.
If it ain't broke, don't fix it.
You can catch more flies with honey than with vinegar.
Don't look a gift horse in the mouth.
Fortune favors the bold.

page 30

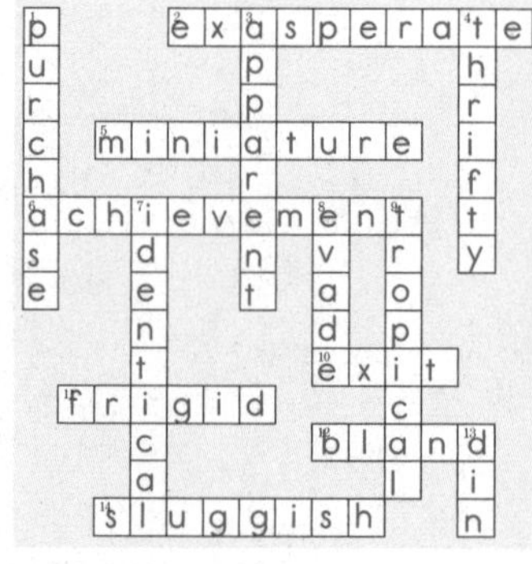

page 32
above the door
at sundown
under the blanket
outside the strike zone
with the eye patch
toward the shipwreck
along the shore
against a rip current
Beyond the mountain
During the Little Ice Age

page 33

under the chair; beneath the blanket; beside the plant; behind the curtain; in his cage

Over the river
through the wood
To Grandfather's house
through the white and drifted snow

page 34

Wow!
Uh-oh!
Stop
Hey
Oops
Ouch
Well
Yikes
Zoinks
Yum

page 35

and
or
but
so
because
unless
Although
if
yet or but
while

page 36

but also
or
nor
as
but
or

Neither a borrower nor a lender be.
Either you are with us or you are against us.

page 37

will have hiked
has been
had graduated
have practiced
has watched
will have solved
had suctioned
will have traveled
has studied
had entered

page 38

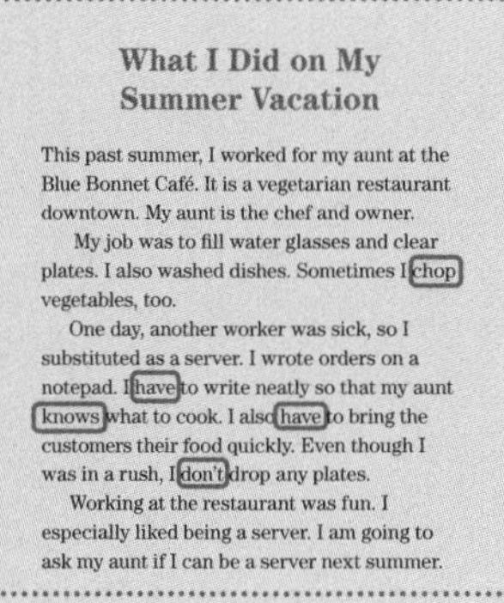

What I Did on My Summer Vacation

This past summer, I worked for my aunt at the Blue Bonnet Café. It is a vegetarian restaurant downtown. My aunt is the chef and owner.

My job was to fill water glasses and clear plates. I also washed dishes. Sometimes I chop vegetables, too.

One day, another worker was sick, so I substituted as a server. I wrote orders on a notepad. I have to write neatly so that my aunt knows what to cook. I also have to bring the customers their food quickly. Even though I was in a rush, I don't drop any plates.

Working at the restaurant was fun. I especially liked being a server. I am going to ask my aunt if I can be a server next summer.

page 39

The longest River in the world is the nile river.

However, the amazon river is the largest river by volume.

From its base, which is far below sea level, to its summit, mauna kea is the tallest mountain in the world.

Measuring from sea level to summit, Mount Everest is the highest Mountain.

With an average temperature of 93°F, the Danakil Desert in ethiopia is the hottest Desert.

The hottest temperature on earth—134°F—was recorded in Death Valley, california.

The record was set on july 10, 2013.

Only two u.s. states have never surpassed 100°F: Alaska and hawaii.

The coldest temperature ever—negative 136°F—was recorded in antarctica.

The coldest town in the world is oymyakon, Russia, where the average temperature is negative 58°F.

page 40

page 41

Living with Lions

What if your neighbors were lions? That is true for the San people of the Kalahari Desert. The San are hunters and gatherers. They work, play, and eat outside. They also share their land with lions. Usually, the San are able to avoid the lions. Lions hunt at night, and the San hunt and gather during the day. The San still sometimes encounter lions by day. In that case, the people calmly walk away from the lions. The lions usually walk away, too.*

At night, lions can be heard roaring, and they sometimes visit the people's camps. The San tell the lions in a stern voice to go away. If the lions do not leave, the people wave flaming branches at the giant cats. This does not hurt the lions, but it scares them off. What about when the San are sleeping? They sleep in shelters made of grass and sticks, so the lions are unable to attack them from behind. This is the lions' preferred method of attack. So the lions tend to leave the San alone even when they are sleeping. The San are afraid of the lions, and it's easy to see why. A lion can easily kill a person. In some situations, groups of lions have been known to attack people. The lions that live with the San rarely attack. By avoiding the lions by day, confronting them with fire in the evening, and sleeping in shelters at night, the San have managed to stay safe. As for the lions, they have learned not to see people as easy prey. For both the San and the lions, being neighbors is a way of life.

*Note: use of a comma before and after too varies. There are 18 commas including a comma before "too."

page 43

Giana and her friend Rose were taking turns going off the high and low diving boards at the same time. Giana did a flip off the low dive after Rose did one off the high dive. Now it was Giana's turn to do a flip off the high dive. But she was scared.

"Let's both jump instead of flipping," said Giana. "I'll jump off the high dive, and then you jump off the low."

"Why? Are you scared to do a flip off the high dive?" asked Rose.

"No," said Gianna.

"It's okay if you're scared," said Rose. "I won't make fun of you. I promise."

"Okay," said Giana. "I'm scared."

"What are you afraid of?" asked Rose.

"I'm afraid of doing a belly flop," said Giana.

"How about you jump this time, but while you're in midair, you picture yourself doing a flip," said Rose. "Then maybe you'll be ready to do a flip next time."

Giana jumped off the high dive, closed her eyes, and pictured herself doing a flip.

Rose asked, "So are you ready to do a flip this time?"

"I think so," Giana said.

She jumped, flipped, and landed on her belly, but it didn't hurt too much.

Now it was Rose's turn to flip off the high dive. She hesitated. "Now I'm scared *I'm* going to land on my belly," she said.

page 44

policemen's coffee
doctors' stethoscopes
pilots' airplanes
ducks' pond

friends' ice creams
referees' whistles
babies' bottles
bears' berries
ants' crumbs

page 45

Dear Diary, ¶ Today, I went to the Centennial Exposition—the first World's Fair ever to be held in America. And to think, it was held right here in Philadelphia! President Ulysses S. Grant, the Emperor of Brazil, and pretty much everybody in Philadelphia were there—not to mention folks who traveled from far and wide. ¶ I can't describe all the exhibits, but I'll tell you the highlights. There was tomato ketchup. Very tasty! I also tasted root beer made with 16 roots and berries. Not only was it delicious, the poster said it is also good for your blood. I'm feeling healthier already! ¶ Second best to the food and drinks was the telephone. This device allows you to talk to your friend without either of you ever leaving home! It was made by Alexander Graham Bell, an American. ¶ Not everything at the World's Fair was American, of course. The Italian exhibition had statues of men, women, and children. They looked so real! ¶ As for the British, they brought bicycles. These are machines with two wheels—a giant one in front and a tiny one in back. The man demonstrating how they worked sped downhill and appeared to be flying! When the wheel hit a tree root, he really did go flying through the air over the bicycle and onto the grass. I wonder if I will ever be so brave as to ride a bike. ¶ As I write, my mind is full of possibilities. I feel like the world must be full of such things as bicycles. I hope to see them all!

page 46

Answers will vary.
If a rat can squeeze through a hole the size of a quarter, then the rat could have come in through this hole in the floor.
Did you know dolphins gossip? They chat about good places to find food.
The bats under the bridge hunt mosquitoes at night.
Most monarch butterflies live only 8 weeks, but the generation that migrates to Mexico each fall lives 8 months.
When ants find crumbs, they notify the other ants in the nest.

page 47

Modern jelly was invented in the Middle Ages, but what we think of as modern peanut butter wasn't invented until the late 19th century. At first, peanut butter was served at fancy parties, and it was not served with jelly, but with pimentos or watercress.

Then a businessperson began to sell peanut butter in jars, and it became affordable for families.
In 1928, sliced bread began being sold, and that enabled kids to make their own sandwiches.
Peanut butter and jelly sandwiches have been popular ever since, but peanut butter also goes with bananas, apples, or bacon on sandwiches.
Many children are allergic to peanuts, so some schools do not allow peanut butter in the lunchroom.
In Europe, children do not eat much peanut butter, but they eat a similar spread made of hazelnuts.

page 48

Name: Conrad Cates
Homeroom: 5H

Opossum Facts

Opossums are the only marsupials that live in north america. Other marsupials, including Kangaroos and Koalas live in australia, new zealand, or south america. All marsupials give birth to extremely small babies twenty baby opossums would fit in a single teaspoon. Once born, baby opossums climb into their mothers pouch, where they drink milk. When they are bigger, they ride around on their Mother's back. Opossums eat a variety of foods, including mice insects birds and slugs. They also scavenge in trash cans for this reason, some people think of opossums as pests. However, usually Raccoons Dogs or Cats knock over the garbage cans opossums just eat what they find afterward. In fact, opossums are so harmless that they usually play dead When they feel threatened.

Capitalize proper nouns. Do not capitalize the names of animals. Do not capitalize words like mother when they are not used as proper names.

page 50

10,000 year-old heart-shaped drawings have been found in caves.
A heart shape appears on an old coin from Cyrene.
The heart from the coin represents the silphium seed.
There are heart-shaped flowers called bleeding hearts.
Greeks and Aztecs believed the heart contained the human soul.

page 51

Answers may vary.
First Paragraph
Main idea: The Sami live in Norway, Sweden, Finland, and Russia.
Supporting detail: They have their own language, style of clothing, and way of making a living.

Second Paragraph
Main idea: The Sami are reindeer herders.
First supporting detail: They follow their reindeer across the Arctic as the reindeer migrate.
Second supporting detail: They sleep in cone-shaped tents.

Third Paragraph
Main idea: The reindeer are the Sami's livelihood.
First supporting detail: They have traditionally eaten the meat.
Second supporting detail: Today, they sell the reindeer meat.

Fourth Paragraph
Main idea: The way of life is changing for the Sami.
First supporting detail: They must build fences.
Second supporting detail: Many have jobs other than reindeer herding.

page 52

Montana, Wyoming, Colorado, New Mexico, North Dakota, South Dakota, Nebraska, Kansas, Oklahoma, Texas, Minnesota, Iowa, Missouri, Arkansas, and Louisiana
the Mississippi River
the eastern half
the Gulf of Mexico
No

page 53

increase
17,063,353
66,573,715
1900
immigration

page 54

coal
hydropower
4.13 percent
19 percent
67 percent

page 55

False, coal forms from trees and other woody plants
True
True
False, coal is formed by swamp plants

page 57

August 27–29, 1776
France promised financial support to the American war effort.
"Give me liberty or give me death!"
April 19, 1775
December 25–26, 1776 and February 27, 1782
financially
1,400
the British
September 3, 1783
nearly one year

page 58

$20,000
the Green Team
through a recycling drive and business sponsorships
It is going to save the school money and teach the students about renewable energy.
"We thought the biggest impact our club could have would be to help our school switch to clean energy."
Magda Kita

page 59

four
Step 4 because onions are optional
one
a knife, a cutting board or plate, a bowl, a mixing spoon or a fork
mash
squeeze

page 61

A. machine base 1; B. motor 2; C. shaver 3; D. shaver lid 4; E. bowl 5

page 62

Answers may vary.
Opinion: The school needs to turn off lights and electronic devices at night.
Supporting Evidence:
Lights and other electronic devices are seen to be left on overnight.
Wasting energy wastes money.
The Seattle School District saved money by turning off beverage machine lights at night.
If all American workers turned off their computers at night, they would save $2.8 billion dollars altogether.

page 63

fact
fact
opinion
fact
fact
fact
fact
fact
opinion
opinion

pages 64–65

chronological order
comparing and contrasting
comparing and contrasting
chronological order

page 66

79 CE
They did not know the mountain was an active volcano.
through Pliny's letters
he was afraid he and his companions would be trampled by the crowd

page 67

Those who fled Herculaneum and Pompeii right away survived.
The surges of gases and ash were the deadliest effect of the volcano.
The people were terrified to see their town buried in ashes.
Pliny's letters would survive for thousands of years.
Men and women were shrieking and yelling.
There was a risk of being trampled as people fled.
A dark cloud spread over the land.
In some places, the temperature during the eruption reached 570°F.

page 69

Jon saw a large man wrestling a bison.
The man survived a violent attack from the bison.
The man was wearing animal fur as clothing.
There were two girls who were big, like the man.
They had spears.

page 71

c; a and c

page 73

Jimmy, Jimmy, Kate, Kate, Jimmy

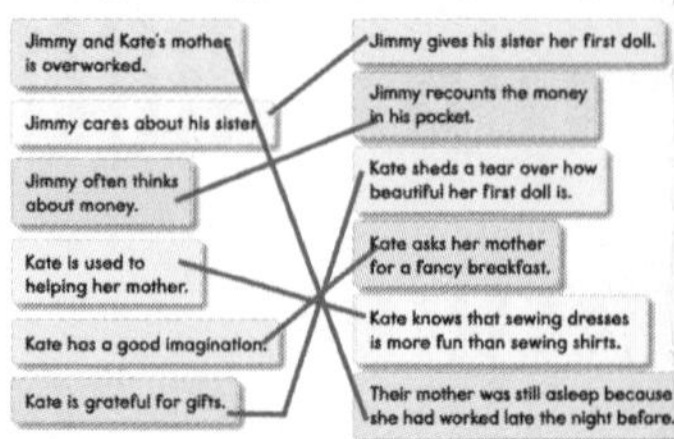

page 75

Pea wants to be left in its pod.
The prince wants to find a real princess.
It's told from the point of view of the pea.
Pea thinks the queen should write a letter to the princess's kingdom to see if she is really a princess.
She thinks, "Let's drag Pea into this mess and make his life miserable!"
Pea says that he slept terribly, and the queen thinks that the princess has said it.

pages 76–77

mystery; science fiction; fantasy; historical fiction; realistic fiction

pages 78–79

actions; actions; she was chosen to sing the solo
words and actions; actions; mild-mannered
words and actions; is talented but lacks confidence

page 80

a
c
b
b

page 81

noon
bees
November
alliteration

page 82

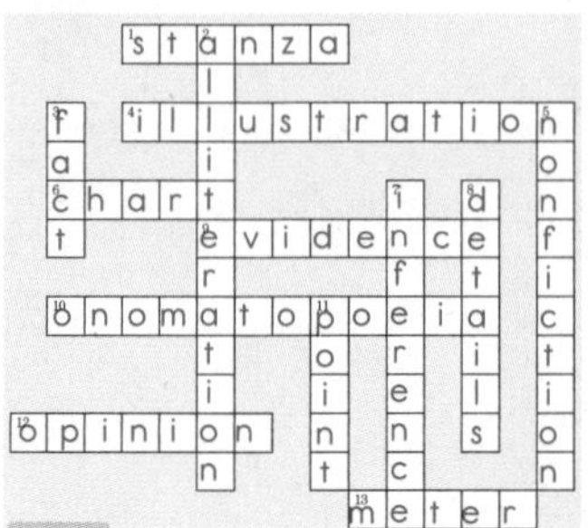

page 84

persuades
entertains
informs

informs
connects people to the human experience

page 85

plan
brainstorm
write
research
revise
proofread

page 102

Answers may vary.
Three pigs build their homes—one with straw, one with sticks, and one with bricks. A wolf blows down the flimsier houses, but the pigs find safety in the brick house.
Impoverished, Jack sells his cow for magic beans. A giant beanstalk grows, and at the top is a giant's castle, where Jack finds a goose that lays golden eggs.
A cursed princess pricks her finger and falls asleep. The kiss of a prince wakes her up.

pages 114–115

unreliable
reliable
reliable
unreliable

page 123

The hive:
Honeybees live in a hive.
Hives are usually in hollow trees.
80,000 bees can live in a hive.

Workers, queens, and drones:
Female bees known as workers find food, build the hive, clean, care for the baby bees, and make honey.
The queen's only job is to lay eggs.
Drones (male bees) mate with the queen.

How and why bees make honey:
Bees drink nectar from flowers.
Back in the hive, the bees regurgitate the nectar into the honeycomb.
The water in the nectar evaporates.
Honey is left behind.
The honey is what the bees eat in the winter, when there are no flowers.

Bee stings:
Bees sting to defend themselves or the hive.
Their stingers are barbed.
The stinger is attached to a venom sac inside the bee.
When the bee stings someone, the venom sac detaches from the bee and kills the bee.
The sting hurts because of the venom.

page 124

Capybaras

Capybaras are the world's largest Rodents. They live in the rainforests and savannas of central america and south america. Weighing 75 to 100 pounds, they are the size of a large dog. The giant rodents are are semi-aquatic. They cool off in the water, graze on aquatic plants, and also use water for protection. predators include jaguars, anacondas and caimans. If a predator threatens a capybara it dives underwater. A capybara can hold its breath underwater for 5 minutes!
Capybarras live in groups of 3 to 30. Together, they their defend territory. Capybaras communicate through scent and sound. They bark to warn each other of trouble. A male's scent indicates his social status and whether whether he is ready to mate.
The closest reltatives to capybaras are guinea pigs. Like guinea pigs, capybaras are easily domesticated. In some places, they are now raised on ranches. Some people even keep them as pets.

page 126

3,275
999,999,999,999
77,777
500,223
800,400,200
45,453,892
703
922,003
202,000,002
33,000

703
3,275
33,000
77,777
500,223
922,003
45,453,892
202,000,002
800,400,200
999,999,999,999

page 127

sixty-four dollars and 50/100
three thousand five hundred six dollars and 33/100
twenty dollars and 10/100

Needs total: $900
Money left over for wants: $83
She can afford dinner out with friends and coffee every morning (or gym membership)

page 128

(8),432	thousands
46(8)	ones
5(8)5	tens
(8)32	hundreds
1,27(8)	ones
4(8)9	tens
(8)73,322	hundred thousands
5,(8)10	hundreds
(8)0,100	ten thousands

Answers will vary: 38; 86; 813; 8,452; 85,603; 845,317

page 129

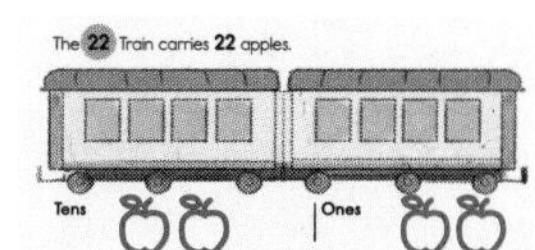

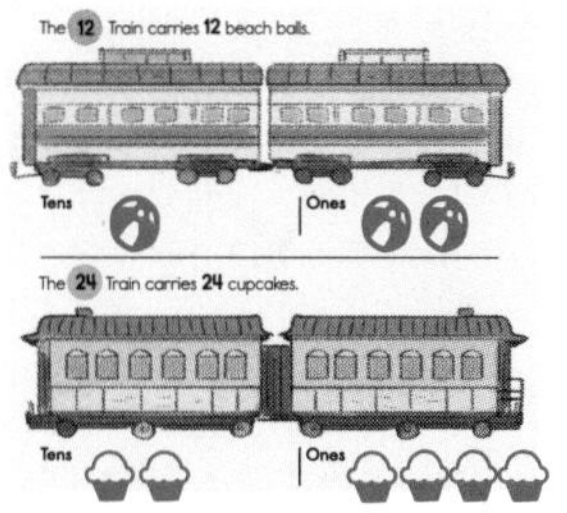

page 130

1,246 = 1,000 + 200 + ← 40 + 6
2,357 = 2,000 + 300 + ← 50 + 7
3,467 = 3,000 + 400 + ← 60 + 7
4,578 = 4,000 + 500 + ← 70 + 8
5,689 = 5,000 + 600 + 80 + 9
6,790 = 6,000 + 700 + 90 + 0
4,219 = 4,000 + 200 + 10 + 9
3,652 = 3,000 + 600 + 50 + 2
5,342 = 5,000 + 300 + 40 + 2
9,243 = 9,000 + 200 + 40 + 3

91,837
46,546
74,359
88,201
29,812
32,784
23,195
55,388
19,234

page 131

10
100
1000
100,000
1,000
1,000
10
10
100
100

page 132

10
100
1,000
10,000
10
100
10
1,000
100
10

page 133

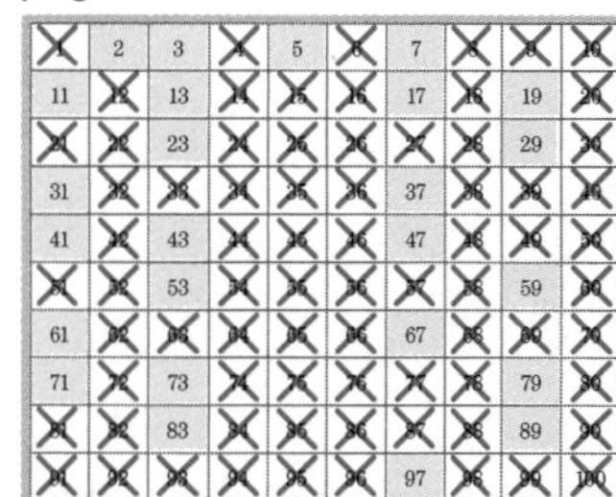

page 134

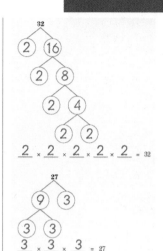

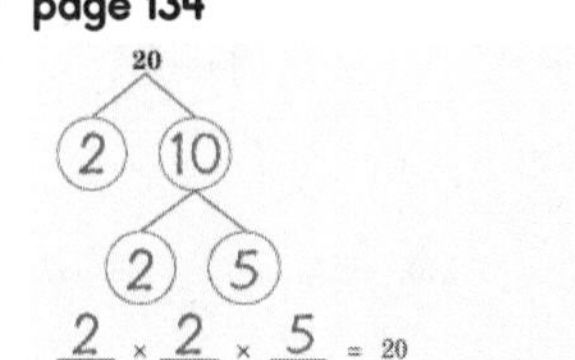

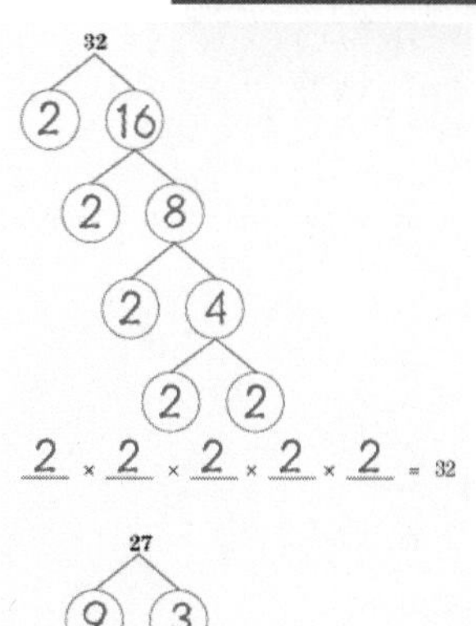

27
(9) (3)
(3) (3)
3 × 3 × 3 = 27

page 136

5 + 5 + 5 + 5 = 20
5 × 4 = 20

8 + 8 + 8 = 24
3 × 8 = 24

3 + 3 + 3 + 3 = 12
3 × 4 = 12

6 + 6 + 6 = 18
3 × 6 = 18

page 137

1 × 12 = 12
2 × 6 = 12
3 × 4 = 12

1 × 14 = 14
2 × 7 = 14

1 × 15 = 15
3 × 5 = 15

1 × 16 = 16
2 × 8 = 16
4 × 4 = 16

1 × 18 = 18
2 × 9 = 18
3 × 6 = 18

pages 138–139

3 × 5 = 15
7 × 6 = 42
9 × 4 = 36
6 × 8 = 48
9 × 12 = 108
8 × 8 = 64
On page 139, the second table has the most cheese.

pages 140–141

6 × 6 = 36
6 × 12 = 72
3 × 7 = 21
4 × 6 = 24
6 × 6 = 36
8 × 9 = 72
4 × 9 = 36
8 × 3 = 24

page 142

774	3,492	7,326
294	4,851	1,872
1,476	5,608	2,776
		2,395

page 143

1,920	1,782	6,244
2,850	774	6,912
5,400	723	2,112

pages 144–145

56,700	22,344
22,776	13,230
	24,318
72,890	20,608
26,077	52,762
9,750	

page 146

17,081
9,215
81,432
34,047
57,218

page 147

36,288
31,832
36,801
23,958
42,054

page 148

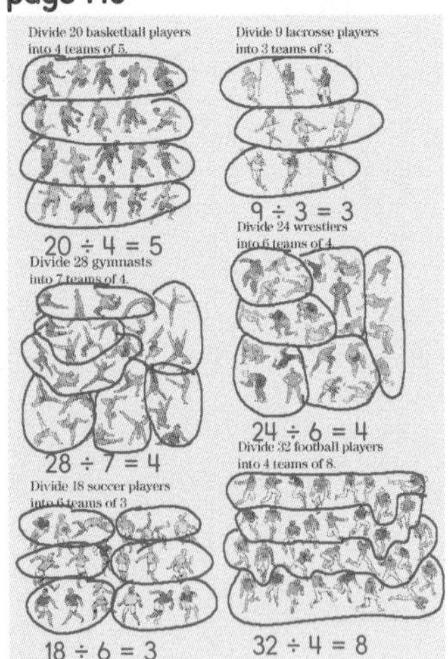
Divide 20 basketball players into 4 teams of 5.
20 ÷ 4 = 5
Divide 9 lacrosse players into 3 teams of 3.
9 ÷ 3 = 3
Divide 28 gymnasts into 7 teams of 4.
28 ÷ 7 = 4
Divide 24 wrestlers into 6 teams of 4.
24 ÷ 6 = 4
Divide 18 soccer players into 6 teams of 3.
18 ÷ 6 = 3
Divide 32 football players into 4 teams of 8.
32 ÷ 4 = 8

page 149

121 ÷ 11 = (11)
56 ÷ 7 = (8)
43 ÷ 6 = (7 R1)
63 ÷ 9 = (7)
66 ÷ 8 = (8 R2)
81 ÷ 9 = (9)
49 ÷ 7 = (7)

page 150

73 R5
53
91 R2
81 R2
47
247

page 151

219
213
28
168
184
212

page 152

118 R2
122 R5
149 R1
82
99 R2
92

page 153

54
64
212
38
132
412

page 154

45 R5	64
87 R2	56
82 R7	26
	251

page 155

469	381	153
147	211	
166	132	
108		

page 156

60 × 50 = 3,000
40 × 40 = 1,600
40 × 80 = 3,200
40 × 80 = 3,200
80 × 30 = 2,400
90 × 30 = 2,700
50 × 100 = 5,000

6,800 ÷ 20 = 340
8,800 ÷ 40 = 220
3,500 ÷ 70 = 50
7,800 ÷ 30 = 260
9,900 ÷ 30 = 330
8,100 ÷ 90 = 90

page 158

$\frac{2}{6}$
$\frac{7}{10}$
$\frac{4}{12}$ (or $\frac{1}{3}$)
$\frac{1}{4}$
$\frac{12}{15}$ (or $\frac{4}{5}$)
$\frac{2}{8}$ (or $\frac{1}{4}$)

page 159

$\frac{1}{5}$
$\frac{2}{3}$
$\frac{1}{2}$

page 160

$\frac{2}{6}$ or $\frac{1}{3}$
$\frac{8}{64}$ or $\frac{1}{8}$
$\frac{9}{81}$ or $\frac{1}{9}$
$\frac{4}{36}$ or $\frac{1}{9}$
$\frac{6}{12}$ or $\frac{1}{2}$
$\frac{9}{45}$ or $\frac{1}{5}$
$\frac{6}{24}$ or $\frac{1}{4}$

page 161

$5\frac{5}{9}$
$9\frac{5}{7}$
$3\frac{1}{3}$
$10\frac{5}{11}$
$7\frac{3}{4}$
$2\frac{1}{11}$
$6\frac{1}{2}$

page 162

$\frac{3}{4}$
$\frac{1}{2}$
$1\frac{2}{5}$
$\frac{3}{7}$
$1\frac{2}{3}$
$1\frac{4}{11}$
$\frac{2}{5}$
$1\frac{5}{7}$
$\frac{1}{3}$

page 163

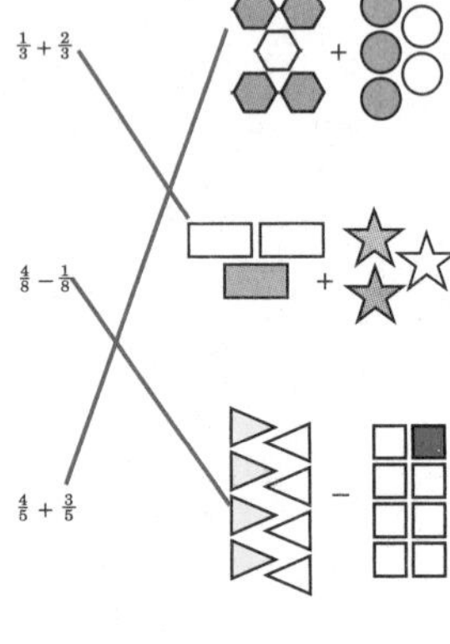
$\frac{1}{3}+\frac{2}{3}$
$\frac{4}{8}-\frac{1}{8}$
$\frac{4}{5}+\frac{3}{5}$
$\frac{3}{4}+\frac{1}{4}$

page 164

$\frac{9}{4}$	$\frac{39}{8}$
$\frac{25}{8}$	$\frac{17}{6}$
$\frac{25}{3}$	$\frac{15}{8}$
$\frac{17}{5}$	$\frac{13}{2}$

page 165

$\frac{21}{80}$	$\frac{7}{10}$
$\frac{3}{10}$	$\frac{1}{4}$
$\frac{8}{15}$	$\frac{5}{12}$
$\frac{27}{40}$	$\frac{21}{64}$
$\frac{3}{7}$	$\frac{1}{3}$

page 166

$\frac{1}{2}$	$\frac{3}{10}$
$\frac{1}{2}$	$\frac{1}{3}$
$\frac{4}{11}$	$\frac{2}{5}$
	$\frac{5}{44}$
	$\frac{7}{16}$
	$\frac{1}{4}$
	$\frac{3}{5}$

page 167

$\frac{7}{16}$	$\frac{1}{2}$
$\frac{5}{6}$	$1\frac{5}{7}$
$1\frac{1}{5}$	$\frac{15}{28}$
$\frac{9}{10}$	$1\frac{1}{5}$
$\frac{8}{15}$	$1\frac{3}{32}$

page 168

$4\frac{2}{3}$	$9\frac{3}{5}$
$\frac{1}{6}$	$\frac{1}{32}$
$10\frac{1}{2}$	$\frac{6}{35}$
27	$12\frac{6}{7}$
	$\frac{9}{20}$
	$3\frac{3}{4}$

page 169

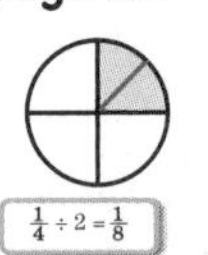
$\frac{1}{4} \div 2 = \frac{1}{8}$
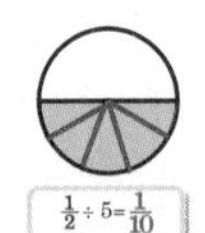
$\frac{1}{2} \div 5 = \frac{1}{10}$
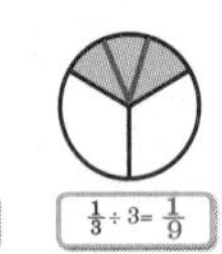
$\frac{1}{3} \div 3 = \frac{1}{9}$

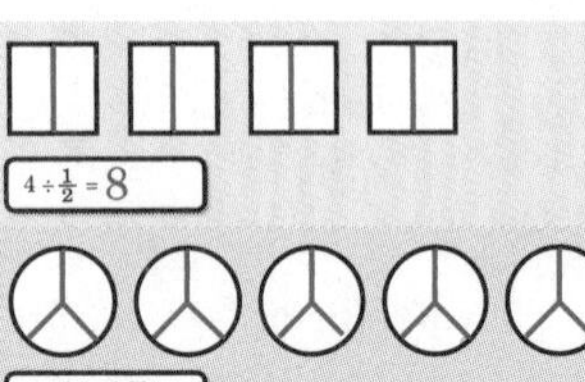
$4 \div \frac{1}{2} = 8$
$5 \div \frac{1}{3} = 15$

$6 \div \frac{1}{4} = 24$

page 170

$1\frac{1}{6}$	$1\frac{1}{2}$
$\frac{7}{8}$	$\frac{13}{14}$
$\frac{9}{10}$	$1\frac{5}{9}$
$\frac{7}{16}$	$1\frac{1}{4}$
$1\frac{1}{10}$	$1\frac{1}{3}$

page 171

0.3	0.11
0.7	0.461
0.57	
9/10	63/1000
777/1000	323/1000
17/100	

page 172

0.75	0.28
0.5	0.58
0.65	0.8
0.12	
0.34	
0.6	

page 173

0.1, 0.312, 0.78
0.006, 0.095, 0.856
0.32, 0.5, 0.613
0.18, 0.454, 0.54
0.19, 0.41, 0.62
0.13, 0.37, 0.4
0.014, 0.11, 0.42
0.09, 0.53, 0.867
0.02, 0.29, 0.523

page 174

<
=
<
<
=
>
>
>
>
>

page 175

40.731 820.2088 13

146.554	0.8918	15.14
184.26	13.403	175.98

page 176

$0.98	($1.10)	$0.42
($1.50)	$0.71	($1.00)

page 177

0.25912
1.0125
24.624
13.76544
706.32
5926.272
0.1344
37.83432
1.74
122.4496

page 178

17/20	47.19	21 2/3
0.09894	77/96	1 ¼
9/10	2 1/12	6

page 180

centimeters
meters
kilometers
meters
centimeters
kilometers

3
4000
5
50
500

page 181

inches
feet/yards
inches
feet/yards
miles
miles

24	3,520	4
2	300	

page 182

100 mL	250 mL
300 mL	450 mL

10 beakers
45,000,000 mL

page 183

2 pints
1 quart
2 loaves
4 cups
1/4 quart
1/8 pint

page 184

32
212
60
150
37
70
5
165

page 185

14 minutes
4 hours, 30 minutes
1 hour, 15 minutes
7 hours, 30 minutes
19 hours
9 hours
6 hours, 45 minutes
83 hours

page 188

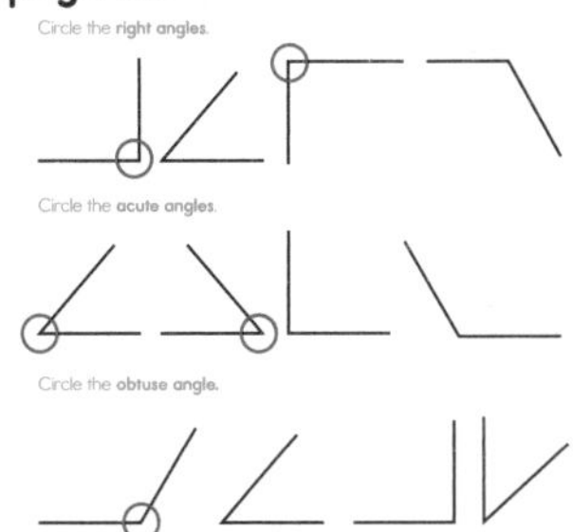

page 189

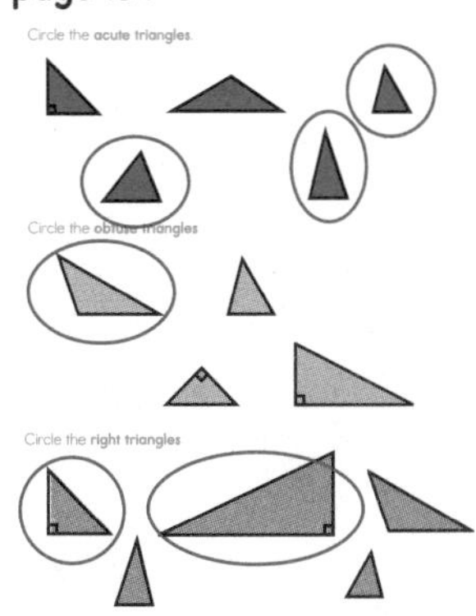

page 190

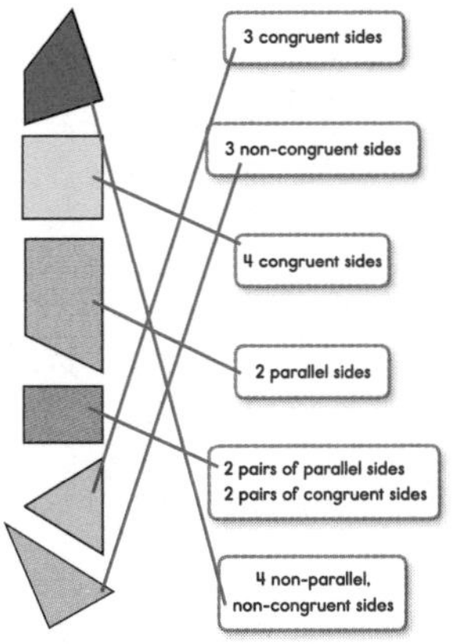

page 191

True
False
True
False
False
True
False
True
False

page 192

20 inches, 25 square inches
44 feet, 120 square feet
32 centimeters, 60 square centimeters
30 kilometers, 50 square kilometers

page 193

96 centimeters
330 square feet
137 inches
84 square meters

page 194

324 cubic inches
864 cubic inches
1728 cubic inches
8 cubic feet
27 cubic feet
256 cubic feet

page 195

81
256
625
1,296
2,401
4,096

page 196

15.7
21.98
12.56
18.84

page 197

25.12
28.26
31.4
34.54

page 198

28.26
50.24
78.5

153.86	113.04
200.96	254.34

page 199

314

page 200

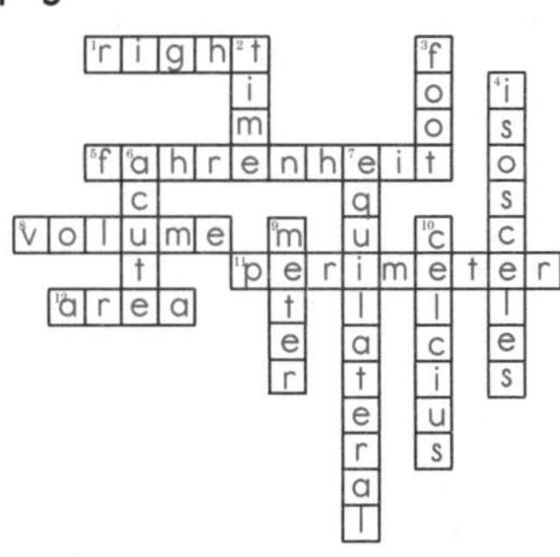

page 203

Chocolate	II	2
Vanilla	IIII	4
Chocolate vanilla swirl	II	2
Lemon	II	2
Peanut butter	I	1
Strawberry	I	1

page 205

$160, 9
January, February, March
$1440, $1450
April
June, July, and August
April, May, June, July, August, and September
4

page 206

0-4	|	1
5-9	||||	4
10-14	||	2
15-19	0	0

page 207

Stem	Leaf
3	2
4	4
8	3, 8
9	2, 5

page 209

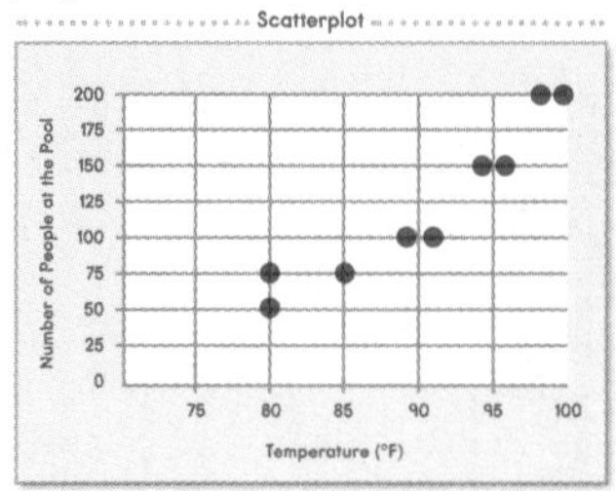

Yes.
The two sets of data are related.

page 211

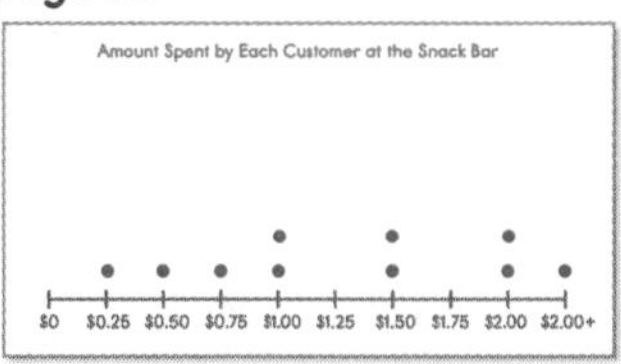

page 212

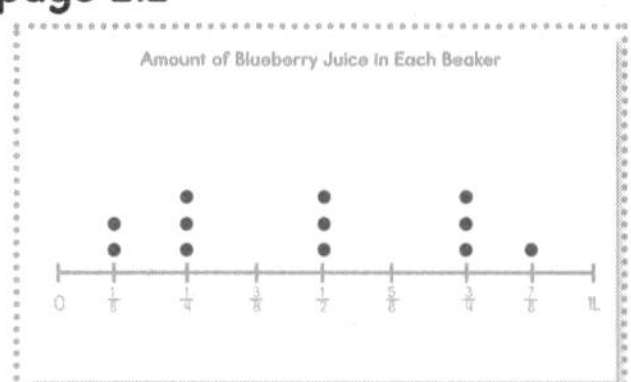

page 213

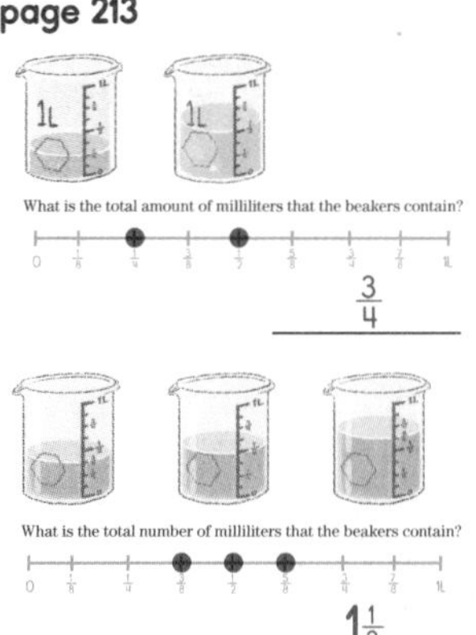

page 216

Square 2 and add that to 4.
Subtract 3 from the sum.

Add 4 plus 5. Divide the sum by 3.

3	7
42	83
50	

page 217

Starting at 0, add 2.
Starting at 0, add 6.
The numbers in the second sequence are 3 times the corresponding numbers in the first.

Starting at 0, add 1.
Starting at 0, add 5.
The numbers in the second sequence are 5 times the corresponding numbers in the first.

Starting at 0, add 1.
Starting at 0, add 4.
The numbers in the second sequence are 4 times the corresponding numbers in the first.

page 218

(0,0) (1,3) (2,16) (3,19) (4,12) (5,15)

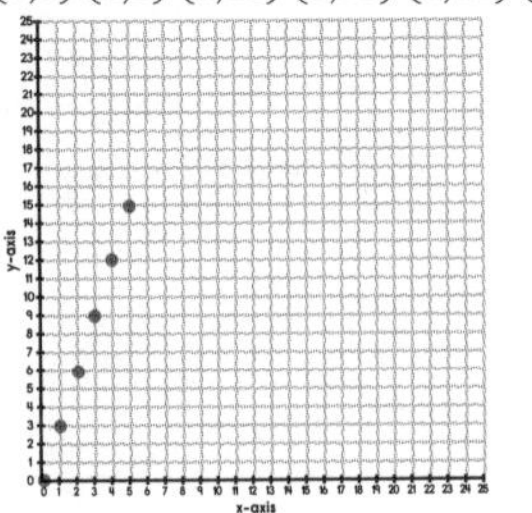

page 219

(0,0) (2,6) (4,12) (6,18) (8,24)

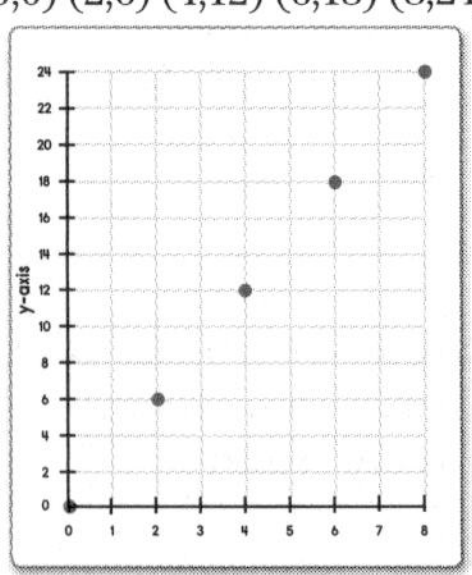

(0,0) (1,4) (2,8) (3,12) (4,16) (5,20)

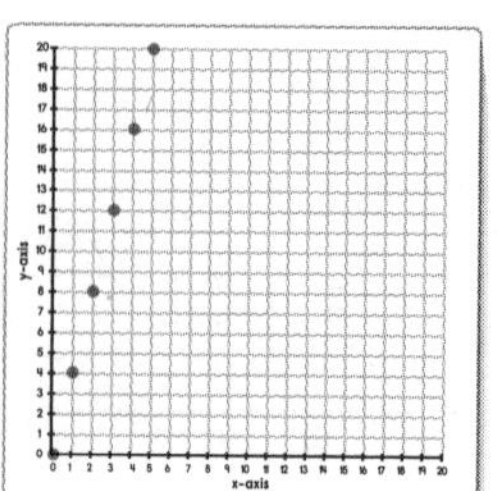

pages 220–221

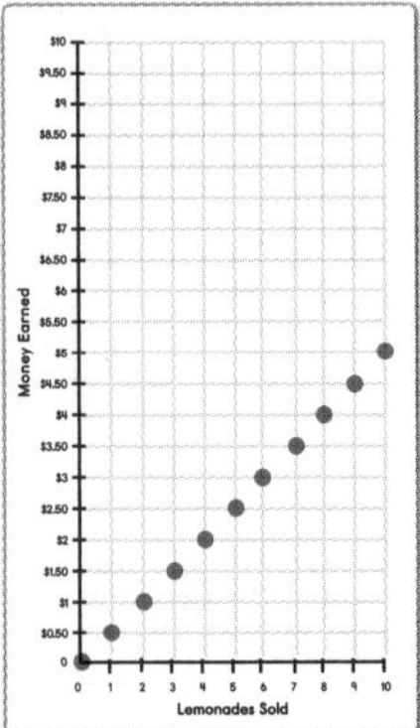

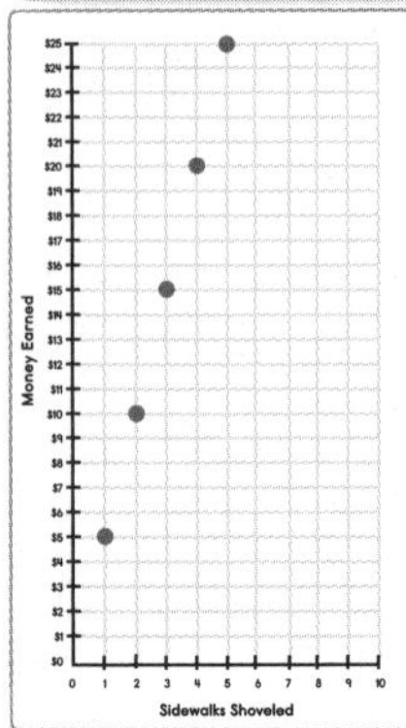

page 222

2 seconds
3.5
7

about 1
7
12
14

page 224

53,127,417,506
$300
4,000+600+80+1
2,468
No
Yes
Yes

page 225

1, 2
70
$40
10
8
2,3,5,7

page 226

348
1,990
1,632
468
1,089

page 227

16,834
9,469
10,114
32,472
1,824

page 228

8
11
6
30
14

page 229

456
127
896
116
344
682

page 230

$235
$391
$263
$266
$422

page 231

34
68
63
3
67

page 232

900
1,800
300
3,500
2,400

page 233

$\frac{3}{8}$
$\frac{18}{24}$ or $\frac{3}{4}$
$\frac{2}{6}$ or $\frac{1}{3}$
$\frac{3}{12}$ or $\frac{1}{4}$
$\frac{2}{24}$ or $\frac{1}{12}$
$\frac{3}{72}$ or $\frac{1}{24}$

page 234

$\frac{5}{8}$
$\frac{17}{20}$
$\frac{3}{8}$
$\frac{5}{12}$
$\frac{2}{5}$
$\frac{29}{30}$

page 235

$\frac{1}{8}$
$\frac{1}{9}$
$\frac{1}{16}$
$\frac{2}{50}$ or $\frac{1}{25}$
$\frac{2}{6}$ or $\frac{1}{3}$
$\frac{3}{20}$

page 236

30.65 mL
5.5 mL
0.85
0.75
$0.82
37.845

page 237

432 square inches
80 square feet
56 square feet
36 feet
252 square feet

page 238

1728 cubic centimeters
1.5 kilometers
38°F
31.4 feet
78.5 square feet
2 gallons

pages 240–241

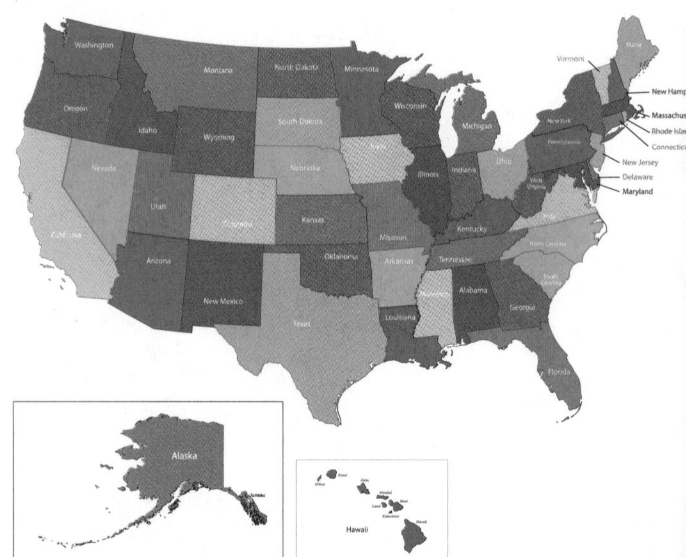

pages 242–243

page 244

Milwaukee
Salt Lake City
Little Rock
Wichita
Baton Rouge
Nashville
Sioux Falls
Juneau

Arizona, Arkansas, Colorado, Georgia, Hawaii, Idaho, Indiana, Iowa, Massachusetts, Mississippi, Ohio, Oklahoma, Rhode Island, South Carolina, Utah, West Virginia, Wyoming

page 249

Northwest Coast, California, Plateau, Great Basin, Southwest, Great Plains, Eastern Woodlands, Southeast

Because food was easily available, not everyone had to gather food. Some could focus on art. One type of art were totem poles.

They irrigated their crops. In lieu of using trees for homes, they built adobe homes.

In the Pacific Northwest, there was a lot of rain. The Southwest was dry. Food from land and sea was abundant in the Pacific Northwest. People in the Southwest had to grow their food using irrigation. People in the Pacific Northwest built their homes with wood. In the Southwest, they used adobe.

Most people on the Plains were farmers.

The prairie grass that thrived in the region fed the bison.

The introduction of the horse to America led to there being more bison hunters.

page 250

caravel
magnetic compass
gunpowder

page 251

3 months and 20 days
Any 3: biscuit powder, ox hides, sawdust, rats
Rats had eaten them, or Worms had eaten them.

page 252

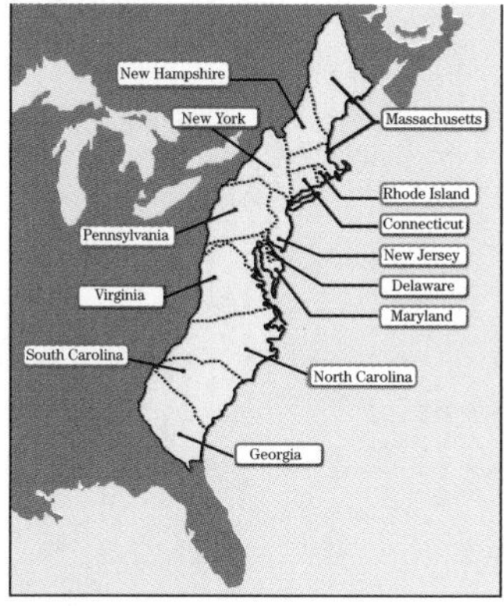

pages 252–253

The Appalachian Mountains
Louisiana
Michigan, Wisconsin, Illinois, and Indiana
Utah
The Gulf of Mexico
Increase

page 255

1607
gold and silver
Any 3: Approximately 14,000 people lived in Tsenacomoco. They lived in villages and grew corn. Their chief was Chief Powhatan. Several chiefdoms had been united by Powhatan to form Tsenacomoco.
It was marshy. There were mosquitos. The drinking water was bad.
3/4
The colonists' crops encroached on the native land. Malaria infected Powhatan's people, making them too sick to fight.

page 257

King George III worked alongside Parliament.
George Washington was talked into running for president.
John Adams was the second U.S. president.
Thomas Jefferson wrote the Declaration of Independence.
Mary Ludwig was nicknamed for her work during the war.
Abigail Adams questioned Massachusetts residents who remained loyal to the Crown.

page 259

Amendment VIII
Amendment I
Amendment VI
Amendment IV
Amendment III

page 261

Louisiana Purchase
Westward Expansion
Manifest Destiny
Missouri Compromise
Bleeding Kansas

pages 262–263

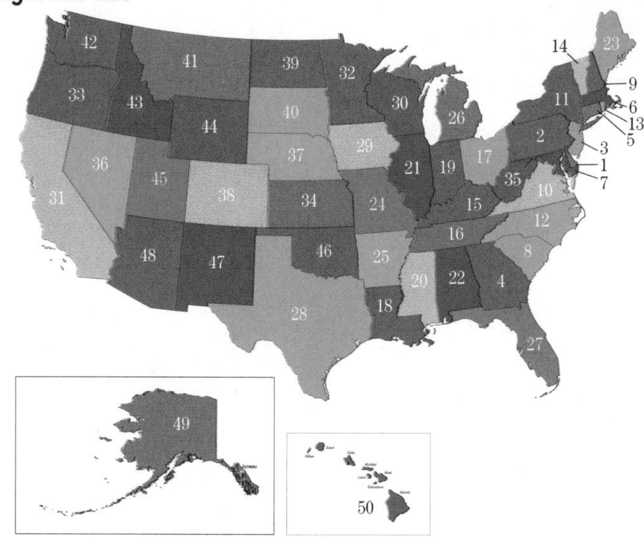

page 267

Seceding from the union means to withdraw from the United States.
South Carolina
South Carolina, Mississippi, Florida, Alabama, Georgia, Louisiana, Texas, Virginia, Arkansas, Tennessee, North Carolina
When Lincoln was elected president, the Southern states feared that he would bring an end to slavery.
He needed troops to fight the Confederate states.
The Confederate States of America
Jefferson Davis
The Union Army cut off supplies from reaching Confederate ports, it defended Washington, D.C., and it captured Alexandria, Virginia.

page 270

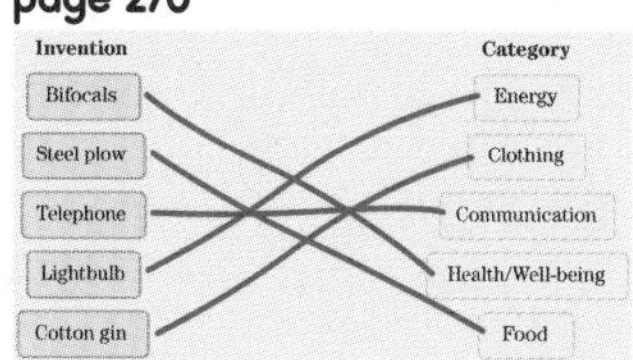

page 271

legislative
executive
judicial

page 272

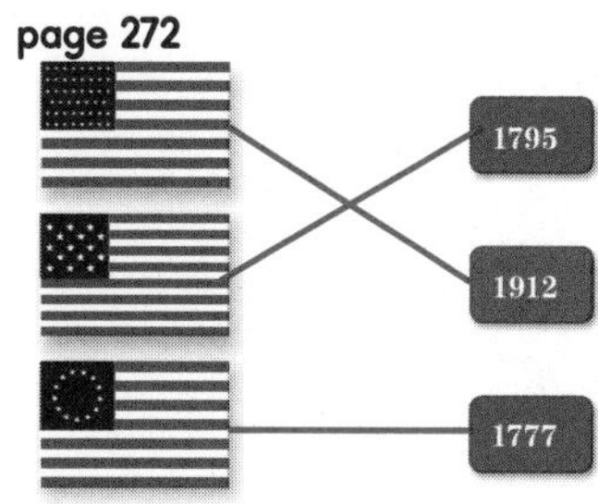

page 273

1892: The Pledge of Allegiance was written by Francis J. Bellamy.
1942: Congress changed the salute to the hand-over-heart gesture.
1954: The words "under God" were added after "one nation."

I pledge allegiance to the flag of the United States of America, and to the republic for which it stands, one nation under God, indivisible, with liberty and justice for all.

page 276

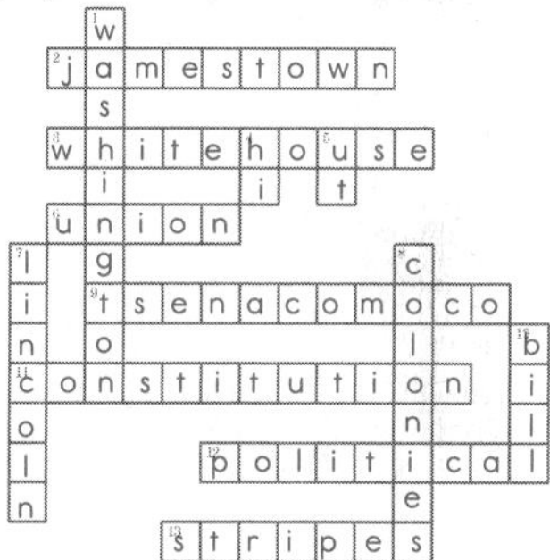

page 279

Both fish and amphibians have gills.
Animals with fur are mammals.
Animals with feathers are birds.
Animals that feed their young milk are mammals. Mammals also have hair.

page 281

Similarities:
Both start out as eggs.
Both are very different as babies and adults.
Both lay several eggs at a time.

Differences:
Frogs lay their eggs in water, and silkworms lay their eggs on land.
Frogs transform from a tadpole to a frog without spinning a cocoon; silkworms spin cocoons.
It takes a frog 5 years to fully mature; it only takes a silkworm weeks.

page 282
Ducks have webbed feet so that they can swim better to catch prey.
Horses have hooves in order to run fast to escape predators.
Eagles have talons so that they can grab and hold on to prey.
Bears have paws so that they can climb trees, dig for food, and grasp prey.

page 283
photosynthesis
herbivores
carnivores
decomposers
bacteria

page 284
They've developed hooves so that they can quickly run away from predators.
Insects pollinate plants, and decompose dead plants and animals into soil, which feeds the grass.
Grassland grasses have deep roots that store water.
Bison grow a thick coat in winter and shed it in the spring

page 285

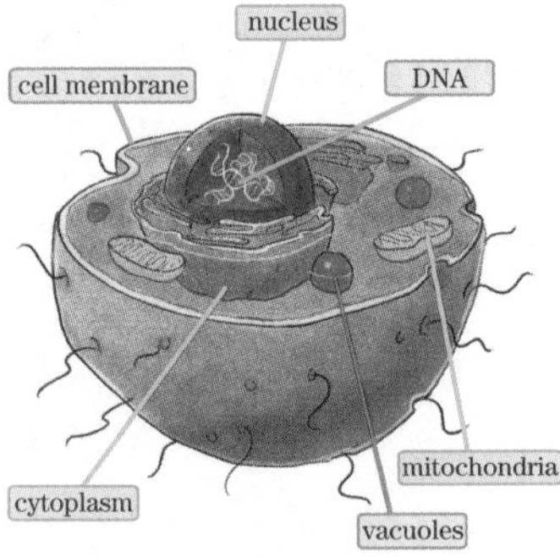

page 286

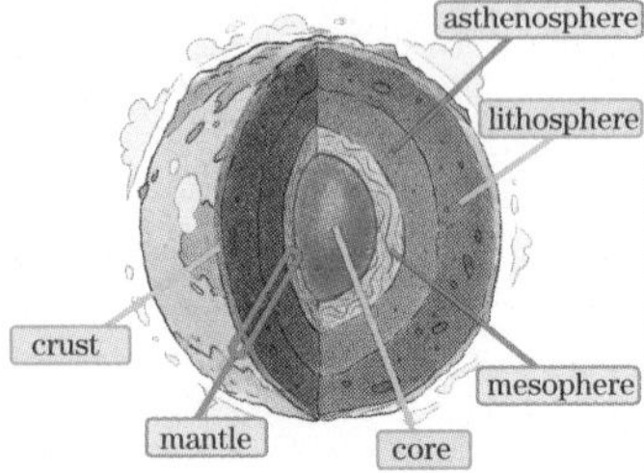

page 287
sedimentary
metamorphic
igneous
sedimentary

page 288

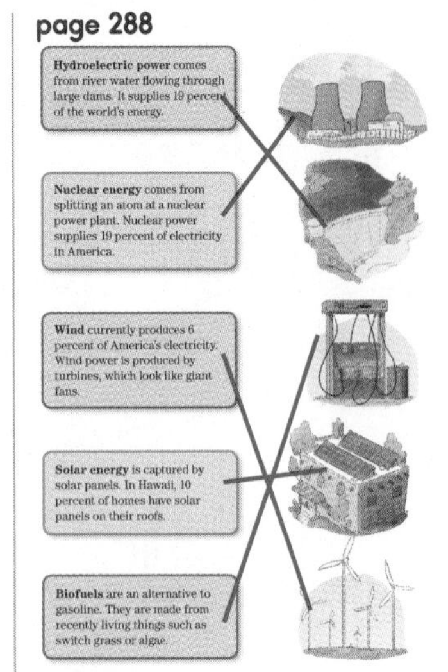

page 289
erosion
deposition
rising sea level
plate tectonics
deposition

page 290
atomic number
mixture
bond
element
compound, atom

page 291
False
False
True
False
True

page 294

molecule
core
reflected
cytoplasm
cell
atom
element
dna
nucleus
hooves
landform
wavelengths

Brain Quest Extras

Congratulations!

You've finished the Brain Quest Workbook!

In this section, you'll find:

Brain Quest Mini-Deck

Cut out the cards and make your own Brain Quest deck.

Play by yourself or with a friend.

Brainiac Certificate

Finish the whole workbook, and you're an official Brainiac!

Congratulations! Write your name on your Braianic Certificate, cut it out, and show it off!

QUESTIONS

What is the suffix of "partition"?

What is the correct spelling: "regretting" or "regreting"?

The "shot heard round the world" started which war?

How many equal sides does an isosceles triangle have?

QUESTIONS

Does "purchase" mean buy or count?

What type of angle is greater than 90 degrees?

How many states contain the word "new"?

In 3,565,287, what number is in the thousandths place?
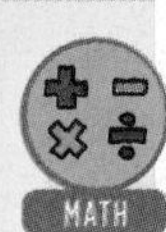

QUESTIONS

Which part of "unfortunate" is the prefix?

Which is the correct spelling: "unmistakeable" or "unmistakable"?

How many sides does a quadrilateral have?

What states start with the letter I?

QUESTIONS

Which is the correct spelling? Mari paid for (their/they're) ice cream.

Mammalogy is the study of what?

What state has the southernmost tip in the United States?

What does congruent mean?

ANSWERS

buy

obtuse

4: New York, New Jersey, New Hampshire, New Mexico

5
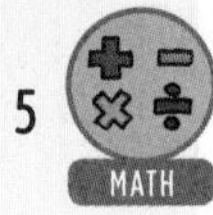

ANSWERS

-tion

regretting

the Revolutionary War

2
MATH

ANSWERS

their

mammals

Hawaii

the same size
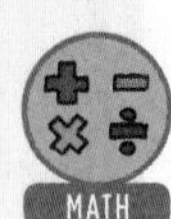

ANSWERS

un-

unmistakable

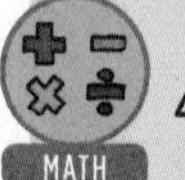

4

Idaho, Illinois, Indiana, Iowa

QUESTIONS

Is “mean as a snake” a simile or metaphor?

What does “the whole enchilada” mean?

What four states touch at their corners?

How many congruent sides does a rhombus have?

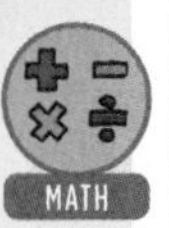

QUESTIONS

Which is not a preposition: to, outside, is, or after?

What part of speech is “Oh, my!”?

True or false: 4°C is warmer than 32°F.

How many pairs of parallel sides does a trapezoid have?

QUESTIONS

What part of speech is “and”?

Which is correct: “J.J. ate a hot dog” or “J.J. ate a Hot Dog”?

What state has the longest ocean coastline?

Simplify $\frac{6}{15}$.

QUESTIONS

Which is correct: Huck Finn rowed down the Mississippi River, or Huck Finn rowed down the Mississippi river?

Fact or opinion: Rainbow sherbet is the most flavorful sherbet.

The cub scouts bought 18 baseball tickets for $11.50 each. How much did they pay total?

What is $56 \times 1{,}000$?

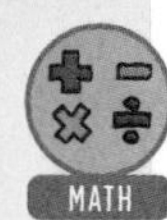

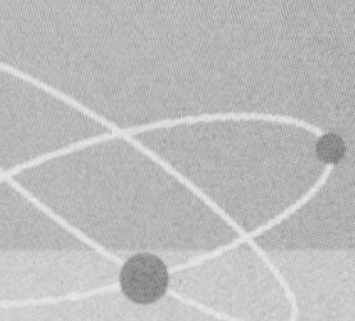

ANSWERS

is

interjection

True

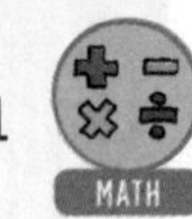

1

ANSWERS

simile

the whole thing/everything

Utah, Colorado, Arizona, New Mexico

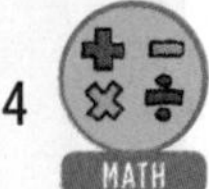

4

ANSWERS

Huck Finn rowed down the Mississippi River.

opinion

$207

56,000

ANSWERS

a conjunction

J.J. ate a hot dog.

Alaska

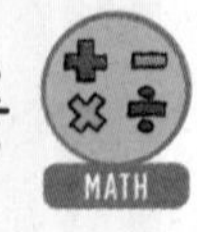

$\frac{2}{5}$

QUESTIONS

Is a letter home from an 1800s immigrant describing Ellis Island an eyewitness or secondhand account?

"I had no choice but to dive into the shark infested water" is written in the first or second person?

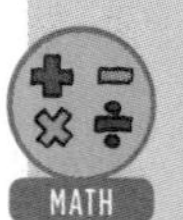

Add $\frac{3}{8} + \frac{5}{16}$.

Which number is not a prime number: 7, 17, 87?

QUESTIONS

What does this proofreading mark ¶ mean?

A synonym for "absurd" is "ridiculous" or "admirable"?

In what year did the Revolutionary War begin?

What is $\frac{5}{8} - \frac{3}{8}$?

QUESTIONS

An "antagonist" is an opponent or friend?

In what year did the Civil War begin?

At what temperature Fahrenheit does water boil?

What is $10 \times \frac{1}{2}$?

QUESTIONS

Is this written in the first or third person: "She blew out the candle and hid"?

Does "abolish" mean "to end" or "to vote"?

What divide separates the rivers that run into the Pacific Ocean and rivers that run into the Atlantic Ocean?

What is $3 \div \frac{1}{3}$?

Start a new paragraph.

ridiculous

1775

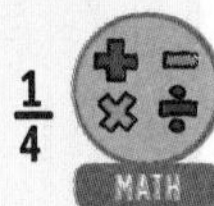

$\frac{1}{4}$

ANSWERS

eyewitness account

opinion

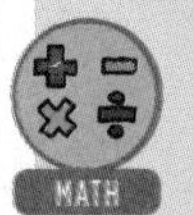

$\frac{11}{16}$

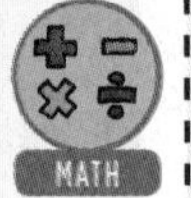

87

ANSWERS

third person

to end

The Continental Divide

9

ANSWERS

opponent

1861

212°F

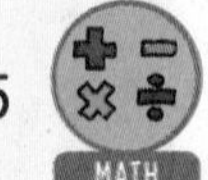

5

QUESTIONS

Does "anxious" mean "worried" or "excited"?

Was the Plymouth Colony founded before or after the Jamestown Colony?

What is $\frac{5}{7} \times \frac{5}{8}$?

Simplify $\frac{8}{64}$.

QUESTIONS

Is "flavorful" or "unfashionable" an antonym for "bland"?

Who was the 4th U.S. president?

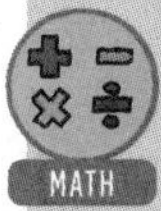

How many cups are in a quart?

Solve by cross canceling $\frac{1}{2} \times \frac{2}{3} \times \frac{3}{4} \times \frac{4}{5} \times \frac{5}{6} \times \frac{6}{7} \times \frac{7}{8}$.

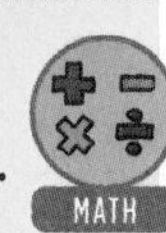

QUESTIONS

Is a concept an idea or an argument?

Which 2 U.S. presidents had sons who also became presidents?

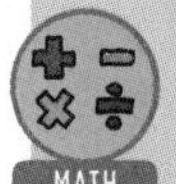

Marianna pays $22 per month for cable for 12 months. How much does she pay in a year?

What is $\frac{3}{4} \div \frac{5}{8}$?

QUESTIONS

Cold is to frigid as hot is to sweltering or damp?

If numbers are declining, are they getting smaller or bigger?

Which is greater, .15 or $\frac{1}{5}$?

What is $7 \div \frac{2}{3}$?

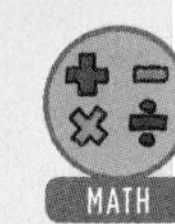

ANSWERS
ENGLISH
flavorful
James Madison
SOCIAL STUDIES
MATH
4
$\frac{1}{8}$
MATH

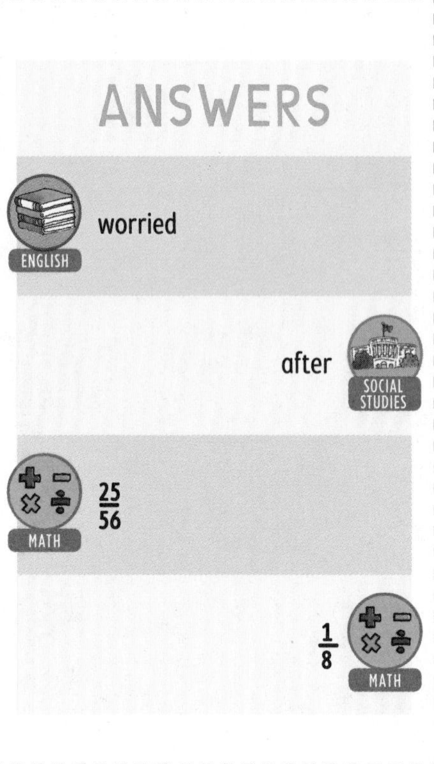
ANSWERS
ENGLISH
worried
after
SOCIAL STUDIES
MATH
$\frac{25}{56}$
$\frac{1}{8}$
MATH

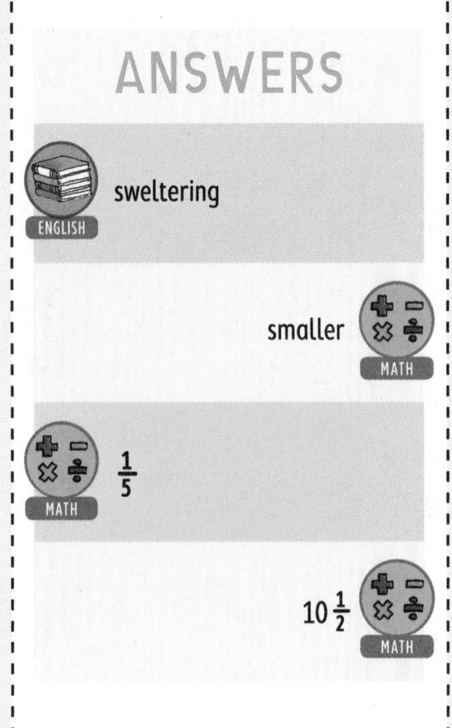
ANSWERS
ENGLISH
sweltering
smaller
MATH
MATH
$\frac{1}{5}$
$10\frac{1}{2}$
MATH

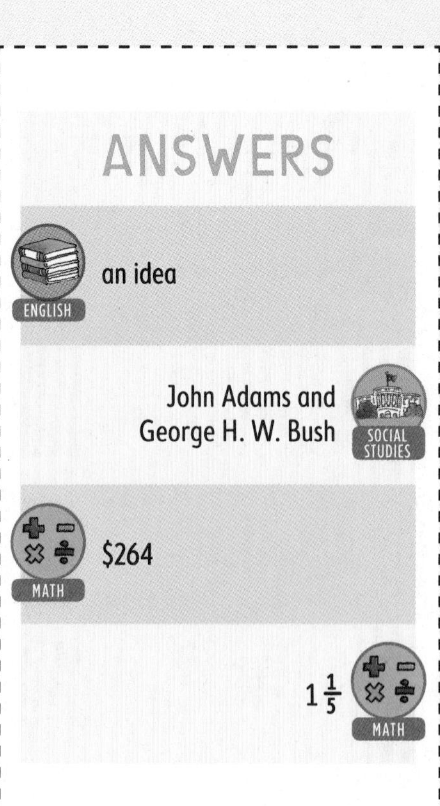
ANSWERS
ENGLISH
an idea
John Adams and George H. W. Bush
SOCIAL STUDIES
MATH
$264
$1\frac{1}{5}$
MATH

QUESTIONS

Is a hardy plant healthy or sick?

Tiny is to miniature as huge is to immense or compact?

What is $\frac{1}{8} \div 4$?

What fraction of the months have 31 days?

QUESTIONS

If people call you "industrious," do they mean that you are "boring" or "hardworking"?

What is the 50th U.S. state?

Find the common denominator to solve $\frac{1}{8} + \frac{1}{2}$.

Change the decimal to a fraction: 0.45.

QUESTIONS

Does "pardon me" mean "help me" or "forgive me"?

Die is to perish as live is to survive or falter?

It was sunny 28 days in August. What fraction of the month was sunny?

Change the fraction to a decimal: $\frac{3}{4}$.

QUESTIONS

Sluggish is to fast as vivid is to bright or drab?

Is the opposite of "seldom" "rarely" or "often"?

What is 0.32 + 0.5?

Round 78 to the nearest 10.
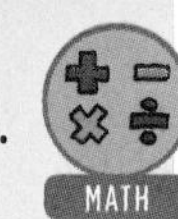

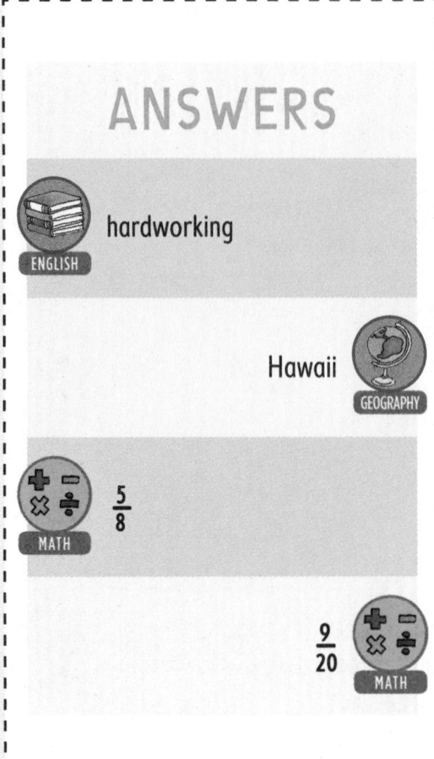

ANSWERS

ENGLISH: hardworking

GEOGRAPHY: Hawaii

MATH: $\frac{5}{8}$

MATH: $\frac{9}{20}$

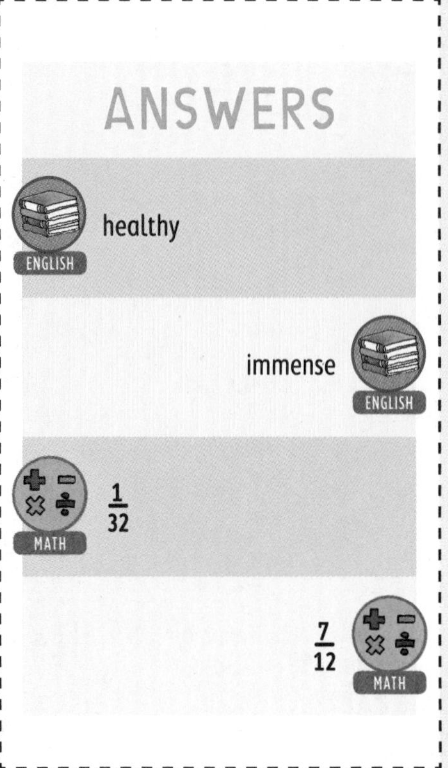

ANSWERS

ENGLISH: healthy

ENGLISH: immense

MATH: $\frac{1}{32}$

MATH: $\frac{7}{12}$

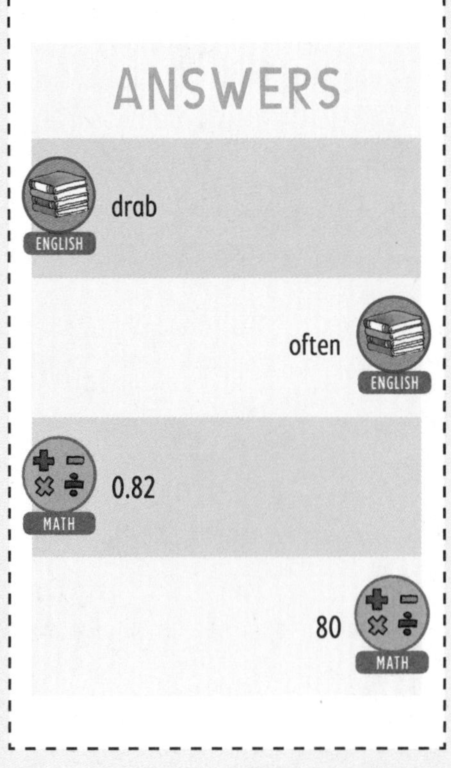

ANSWERS

ENGLISH: drab

ENGLISH: often

MATH: 0.82

MATH: 80

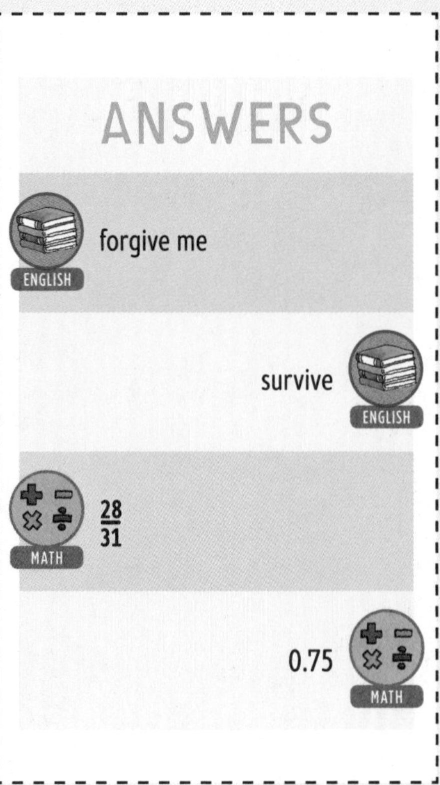

ANSWERS

ENGLISH: forgive me

ENGLISH: survive

MATH: $\frac{28}{31}$

MATH: 0.75

QUESTIONS

Spell the word that sounds like "rain" but means "to rule."

Is magnesium sulphate ($MgSO_4$) an element or compound?

What is 342 × 18?

Mary worked from 7:01 a.m. to 8:03 p.m. How much time passed?

QUESTIONS

Spell the word that sounds like "team" but means "to have lots of."

Where should the comma go: "You toast the marshmallows and I'll break the chocolate bars in half"?

What is 420 ÷ 5?

Find the numbers that are multiples of 7: 14, 23, 28, 37.

QUESTIONS

Does "gravy train" mean "an easy way to make a living" or "a dishonest way to make a living"?

True or false: "have swum" is in the perfect tense.

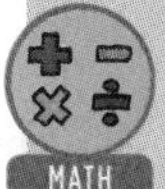
What is the perimeter of a square with 5 foot sides?

Estimate the product by rounding the numbers 49 × 32 to the nearest 10.

QUESTIONS

Does "have a cow" mean "spend too much" or "get upset"?

Where should the comma go in "Text me later Kaitlyn"?

What is the volume of a box that is 8 centimeters high, 100 centimeters long, and 50 centimeters wide?

What is pi to the nearest $\frac{1}{1000}$th?
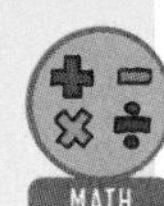

ANSWERS

 teem

after "marshmallows" 

 84

14, 28 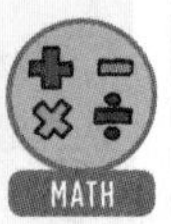

ANSWERS

 reign

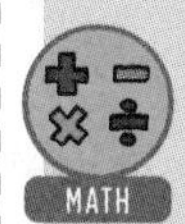 6,156

13 hours and 2 minutes 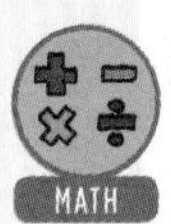

ANSWERS

 get upset

after "later" 

 40,000 square centimeters or 400 square meters

3.14 

ANSWERS

 an easy way to make a living

True 

 20 feet

1,500 

Brainiac Award!

You have completed the entire Brain Quest Workbook! Woo-hoo! Congratulations! That's quite an achievement.

Write your name on the line and cut out the award certificate.

Show your friends. Hang it on your wall! You're a certified Brainiac!

Presented to:

____

for successfully completing all thirteen chapters of

BRAIN QUEST 5TH GRADE WORKBOOK